PARENTS' ANSWER BOOK

■ ■ ■

DR. JAMES DOBSON

PARENTS' ANSWER BOOK

TYNDALE HOUSE PUBLISHERS, INC.
WHEATON, ILLINOIS

Visit Tyndale's exciting Web site at www.tyndale.com

First printing of *Parents' Answer Book*, 2003. All rights reserved.

Cover photograph copyright © 2002 by Harry Langdon. All rights reserved.

Living Books is a registered trademark of Tyndale House Publishers, Inc.

Designed by Julie Chen

Taken from *Complete Marriage and Family Home Reference Guide*, copyright © 2000 by James Dobson, Inc.; originally published as *Solid Answers*, copyright © 1997 James Dobson, Inc. All rights reserved.

ISBN 0-8423-8716-1

Printed in the United States of America

09 08 07 06 05
7   6   5   4

TABLE OF CONTENTS

Appreciation Page . . . . *ix*
Introduction . . . . *xi*

1 UNDERSTANDING THE NATURE OF CHILDREN 1
The Influence of Culture, 1–2 ❈ Temperament, 2–15 ❈ The Innate
Disobedient Nature, 15–17 ❈ Testing Authority, 17–20

2 RAISING THE PRESCHOOL CHILD 21
Fussy Babies, 21–22 ❈ Mental Stimulation, 22–24 ❈ Answering
Difficult Questions, 24–25 ❈ Disruptiveness in Church, 25–26
❈ Lying, 26–27 ❈ Violent Entertainment, 28–29 ❈ Teaching
Politeness, 29–30 ❈ Encouraging Responsibility, 30

3 DISCIPLINING THE PRESCHOOL CHILD 31
Permissiveness, 31–34 ❈ Balancing Love and Control, 34–36
❈ Instilling Respect, 36–37 ❈ Age-Appropriate Discipline and
Responsibility, 37–41 ❈ Fussy Babies and Toddlers, 41–45 ❈ Toilet
Training, 45–46 ❈ Discipline, 46–51 ❈ The "Terrible Twos," 51–52
❈ Avoiding Confrontation, 52–53 ❈ Anticipating the Future, 53–54

4 CHILDREN'S HEALTH AND WELL-BEING 55
Sudden Infant Death Syndrome, 55–56 ❈ Failure to Grow, 56–57
❈ Battles over Food, 57–59 ❈ Bed-Wetting, 59–61 ❈ Cruelty to
Animals, 61–62 ❈ Nightmares and Night Terrors, 62–64 ❈ Dangers
of Marijuana, 64–65 ❈ Alcohol during Pregnancy, 65–66 ❈ Eating
Disorders, 66–67 ❈ Childhood Depression, 67–68 ❈ Long-Term
Effects of Childhood Trauma, 68–70 ❈ Childhood Obesity, 70–71
❈ Stuttering, 71–72 ❈ Preparing for Adolescence, 72 ❈ Parental
Rights vs. Adolescent's Right to Privacy, 73–74

5 ATTENTION DEFICIT DISORDER
IN CHILDREN AND ADULTS 75
Recognizing Attention Deficit Disorder (ADD), 75–77 ❈ ADD without
Hyperactivity, 78–79 ❈ Cause of ADD, 79 ❈ ADD as a Lifelong
Condition, 79–80 ❈ Positive Features of ADD, 81 ❈ Treatment of
ADD, 81–83 ❈ Disciplining/Managing the ADD Child, 83–86

6 EFFECTIVE PARENTING TODAY 87
Prioritizing Parenting, 87–89 ❈ The Challenge of Parenting, 89–93
❈ Research on Parenting, 94–95 ❈ Discerning a Child's Needs,
95–96 ❈ Dealing with Grandparents, 96–97 ❈ Choosing Clothes, 97
❈ Contemporary Music, 97 ❈ Teaching Courtesy in Addressing

Adults, 98–99 ✹ Family Activities, 99–100 ✹ Raising the Adopted
Child, 100–106 ✹ Dealing with Negative Feelings toward Your
Children, 106 ✹ Gender Differences, 106–107 ✹ Importance of the
Father-Daughter Relationship, 107–108 ✹ Sexual Attitudes and
Behavior, 108–110 ✹ Television, 110–113 ✹ Video Games, 113–114
✹ Violence in Media, 114–115 ✹ Protecting Your Children, 115–117

7 DISCIPLINING THE ELEMENTARY SCHOOL CHILD . . 119
Guidelines for Discipline, 119–121 ✹ Shaping the Will without
Breaking the Spirit, 121–123 ✹ Setting and Enforcing Boundaries,
123–128 ✹ Mutual Respect, 128–129 ✹ Presenting a United Front,
129–130 ✹ External Discipline vs. Internal Control, 130–131
✹ Recognizing the Origin of Negative Behavior, 131–132 ✹ Venting
Feelings, 132–133 ✹ Inappropriate Parental Anger, 133–135 ✹ Dealing
with Your Mistakes, 135 ✹ Teaching Respect without Instilling Undue
Fear, 135–136 ✹ The Habit of Saying No, 136–137 ✹ Disciplining
Other People's Children, 137–138 ✹ Discipline in Single-Parent
Families, 138 ✹ Shaping Moods/Attitudes, 139–142 ✹ The Timing of
Negative Consequences, 142–143 ✹ Confronting Disrespectful
Behavior, 143–144 ✹ Connecting Behavior with Consequences,
144–146 ✹ Dealing with Morning Dawdling, 146–148 ✹ Reinforcing
Positive Behavior with Rewards, 148–151 ✹ Whining, 151–152
✹ Teaching Responsibility, 152–153 ✹ The Scriptural Basis for
Discipline, 153–155 ✹ Listening to Children, 155 ✹ Swearing, 155
✹ Setting Boundaries on Family Vacations, 155–156 ✹ Apologizing to
Children, 156–157 ✹ Avoiding Adolescent Rebellion, 157–158
✹ The Bottom Line in Parenting, 158–159 ✹ Advice to Parents of
Strong-Willed Children, 159

8 TO SPANK OR NOT TO SPANK 161
Effects of Spanking, 161–163 ✹ Dangers of Extremes, 164–166
✹ Guidelines for Spanking, 166–172 ✹ Corporal Punishment and the
Law, 172

9 WHAT'S A MOTHER TO DO? 173
Creating a Network, 173–174 and 175–176 ✹ Child-Care Centers,
174–175 ✹ Full-Time Mothering vs. Career, 176–181 ✹ Dealing with
Fears, 181–182

10 EDUCATION: PUBLIC, PRIVATE,
AND HOMESCHOOLING. 183
Teacher-Led vs. Student-Led Education, 183–185 ✹ Public Schools,
185–188 ✹ Corporal Punishment in Schools, 188 ✹ Class Discipline,
188–189 ✹ Work/Play Balance, 189–190 ✹ Curriculum Issues,
190–191 ✹ Intellectual Potential, 191–193 ✹ Self-Esteem, 194–195

⊗ Developmental Issues, 195–198 ⊗ Repeating Grades, 198–199 ⊗ Benefits of Formal Education, 199 ✳ Disorganization, 200 ⊗ Writing Skills, 201–202 ⊗ "The Class Clown," 202–203 ⊗ School Choice, 203–205 ⊗ Early Reading, 205–206 ⊗ Grades, 206–207 ⊗ Chaotic Classrooms, 207 ✳ Year-Round Schools, 207–208 ⊗ Homework, 208–210 ⊗ Underachievers, 210–213 ⊗ Memorization, 213–214 ⊗ Teaching Respect for Other Ethnic Groups, 214–215 ⊗ Homeschooling, 215–218 ✳ Voluntary School Prayer, 218–219

11 SEX EDUCATION: WHERE, WHEN, AND HOW . . . 221

Impact of Sex Education Programs, 221–222 ⊗ Coed Sex Education, 222–223 ⊗ Parental Involvement in Sex Education, 223–227 ✳ Timing of Sex Education, 227–229 ⊗ Encouraging Abstinence, 229–230 ⊗ When to End Formal Sex Education, 230–231 ⊗ "Safe Sex," 231–233 ⊗ Obstacles to Abstinence Education, 233–235 ⊗ What's Missing from Sex Education Programs, 235–236 ⊗ Teaching Morality, 236–237 ⊗ Sexually Transmitted Diseases, 237–242

12 SPIRITUAL LIFE OF THE FAMILY 243

Cultural Influences, 243–245 ⊗ Parents' Responsibility to Teach Spiritual Values, 245–246 ⊗ Family Devotions, 246 ⊗ Conceptualizing God for Children, 246–248 ⊗ A Critical Period in Spiritual Training, 248–249 ⊗ Santa Claus, 249–250 ⊗ Halloween, 250 ⊗ "Forcing" Religion on Children, 251–252 ✳ Rebellion against Childhood Spiritual Training, 252–257 ⊗ Praying for the Spiritual Welfare of Children, 257–264 ⊗ Dealing with Past Mistakes, 264–265 ⊗ The Role of Grandparents, 265–267

13 SIBLING RIVALRY 269

The Inevitability of Rivalry, 269–270 ⊗ Minimizing the Rivalry, 270–274 ⊗ Fighting to Attract Attention, 274–275 ⊗ Establishing a "System of Justice," 275–277

14 HELP FOR SINGLE PARENTS AND STEPPARENTS . . 279

Encouragement for Single Parents, 279–281 ✳ Blended Families, 281–283 ⊗ Time Away, 283–284 ✳ Challenges of Noncustodial Parents, 284–285 ✳ Help for Single Mothers Raising Sons, 285–286 ⊗ Visitation, 286–287 ⊗ Helping Single Parents, 287–289

15 LIVING WITH A TEENAGER 291

Causes of Promiscuity, 291–292 ⊗ Development Rates, 293–294 ⊗ Challenges of Early Adolescence, 294–297 ⊗ Power Issues, 297–303 ⊗ Fatigue, 303–304 ⊗ Self-Consciousness/Body Image,

304–305 ❋ Communication "Blackouts," 305–308 ❋ Hormonal Influences, 308–310 ❋ Channeling Energy Positively, 310 ❋ Parental Influence on Smoking/Drug Abuse, 311 ❋ Masturbation, 312–315 ❋ Dating vs. "Courtship," 315–316 ❋ Gender Roles, 316–318 ❋ Causes of Disrespectful Behavior, 318–320 ❋ Influences of Modern Music/Media, 320–323 ❋ Preparing Teens for Independence, 323–325 ❋ Picking Your Battles, 325–329 ❋ The Bottom Line on Surviving the Teen Years, 329 ❋ Absentee Fathers, 329–330 ❋ Creating a Father-Son Bond, 330–332 ❋ The Father-Daughter Relationship, 333–334 ❋ Mother-Daughter Friction, 334–336 ❋ Drawing the Line on Negative Behavior, 336–337 ❋ Teen Violence, 337–340 ❋ Motivating Teenagers, 340–343 ❋ Using Action, Not Anger, 343–345 ❋ Responding to a Teenage Pregnancy, 345–346 ❋ Symptoms of Drug Abuse, 346–347 ❋ Pros and Cons of "Privacy," 347–348 ❋ Harmful Cultural Trends, 348–349 ❋ Moms at Home during Adolescence? 349–351

16 BUILDING SELF-CONFIDENCE IN
CHILDREN AND TEENS 353
Causes of Low Self-Esteem, 353–354 ❋ Physical Attractiveness and Self-Esteem, 354–355 ❋ Intelligence and Self-Esteem, 355–356 ❋ Parental Influence in Self-Esteem, 356–358 ❋ Values That Support Self-Esteem, 358–360 ❋ The Influence of Painful Experiences, 360–361 ❋ The Influence of Toys and Culture, 361–363 ❋ Challenges of the Middle Child, 363–364 ❋ Negative Expectations, 364–365 ❋ Mental Blocks, 365–366 ❋ The Role of Teachers, 366–370 ❋ Teaching Empathy, 370–371 ❋ Self-Esteem and Sibling Rivalry, 371–372 ❋ Early Teen Issues, 372 ❋ Accepting Your Child's Basic Personality, 373–374 ❋ Humor vs. Ridicule, 374

17 THE DELICATE ART OF LETTING GO. 375
Impact of the Empty Nest on Fathers, 375–376 ❋ Parental Reluctance to Let Go, 376–378 ❋ When Adult Children Return Home, 378–379 ❋ Easing the Transition to College, 379

Endnotes. 381
Index. 387
Index of Scripture References 409

APPRECIATION

Because of the breadth of family-related topics addressed in this book, a considerable amount of support was needed for research, computer technology, aesthetic design, and administrative assistance. Fortunately, I was blessed to have the assistance of a highly professional and dedicated team throughout this project. These gifted people worked tirelessly to help me review current literature, to identify the common questions submitted through the years to Focus on the Family, and to validate my own responses in consultation with specialists in medicine, education, psychology, and other fields. Without the diligence of all these individuals, this book would not yet be off the presses.

Great appreciation is hereby expressed to Craig Osten, Steve Johnson, Karen Bethany, Kevin Triguero, Athena MacMillan, Jim Ware, Jeff Stoddard, Ken Janzen, John Perrodin, Kurt Bruner, Diane Passno, and Tricia Jones. Though you can't see their fingerprints on the pages of this book, I assure you that they are there.

This book is dedicated to these very special friends and colleagues.

INTRODUCTION

Few endeavors are as intimidating as parenting. Thirty years ago Dr. Benjamin Spock, author of *Baby and Child Care,* wrote about the insecurity that often hits mothers as they prepare to leave the hospital maternity ward. "I can remember mothers who cried on the morning they were to take their baby home. 'I won't know what to do,' they wailed."*

It hasn't always been this way. When a child was born during or before the 1900s, the new mother was tended by many friends and relatives, who hovered around her to offer their advice and help. These aunts, grandmothers, and neighbors hadn't read many books on child rearing, but they didn't need them. They were guided by a certain traditional wisdom that gave them confidence in handling babies and children. They had answers, whether right or wrong, for every question, and they were willing to share what they knew with those they loved. So a new mother was undergirded by older women who had many years' experience in caring for babies and children.

That loving support system has all but disappeared in recent decades. Many women live in a mobile society in which neighbors are often strangers. Their own mothers, aunts, and sisters have moved far away to Detroit or Dallas or Portland—and they might not be trusted even if

*Dr. Benjamin Spock, "How Not to Bring Up a Bratty Child." *Redbook* (February 1974): 31.

they were available for help. This isolation has shaken the confidence of new mothers who are aware that there is too much they don't know about kids.

Today's moms and dads not only lack family support; millions are guided by no underlying philosophy of child rearing. After all, everything seems more complicated now than in the old days when life was slow and predictable. New challenges and troubling ethical questions spring up faster than we can resolve them. And all the old rules are under assault as revolutionary change flows through our lives.

The resulting anxiety has brought parents rushing to the "experts" for information and advice. They turn to pediatricians, psychologists, psychiatrists, and educators for answers to their questions about the complexities of parenthood. Consequently, increasing numbers of children in Western nations since the 1920s have been reared according to this professional consultation. In fact, no country on earth has embraced the teachings of child psychology and the offerings of family specialists more than has the United States.

It is now appropriate that we ask, "What has been the effect of this professional influence?" One would expect that the mental health of our children would exceed that of individuals raised in nations not having this technical assistance. Such has not been the case. Juvenile delinquency, drug abuse, alcoholism, unwanted pregnancies, mental illness, and suicide are rampant among the young and continue their steady rise. In many ways, we have made a mess of parenthood! Of course, I would not blame all these woes on the bad advice of the "experts," but I believe they played a role in creating the problem. Why? Because in general, behavioral scientists have disregarded the Judeo-Christian ethic and the timeless wisdom that it offers.

Instead, the twentieth century spawned a generation of professionals who ignored the parental attitudes and practices of more than two thousand years, substituting their own wobbly-legged insights of the moment. Each authority, writing from his own limited experience and reflecting his own unique biases, has sold us his guesses and suppositions as though they represented Truth itself.

These false teachings have included the notions that loving discipline is damaging, religious instruction is hazardous, defiance is a valuable ventilator of anger, authority is dangerous, chaos produces creativity, and on and on it goes. In more recent years, this humanistic perspective has become even more extreme and anti-Christian, from homosexual propaganda taught to children to safe-sex indoctrination of today's teenagers.

This is where moral relativism leads—this is the ultimate product of a human endeavor that accepts no standards, honors no cultural values, acknowledges no absolutes, and serves no god except the human mind. King Solomon wrote about such foolish efforts in Proverbs 14:12: "There is a way which seemeth right unto a man, but the end thereof are the ways of death" (KJV).

Now admittedly, the book you are reading also contains many suggestions and perspectives that I have not attempted to prove. How do my writings differ from the unsupported recommendations of those whom I have criticized? There is a single answer. The advice I've offered is more than a reflection of my own guesses and suppositions about this and that. Nestled behind and below most of these responses is a guiding philosophy that has been drawn from two reliable and time-honored sources.

The first comes from the wisdom of the ages. I have drawn heavily from the traditional approach to parenthood that was born of two thousand years' experience. It has been handed down generation to generation as the centuries unfolded. Surely something of value was learned by all those men and women who have gone before. We should consider how they did things and what they believed before we abandon their secure moorings.

The second foundation for this book emanates from the Judeo-Christian system of values. There are numerous principles woven into the Holy Scriptures that apply to everyday family life. They were inspired by the Creator Himself, who is the originator of the institutions of marriage and parenthood. Whether or not it is obvious, those concepts have provided the basis for many of the answers I have provided. And within that scriptural foundation lies the confidence of which I spoke.

The eternal plan for the family, as I understand it, begins with a lifelong commitment between a man and a woman, undergirded by absolute loyalty and fidelity to one another. The husband then devotes himself to the best interests of his wife, providing for her needs and protecting her to the point of death if necessary. The wife honors her husband, devotes herself to him, and respects his leadership in the family. If they are blessed with children, those children are recognized to have inestimable worth and dignity—not for what they produce or accomplish, but for who they are as

God's own handiwork. They are taught while very young to yield to the authority of their parents. Boundaries of behavior are established in advance and then enforced with reasonable firmness. They learn honesty, integrity, humility, self-control, personal responsibility, sexual purity, concern for others, the work ethic, and the fundamentals of their faith. They are never subjected to humiliation, rejection, sexual exploitation, or abuse of any kind. Instead, they enjoy unconditional love and are raised "in the fear and admonition of the Lord."

Let me leave you with this thought: When you and I have reached the end of our brief journey on this earth, nothing will matter more to us than the quality of our families and the depth of our relationship with God. "Meaning" in this human experience is drawn essentially from these two sources. If that is true, then should we not live by those priorities every day that remains to us? It is my prayer that the advice in this book will be helpful in building both a warm and satisfying family and a personal relationship with Jesus Christ.

James C. Dobson

James C. Dobson, Ph.D.

UNDERSTANDING THE
NATURE OF CHILDREN

Q1 I took a class in child development, and the professor emphasized the influence of culture in shaping the human personality. He said, "All behavior is caused by what we experience." What does that mean, and do you agree with it?

It means that children are merely responders to environmental influences occurring in a lifetime and that if all those experiential factors were known, every behavior (and misbehavior) would be explained. Do I agree with this view? Not for a minute. It is a mechanistic, deterministic theory that makes robots out of human beings. If it were valid, we would never be capable of independent action, free choice, or discernment of right and wrong. This is an unbiblical theory that strikes at the heart of the God-man relationship. We are morally accountable because the Creator put within us the ability to think, to choose, to judge, and even the freedom to do evil. We are capable of rational thought that is greatly influenced, but not "caused," by what we experience. There are other influences that come from within—including those related to the temperament with which we arrive in the delivery room. Human behavior is far more complicated than believed in the past, yet some learned people still think we are the sum total of our experiences.

The psychologist who spoke at your school was expressing a historic tenet of his (and my) profession. I just happen to disagree with it emphatically.

Q2 Talk more about the inborn temperament in babies. What do we know about their little personalities before they have interacted with the world at all?

Philosophers Locke and Rousseau told us in the seventeenth and eighteenth centuries that babies came into the world as *tabulae rasae,* or "blank slates," upon which society and the environment wrote the fundamentals of personality.[1] But they were also wrong. Every newborn is unique from every other baby, even from the first moments outside the womb. Except for identical twins, triplets, etc., no two are alike in biochemistry or genetics.

How foolish of philosophers and behavioral scientists to have thought otherwise. If God makes every grain of sand unique and every snowflake like no other, how simplistic to have believed He massproduces little human robots. That is nonsense. We are, after all, made in His image.

Just ask the real experts—the mothers who understand their babies better than anyone. They'll tell you that each of their infants had a different "feel"—a different personality—from the first moment they were held. If these mothers are eventually blessed with six or eight or even twenty children, they will continue to say emphatically that every one of them was unique and distinct from the others when only one hour old. They are right—and their perceptions are being confirmed by scientific inquiry.

Q3 What does research tell us about the personalities of newborns?

One of the most ambitious studies yet conducted took a period of three decades to complete. That investigation is known in professional literature as the New York Longitudinal Study. The findings from this investigation, led by psychiatrists Stella Chess and Alexander Thomas, were reported in their excellent book for parents entitled *Know Your Child*.

Chess and Thomas found that babies not only differ significantly from one another at the moment of birth, but those differences tend to be rather persistent throughout childhood. Even more interestingly, they observed three broad categories, or patterns of temperaments, into which the majority of children can be classified. First they referred to "the difficult child," who is characterized by negative reactions to people, intense mood swings, irregular sleep patterns and feeding schedules, frequent periods of crying, and violent tantrums when frustrated.

Does that sound familiar? I described those individuals many years ago as "strong-willed" children.

The second pattern is called "the easy child," who manifests a positive approach to people, quiet adaptability to new situations, regular sleep patterns and feeding schedules, and a willingness to accept the rules of the game. The authors concluded, "Such a youngster is usually a joy to his or her parents, pediatrician and teachers."[2] Amen.

My term for the easy child is "compliant."

The third category was given the title "slow-to-warm-up" or "shy." These youngsters respond negatively to new situations, and they adapt slowly. However, they are less intense than difficult children, and they tend to have regular sleeping and feeding schedules. When they are upset or frustrated, they typically withdraw from the situation and react mildly, rather than explode with anger and rebellion.

Not every child fits into one of these categories, of course, but approximately 65 percent do. Drs. Chess and Thomas also emphasized that babies are fully human at birth, being able immediately to relate to their parents and learn from their environments. I doubt if that news will come as a surprise to most mothers, who never believed in the "blank slate" theory, anyway.

It should not be difficult to understand why these findings from longitudinal research have been exciting to me. They confirm my own clinical observations, not only about the wonderful complexity of human beings, but also about the categories of temperament identified by Drs. Chess and Thomas.

Q4 **Tell me why some kids with every advantage and opportunity seem to turn out bad, while others raised in terrible homes become pillars in the community. I know one young man who grew up in squalid circumstances, yet he is such a fine person today. How did his parents manage to raise such a responsible son when they didn't even seem to care?**

That illustrates just the point I have been trying to make. Neither heredity nor environment will account for all human behavior. There is something else there—something from within—that also operates to make us who we are. Some behavior is caused, and some plainly isn't.

Several years ago, for example, I had dinner with two parents who had unofficially "adopted" a thirteen-year-old boy. This youngster followed their son home one afternoon and asked if he could spend the night. As it turned out, he stayed with them for almost a week without so much as a phone call coming from his mother. It was later learned that she works sixteen hours a day and has no interest in her son. Her alcoholic husband divorced her several years ago and left town without a trace. The boy had been abused, unloved, and ignored through much of his life.

Given this background, what kind of kid do you think he is today—a druggie? a foulmouthed delinquent? a lazy, insolent bum? No. He is polite to adults; he is a hard worker; he makes good grades in school and enjoys helping around the house. This boy is like a lost puppy who desperately wants a good home. He begged the family to adopt him officially so he could have a real father and a loving mother. His own mom couldn't care less.

How could this teenager be so well disciplined and polished despite his lack of training? I don't know. It is simply within him. He reminds me of my wonderful friend David Hernandez. David and his parents came to America illegally from Mexico more than fifty years ago and nearly starved to death before they found work. They eventually survived by helping to harvest the potato crop throughout the state of California. During this era, David lived under trees or in the open fields. His father made a stove out of an oil drum half-filled with dirt. The open campfire was the centerpiece of their home.

David never had a roof over his head until his parents finally moved into an abandoned chicken coop. His mother covered the boarded walls with cheap wallpaper, and David thought they were living in luxury. Then one day, the city of San Jose condemned the area, and David's "house" was torn down. He couldn't understand why the community would destroy so fine a place.

Given this beginning, how can we explain the man that David Hernandez became? He graduated near the top of his class in high school and was granted a scholarship to college. Again, he earned high marks and four years later entered Loma Linda University School of Medicine. Once more, he scored in the top 10 percent of his class and continued in a residency in obstetrics and gynecology. Eventually, he served as a professor of OB-GYN at both Loma Linda University and the University of Southern California medical schools. Then, at the peak of his career, his life began to unravel.

I'll never forget the day Dr. Hernandez called me on the telephone. He had just been released from the hospital following a battery of laboratory tests. The diagnosis? Sclerosing cholangitis, a liver disorder that was invariably fatal at that time. We lost this fine husband, father, and friend six years later at the age of forty-three. I loved him like a brother, and I still miss him today.

Again, I ask, how could such discipline and genius come from these infertile circumstances? Who would have thought that this deprived Mexican boy sitting out there in the dirt would someday become one of the most loved and respected surgeons of his era? Where did the motivation originate? From what bubbling spring did his ambition and thirst for knowledge flow? He had no books, took no educational trips, knew no scholars. Yet he reached for the sky. Why did it happen to David Hernandez and not the youngster with every advantage and opportunity?

Why have so many children of prominent and loving parents grown up in ideal circumstances only to reject it all for the streets of Atlanta, San Francisco, or New York? Good answers are simply not available. It apparently comes down to this: God chooses to use individuals in unique ways. Beyond that mysterious relationship, we must simply conclude that some kids seem born to make it and others are determined to fail. Someone reminded me recently that the same boiling water that softens the carrot also hardens the egg. Likewise, some individuals react positively to certain circumstances and others negatively. We don't know why.

Two things are clear to me from this understanding. First, parents have been far too quick to take the credit or blame for the way their children turn out. Those with bright young superstars stick out their chests and say, "Look what we accomplished." Those with twisted and irresponsible kids wonder, "Where did we go wrong?" Well, neither is entirely accurate. No one would deny that parents play an important role in the development and training of their children. But they are only part of the formula from which a young adult is assembled.

Second, behavioral scientists have been far too simplistic in their explanation of human behavior. We are more than the aggregate of our experiences. We are more than the quality of our nutrition. We are more than our genetic heritage. We are more than our biochemistry. And certainly, we are more than our parents' influence. God has created us as unique individuals, capable of independent and rational thought that is not attributable to any source. That is what makes the task of parenting so challenging and rewarding. Just when you think you have your kids figured out, you had better brace yourself! Something new is coming your way.

Q5 Does Scripture confirm that babies have temperaments or personalities before birth?

Yes, in several references we learn that God knows and relates to unborn children as individuals. He said to the prophet Jeremiah, "Before I formed you in the

womb I knew you, and before you were born I conse-
crated you; I appointed you a prophet to the nations"
(Jeremiah 1:5, RSV). The apostle Paul said he was also
chosen before birth (see Ephesians 1:4). And in a remarkable account, we are told of the prenatal development of the twins Jacob and Esau. As predicted
before their births, one turned out to be rebellious
and tough while the other was something of a mama's
boy. They were fighting before they were born and
continued in conflict through much of their lives (see
Genesis 25:22-27). Then later, in one of the most
mysterious and disturbing statements in the Bible, the
Lord said, "Jacob have I loved, but Esau have I hated"
(Romans 9:13, KJV). Apparently, God discerned a rebellious nature in Esau before he was born and knew
that he would not be receptive to the divine Spirit.

These references tell us that unborn children are
unique individuals with whom God is already acquainted. These examples also confirm for me, at
least, the wickedness of abortion, which destroys
those embryonic little personalities.

Q6 I have two children who are as different as night
and day. In fact, they conform perfectly to your
description of "strong-willed" and "compliant" children.
One is a spitfire, and the other is a sweetheart. I am very
interested in knowing more about what this means for
them long-term. Beyond everyday issues of discipline and
relating within a family, what can you tell me about these
kids?

You'll be interested to know that more than thirty-
five thousand parents participated in a study I conducted to answer those specific questions. It is described in detail in my book *Parenting Isn't for
Cowards,* but let me boil down eleven of the most important findings. Remember that these conclusions

represent common traits and characteristics that may or may not apply to your two children. These descriptions represent what typically happens with very strong-willed children (SWC) and very compliant children (CC) as the years unfold.

Conclusion 1: In the human family, there are nearly three times as many SWCs as CCs. Nearly every family with multiple children has at least one SWC.

Conclusion 2: Male SWCs outnumber females by about 5 percent, and female CCs outnumber males by about 6 percent. Thus, there is a slight tendency for males to have tougher temperaments and for females to be more compliant, but it can be, and often is, reversed.

Conclusion 3: The birth order has nothing to do with being strong-willed or compliant. These elements of temperament are basically inherited and can occur in the eldest or in the baby.

Conclusion 4: Most parents know they have an SWC very early. One-third can tell it at birth. Two-thirds know by the first birthday, and 92 percent are certain by the third birthday. Parents of compliant children know it even earlier.

Conclusion 5: The temperaments of children tend to reflect those of their parents. Although there are many exceptions, two strong-willed parents are more likely to produce tough-minded kids and vice versa.

Conclusion 6: What can parents expect from SWCs in the teen years? The answer? A battle! Fully 74 percent of SWCs rebel significantly during adolescence.

Conclusion 7: Incredibly, only 3 percent of CCs experience severe rebellion in adolescence, and just 14 percent even go into mild rebellion. They start out life with a smile on their face and keep it there into young adulthood.

Conclusion 8: The best news for parents of SWCs is the rapid decrease in their rebellion in young adulthood. It drops almost immediately in the early twenties and then trails off even more from there. Some are still angry into their twenties and early thirties, but the fire is gone for the majority. They peacefully rejoin the human community.

Conclusion 9: The CC is much more likely to be a good student than the SWC. Nearly three times as many SWCs made Ds and Fs during the last two years of high school as did CCs. Approximately 80 percent of CCs were A and B students.

Conclusion 10: The CC is considerably better adjusted socially than the SWC. It would appear that the youngster who is inclined to challenge the authority of his parents is also more likely to behave offensively with his peers.

Conclusion 11: The CC typically enjoys much higher self-esteem than the SWC. It is difficult to overestimate the importance of this finding. Only 19 percent of compliant teenagers either disliked themselves (17 percent) or felt extreme self-hatred (2 percent). Of the very strong-willed teenagers, however, 35 percent disliked themselves, and 8 percent experienced extreme self-hatred.

Those were the primary findings from our study. It yielded a picture of the compliant child as being someone more at peace with himself or herself, as well as with parents, teachers, and peers.

The strong-willed child, by contrast, seems compelled from within to fuss, fight, test, question, resist, and challenge. Why is he or she like that? It is difficult to say, except to affirm that they are more unsettled in every aspect of their lives. We do know that lower self-esteem is related to the excessive peer dependency, academic difficulties, social problems, and even rebellion we have seen. Acceptance of one's intrinsic worth is the core of the personality. When it is unsteady, everything else is affected.

Q7 What are the long-range implications of raising a strong-willed child? What can we expect as the years go by?

Well, I can give you a few encouraging conclusions from our study. The tendency of strong-willed children is to return to parental values when they reach adulthood. Parents told us that 85 percent of their grown SWCs (twenty-four years of age and older) came back to what they had been taught—entirely or at least "somewhat." That is good news. Only 15 percent were so headstrong that they rejected their family's core values in their mid-twenties. In those exceptional cases, I'll wager that other problems and sources of pain were involved.

What this means, first of all, is that these tough-minded kids will argue and fight and complain throughout their years at home, but the majority will turn around when they reach young adulthood and do what their parents most desired. That should be reassuring. Furthermore, if we could have evaluated these individuals at thirty-five instead of twenty-four years of age, we would have seen that even fewer were still in rebellion against parental values.

Second, raising a strong-willed child (or a houseful of them) can be a lonely job for parents. You can begin to feel like yours is the only family that has gone through these struggles. Don't believe it. In another study of three thousand parents, we found that 85 percent of families had at least one strong-willed child. *This is parenthood. This is human nature.*

Third, I urge you as parents of strong-willed children not to feel "cheated" or depressed by the assignment of raising such individuals. You are not an exception or the butt of some cruel cosmic joke. All human beings, including the very compliant child, arrive with a generous assortment of flaws. Yes, it is more difficult to raise an independent little fellow or gal, but you can do it! You can, through prayer and supplication before the Lord, bring him or her to that period of harmony in early adulthood that makes the effort worthwhile. I also believe that you can increase the odds of transmitting your values to these individuals by following some time-honored principles found in Scripture. So hang in there! Nothing of value in life comes easy anyway, except the free gift of salvation from Jesus Christ.

Hold tightly to Solomon's encouraging words, "Train up a child in the way he should go: and when he is old, he will not depart from it" (Proverbs 22:6, KJV).

Q8 Okay, I understand the strong-willed child better than I did. But tell me how to get our son through these tough years. He is tough as nails. What specific suggestions do you have for us?

Here is a summary of some approaches or ideas that I think are important:

1. You should not blame yourself for the temperament with which your child was born. He (or she) is simply a tough kid to handle, and your task is to rise to the challenge.
2. He is in greater danger because of his inclination

to test the limits and scale the walls. Your utmost diligence and wisdom will be required to deal with him.

3. If you fail to understand his lust for power and independence, you can exhaust your resources and bog down in guilt. It will benefit no one.

4. For parents who have just begun, take charge of your babies. Hold tightly to the reins of authority in the early days, and build an attitude of respect during your brief window of opportunity. You will need every ounce of "awe" you can get during the years to come. Once you have established your right to lead, begin to let go systematically, year by year.

5. Don't panic, even during the storms of adolescence. Better times are ahead.

6. Don't let your son get too far from you emotionally. Stay in touch. Don't write him off, even when every impulse is to do just that. He needs you now more than ever before.

7. Give him time to find himself, even if he appears not to be searching.

8. Most important, I urge you to hold your children before the Lord in fervent prayer throughout their years at home. I am convinced that there is no other source of confidence and wisdom in parenting. There is not enough knowledge in the books, mine or anyone else's, to counteract the evil that surrounds our kids today. Teenagers are confronted by drugs, alcohol, sex, and foul language wherever they turn. And, of course, the peer pressure on them is enormous. We must bathe them in prayer every day of their lives. The God who made your children will hear your petitions. He has promised to do so. After all, He loves them more than you do.

And a concluding word: Remember that anyone can raise the easy kid. Guiding an SWC through the rebellious years takes a pro with a lot of love to give. I'll bet you're up to the task!

Q9 What are the special needs of a compliant kid— one that goes along to get along? Does he have any special needs?

That's a great question, and the answer is yes. When one child is a stick of dynamite and the other is an all-star sweetheart, the cooperative, gentle individual can easily be taken for granted. If there's an unpleasant job to be done, he may be expected to do it because Mom and Dad just don't have the energy to fight with the tiger. When it is necessary for one child to sacrifice or do without, there's a tendency to pick the one who won't complain as loudly. Under these circumstances, the compliant boy or girl comes out on the short end of the stick.

The consequences of such inequity should be obvious. The responsible child often becomes angry over time. He has a sense of powerlessness and resentment that simmers below the surface. He's like the older brother in the parable of the Prodigal Son told by Jesus. He didn't rebel against his father. He stayed behind and ran the farm while his irresponsible brother squandered his money on fun and games. Who could blame him for resenting little bro? His response is typical of the compliant, hardworking sibling.

I strongly recommend that parents seek to balance the scales in dealing with the compliant child. Make sure he gets his fair share of parental attention. Help him find ways to cope with his overbearing sibling. And, within reason, give him the right to make his own decisions.

There's nothing simple about raising kids, is

there? Even the "easiest" of them needs our very best effort.

Q10 How can you say that precious little newborns come into the world inherently evil? I agree with the experts who say that babies are born good and they only learn to do wrong later.

Please understand that the issue here is not with the purity or innocence of babies. No one would question their preciousness as creations of God. The point of disagreement concerns the tendencies and inclinations they have inherited. People who believe in "innate goodness" would have us believe that human beings are naturally unselfish, honest, respectful, kind to others, self-controlled, obedient to authority, etc. Children, as you indicated, then subsequently learn to do wrong when they are exposed to a corrupt and misguided society. Bad *experiences* are responsible for bad behavior. To raise healthy kids, then, it is the task of parents to provide a loving environment and then stay out of the way. Natural goodness will flow from within.

This is the humanistic perspective on childish nature. Millions of people believe it to be true. Most psychologists have also accepted and taught this notion throughout the twentieth century. There is only one thing wrong with the concept. It is entirely inaccurate.

Q11 How can you be so sure about the nature of children? What evidence do you have to support the belief that their tendency is to do wrong?

We'll start with what the "Owner's Manual" has to say about human nature. Only the Creator of children can tell us how He made them, and He has done that in Scripture. It teaches that we are born in sin, having inherited a disobedient nature from Adam.

King David said, "In sin did my mother *conceive* me" (Psalm 51:5, KJV, italics added), meaning that this tendency to do wrong was transmitted genetically. Paul tells us it has infected every person who ever lived. "For *all* have sinned, and come short of the glory of God" (Romans 3:23, KJV, italics added). Therefore, with or without bad associations, children are naturally inclined toward rebellion, selfishness, dishonesty, aggression, exploitation, and greed. They don't have to be taught these behaviors. They are natural expressions of their humanness.

Although this perspective is viewed with disdain by the secular world today, the evidence to support it is overwhelming. How else do we explain the pugnacious and perverse nature of every society on earth? Bloody warfare has been the centerpiece of world history for more than five thousand years. People of every race and creed around the globe have tried to rape, plunder, burn, blast, and kill each other century after century. Peace has been but a momentary pause when they stopped to reload! Plato said more than 2,350 years ago, "Only dead men have seen an end to war."[3] He was right, and it will continue that way until the Prince of Peace comes.

Not only have nations warred against each other since the beginning of time, we also find a depressing incidence of murder, drug abuse, child molestation, prostitution, adultery, homosexuality, and dishonesty among individuals. How would we account for this pervasive evil in a world of people who are naturally inclined toward good? Have they really drifted into these antisocial and immoral behaviors despite their inborn tendencies? If so, surely one society in all the world would have been able to preserve the goodness with which children are born. Where is it? Does such a place exist? No, although admittedly some societies are more moral than others. Still, none reflect the harmony that might be expected from the natural-goodness theorists. Why not? Because their basic premise is wrong.

Q 12 What, then, does this biblical understanding mean for parents? Are they to consider their babies guilty before they have done anything wrong?

Of course not. Children are not responsible for their sins until they reach an age of accountability—and that time frame is known only to God. On the other hand, parents should not be surprised when rebellious or mischievous behavior occurs. It *will* happen, probably by the eighteenth month or before. Anyone who has watched a toddler throw a temper tantrum when she doesn't get her way must be hard-pressed to explain how that expression of "innate goodness" got so mixed up! Did her mother or father model the tantrum for her, falling on the floor, slobbering, kicking, crying, and screaming? I would hope not. Either way, the kid needs no demonstration. Rebellion comes naturally to his and her entire generation—although in some individuals it is more pronounced than in others.

For this reason, parents can and must train, mold, correct, guide, punish, reward, instruct, warn, teach, and love their kids during the formative years. Their purpose is to shape that inner nature and keep it from tyrannizing the entire family. Ultimately, however, only Jesus Christ can cleanse it and make it "wholly acceptable" to the Master. This is what the Bible teaches about people, and this is what I firmly believe.

Q 13 Why can't parents get children to obey just by explaining what they want them to do? Why is it so often necessary to punish or raise our voices to get

**them to cooperate? Why can't they just accept a few
reasonable rules and avoid all that conflict? It just doesn't
add up to me.**

After working with children for years, I'm convinced that their challenging behavior is motivated in
part by the desire for power that lies deep within the
human spirit. From a very early age, they just don't
want anyone telling them what to do. They are also
great admirers of strength and courage. Maybe this is
why mythical characters like Superman, Robin
Hood, and Wonder Woman have been so prominent
in the folklore of children. Perhaps it is also why kids
brag that "My dad can beat up your dad!" (One child
said in reply, "That's nothing; my mom can beat up
my dad, too!")

It is a fact that most boys, and some girls, care
about the issue of "who's toughest." Whenever a
youngster moves into a new neighborhood or a new
school district, he often has to fight, either verbally
or physically, to establish himself on the hierarchy of
strength. There is usually a "top dog" in a group of
children, who bosses everyone else around. There is
also a little defeated pup at the bottom of the heap,
who takes the brunt of everyone's abuse. And each
child between those extremes usually knows where
he or she ranks in relation to the others.

I believe this admiration for power also makes
children want to know how tough their leaders are.
They will occasionally disobey adults for the precise
purpose of testing their determination and courage.
Thus, whether you are a parent or grandparent or
Boy Scout leader or bus driver or Brownie leader or
schoolteacher, I can guarantee that sooner or later,
one of the children under your authority will clench
his little fist and challenge your leadership. He will
convey this message by his disobedient manner: "I

don't think you are tough enough to make me do what you say." The way you handle that confrontation is being watched closely by every child in the group. Your reaction will determine how soon another occurs and with what intensity it is driven.

Q14 My wife and I have two very strong-willed kids who are hard to handle. They seem to need to test us, and they're the happiest and most contented when we are the toughest on them. Why do they insist on making us growl at them and even punish them more than we'd like to?

It is curious, isn't it, that some children seem to enjoy fighting with their parents. It's a function of the pugnacious temperament with which they are born. Many kids just like to run things and seem to enjoy picking fights.

There is another factor that is related to a child's sense of security. Let me illustrate it this way. Imagine you're driving a car over the Royal Gorge Bridge in Colorado, which is suspended hundreds of feet above the canyon floor. As a first-time traveler, you're pretty tense as you drive across. It is a scary experience. I knew one little fellow who was so awed by the view over the side of the bridge that he said, "Wow, Daddy! If you fell off of here, it'd kill you constantly!"

Now suppose there were no guardrails on the side of the bridge. Where would you steer the car? Right down the middle of the road. Even though you don't plan to hit those protective railings along the side, you just feel more secure knowing that they're there.

It's the same way with children. There is security in defined limits. They need to know precisely what the rules are and who's available to enforce them.

Whenever a strong-willed child senses that the boundaries may have moved, or that his or her parents may have lost their nerve, he or she will often precipitate a fight just to test the limits again. They may not admit that they want you to be the boss, but they breathe easier when you prove that you are.

2

RAISING THE
PRESCHOOL CHILD

Q15 I have a very fussy eight-month-old baby who cries whenever I put her down. My pediatrician says she is healthy and that she cries just because she wants me to hold her all the time. I do give her a lot of attention, but I simply can't keep her on my lap all day long. How can I make her less fussy?

The crying of infants is an important form of communication. Through their tears we learn of their hunger, fatigue, discomfort, or diaper disaster. Thus, it is important to listen to those calls for help and interpret them accordingly. On the other hand, your pediatrician is right. It is possible to create a fussy, demanding baby by rushing to pick her up every time she utters a whimper or a sigh. Infants are fully capable of learning to manipulate their parents through a process called reinforcement, whereby any behavior that produces a pleasant result will tend to recur. Thus, a healthy baby can keep her mother hopping around her nursery twelve hours a day (or night) by simply forcing air past her sandpaper larynx. To avoid this consequence, it is important to strike a balance between giving your baby the attention she needs and establishing her as a tiny dictator. Don't be afraid to let her cry for a reasonable period of time (which is thought to be healthy for the lungs), although it is necessary to listen to the tone of her voice for the difference between random discontent and genuine distress. Most mothers learn to recognize this distinction very quickly.

When my daughter was one year of age, I used to stand out of sight at the doorway of her nursery for four or five minutes, awaiting a momentary lull in the crying before going to pick her up. By so doing, I reinforced the pauses rather than the tears. You might try the same approach.

Q 16 We have a one-year-old daughter, and we want to raise her right. I've heard that parents can increase the mental abilities of their children if they stimulate them properly during the early years. Is this accurate, and if so, how can I accomplish this with my baby?

Research has shown that parents can, indeed, increase the intellectual capability of their children. This conclusion was first reached through the renowned Harvard University Preschool Project. A team of researchers led by Dr. Burton White studied young children aged eight to eighteen months over a ten-year period, hoping to discover which experiences in the early years of life contribute to the development of healthy, intelligent human beings. The results of this important study are summarized below.

a) It is increasingly clear that the origins of human competence are to be found in a critical period of development between eight and eighteen months of age. The child's experiences during these brief months do more to influence future intellectual competence than any time before or after.

b) The single most important environmental factor in the life of the child is his or her mother. "She is on the hook," said Dr. White, and exercises more influence on her child's experiences than any other person or circumstance.

c) The amount of live language directed to a child (not to be confused with television, radio, or overheard conversations) is vital to his or her development of fundamental linguistic, intellectual, and social skills. The researchers concluded, "Providing a rich social life for a twelve- to fifteen-month-old child is the best thing you can do to guarantee a good mind."

d) Those children who were given free access to living areas of their homes progressed much faster than those whose movements were restricted.

e) The nuclear family is the most important educational delivery system. If we are going to produce capable, healthy children, it will be by strengthening family units and by improving the interactions that occur within them.

f) The best parents were those who excelled at three key functions:

1. They were superb designers and organizers of their children's environments.

2. They permitted their children to interrupt them for brief, thirty-second episodes, during which personal consultation, comfort, information, and enthusiasm were exchanged.

3. They were firm disciplinarians while simultaneously showing great affection for their children.[4]

Occasionally, information comes along that needs to be filed away for future reference. These findings from the Harvard University Preschool Project are that significant. You will not want to forget these six findings. I believe they hold the keys to raising healthy children.

Q.17 Can the findings from Dr. White's study be applied by parents whose children are placed in child-care centers?

Of course. It is just more difficult and challenging when an employee substitutes for a mother and father during the prime-time hours of the day.

Q.18 At age twenty-one, I became pregnant and had a baby girl. The father and I never married. My daughter is almost three years old now, and I know she will soon be asking questions about her daddy. How should I explain this situation to her, and when should that explanation be given?

Eventually, you will want to tell your daughter the whole story about her father and describe your relationship with him, but now is not the time to do that. She must be mature and emotionally ready to deal with those details. On the other hand, you don't want to treat the subject as a dark secret that haunts the two of you. Neither do you want to be untruthful and tell yarns that will later have to be admitted.

At this early stage, I'd suggest that you respond confidently and lovingly to the inevitable questions about "Daddy." When the appropriate occasions surface, begin giving her vague explanations that are based in truth but are short of the whole story. You may wish to say something like this, "Your daddy went away before you were born. He didn't want to live with me. I'm not sure why. Maybe he had some problems that made it hard to be a husband. I don't know. I'm sure if he had ever met you, he'd have loved you very much. But he left before you were born. Do you know what I think? I think we should start praying that the Lord will send us another man to be my husband and your daddy. Would you like that?"

I recognize that there are potential problems with a reply of this nature and that it may not be entirely appropriate for every case. It simply attempts to lay the foundation for the more in-depth discussions to follow. Just as important, it likely will defuse the situation early on while conveying a sense of affirmation, security, and mutual reliance upon the Lord. And once you've achieved that, take a deep breath and let it rest for a while! If you're at peace, your daughter will be, too—and there will be ample time to add detail to the picture as God directs.

Q19 I get very upset because my two-year-old boy will not sit still and be quiet in church. He knows he's not supposed to be noisy, but he hits his toys on the pew and sometimes talks out loud. Should I reprimand him for being disruptive?

With all respect, your question reveals a rather poor understanding of the nature of toddlers. Most two-year-olds, those who are normally active, can no more fold their hands in church and listen to a sermon intended for adults than they could swim the Atlantic Ocean. They squirm and churn and burn because they must. You just can't hold a toddler down. All their waking hours are spent in activity, and that's normal for this stage of development. So I do not recommend that your child be punished for this behavior. I think he should be left in the church nursery, where he can shake the foundations without disturbing the worship service. If there is no nursery, I suggest, if it is possible from a financial point of view, that he be left at home with a sitter until he is at least three years of age.

Q.20 My five-year-old is developing a problem with lying, and I don't know how to handle it. What can I do to get him to tell the truth?

Lying is a problem with which every parent must deal. All children distort the truth from time to time, and some become inveterate liars. Responding appropriately is a task that requires an understanding of child development and the characteristics of a particular individual. I'll offer some general advice that will have to be modified to fit specific cases.

First, understand that a young child may or may not fully comprehend the difference between lies and the truth. There is a very thin line between fantasy and reality in the mind of a preschool boy or girl. So before you react in a heavy-handed manner, be sure you know what he understands and what his intent is.

For those children who are clearly lying to avoid unpleasant consequences or to gain an advantage of some sort, parents need to use that circumstance as a "teachable moment." The greatest emphasis should be given to telling the truth in all situations. It is a virtue that should be taught—not just when a lie has occurred, but at other times as well. In your personal devotions with the children, turn to Proverbs 6:16-19 and read that insightful passage together. It says, "There are six things the Lord hates, seven that are detestable to him: haughty eyes, a lying tongue, hands that shed innocent blood, a heart that devises wicked schemes, feet that are quick to rush into evil, a false witness who pours out lies and a man who stirs up dissension among brothers."

These are insightful verses around which to structure devotional periods with children. Explain who Solomon was, why his teachings are so important to us, and why the Scripture is our friend. It is like a flashlight on a dark night, guiding our footsteps and keeping us on the right path. It will even protect us while we are asleep, if we will bind it on our heart forever. Memorize the passage in Proverbs together so it can be referred to in other contexts. Use it as a springboard to discussions of virtues and behavior that will please God. Each verse can be applied to everyday situations so that a child can begin to feel accountable for what he does and says.

Returning to the specific issue of lying, point out to the child that in a list of seven things the Lord hates most, two of them deal with dishonesty. Telling the truth is something God cares about, and therefore it should matter to us. This will explain why you are going to insist that your son or daughter learn to tell the truth even when it hurts to do so. Your goal is to lay a foundation that will help you underscore a commitment to honesty in the future.

The next time your child tells a blatant lie, you can return to this discussion and to the Scripture on which it was based. At some point, when you feel the maturity level of the youngster makes it appropriate, you should begin to insist that the truth be told and to impose mild punishment if it isn't. Gradually, over a period of years, you should be able to teach the virtue of truthfulness to your sons and daughters.

Of course, you can undermine everything you're trying to establish by your own dishonesty in front of your kids. Believe me, they will note it and behave likewise. If Daddy can twist the truth, he'll have little authority in preventing them from doing the same.

Q.21 I'm concerned about the violent content of some children's cartoon shows and the toys and other products connected with them. My husband thinks they're harmless. What's your point of view?

I share your misgivings. There's a trend toward a brand of violence in some of today's cartoons and toys that I see as a dangerous departure from the more traditional combat-type games in which boys have always engaged. For one thing, the characters tend to be adults involved in adult activities, some of which are highly questionable. I don't feel that they are appropriate role models for impressionable young children. In addition, there's an occult or New Age flavor to many of these programs and products. The settings are mythical or futuristic, and the action often revolves around superstition, sorcery, and magic. For these reasons they concern me for spiritual as well as psychological reasons.

The electronic media has incredible power to "sell" these dubious heroes and their exploits to our children. Studies have measured actual physiological changes that occur when kids are watching a violent television program or movie: the pulse rate quickens, the eyes dilate, the hands sweat, the mouth goes dry, and breathing accelerates. It should be obvious that this kind of "entertainment" has a dramatic emotional impact—especially if it's repeated often enough. And the toys that are marketed as "spin-offs" from such programs only serve to reinforce or extend those negative effects. What's more, there's no balancing positive, healthy, or educational component to these products.

That's why our organization, Focus on the Family, and others have made major investments in high-quality videos and other materials for children. We must provide alternatives for families that want their kids to have wholesome entertainment but are determined to protect them from the popular culture. We will continue to do what we can to meet that need.

Q.22 **Do you think a child should be required to say "thank you" and "please" around the house?**

I sure do. Requiring these phrases is one method of reminding the child that his is not a "gimme-gimme" world. Even though his mother is cooking for him and buying for him and giving to him, he must assume a few attitudinal responsibilities in return. Appreciation must be taught, and this instructional process begins with fundamental politeness at home.

Q.23 **I have a friend whose children drive me crazy when I'm around them. They are the most undisciplined brats I've ever seen. We can't even talk when they are around. I would love to help my friend with a few disciplinary tips. How can I do this without offending her?**

When you want to point out a flaw or shortcoming in someone else's behavior or character, you do it the way porcupines make love: very, very carefully. Otherwise, you're likely to lose a friend.

Pointing out parenting mistakes in others is even riskier. You're liable to get your ears pinned back for trying it—even when your motives are honorable and you have a child's interest at heart. That's why I never offer unsolicited advice about other people's children, no matter how badly I think it is needed.

If you insist on telling the other mother what she doesn't want to hear, let me suggest that you first invest some time and effort in your friend. When a relationship of confidence has been carefully constructed, you'll have then earned the right to offer her some gentle advice.

There are no shortcuts to this process.

Q24 My children love to do things for themselves, but they make such messes that it's easier for me to do things for them. I just don't have the patience to see them fumble with stuff. Do you think I'm wrong to step in and do things for them?

I think you *are* wrong, even though I understand how you feel. I heard a story about a mother who was sick in bed with the flu. Her darling daughter wanted so much to be a good nurse. She fluffed the pillows and brought a magazine to read. And then she even showed up with a surprise cup of tea.

"Why, you're such a sweetheart," the mother said as she drank the tea. "I didn't know you even knew how to make tea."

"Oh, yes," the little girl replied. "I learned by watching you. I put the tea leaves in the pan, and then I put in the water, and I boiled it, and then I strained it into a cup. But I couldn't find a strainer, so I used the flyswatter instead."

"You what?" the mother screamed.

And the little girl said, "Oh, don't worry, Mom. I didn't use the new flyswatter. I used the old one."

Well, when kids try their hardest and they get it all wrong in spite of themselves, what's a parent to do? What mothers and fathers often do is prevent their children from carrying any responsibility that could result in a mess or a mistake. It's just easier to do everything for them than to clean up afterward. But I urge parents not to fall into that trap.

Your child needs her mistakes. That's how she learns. So go along with the game every now and then . . . even if the tea you drink tastes a little strange.

3

DISCIPLINING THE
PRESCHOOL CHILD

Q.25 You have been very critical of behavioral scientists and other writers who recommend a more permissive approach to child rearing. Explain why this concerns you. Why is it ever wrong to be kind and merciful to a boy or girl?

The issue is not one of kindness and mercy. It is one of loving authority and leadership at home, which is in the child's best interest. The majority of books and seminars since 1950 on child raising have effectively stripped parents of the ability to deal with willful defiance when it occurs. First, they haven't admitted that such behavior happens, and second, they have given parents no tools with which to confront it. This bad advice has led to a type of paralysis in dealing with kids. In the absence of "permission" to step in and lead, parents were left with only their anger and frustration in response to defiant behavior.

Let me give an example from a parenting text entitled *Your Child from Two to Five,* published during the permissive 1950s. In it was a bit of characteristic advice from that era, paraphrased from the writings of a Dr. Luther Woodward as follows:

> What do you do when your preschooler calls
> you a "big stinker" or threatens to flush you

down the toilet? Do you scold—punish—or
sensibly take it in your stride? Dr. Woodward
recommends a positive policy of understanding as the best and fastest way to help a
child outgrow this verbal violence. When parents fully realize that all little tots feel angry
and destructive at times, they are better able to
minimize these outbursts. Once the preschooler gets rid of his hostility, the desire to
destroy is gone and instinctive feelings of love
and affection have a chance to sprout and
grow. Once the child is six or seven, parents
can rightly let the child know that he is expected to be outgrowing sassing his parents.[5]

Having recommended that passive approach, with
which I disagree strongly, Dr. Woodward then told
parents to brace themselves for unjust criticism. He
wrote, "But this policy [of letting children engage in
defiance] takes a broad perspective and a lot of com-
posure, especially when friends and relatives voice
disapproval and warn that you are bringing up a
brat."[6]

In this case, your friends and relatives will be
right: You will be bringing up a bratty kid—and
maybe a houseful of them! Dr. Woodward's recommendation encourages parents to stand passively
through the formative years when respect for authority can so easily be taught. His philosophy is
based on the simplistic notion that children will develop sweet and loving attitudes if adults will permit
and encourage their temper tantrums during childhood. According to the optimistic Dr. Woodward,
the tot who has been calling his mother a "big
stinker" for six or seven years can be expected to
transform, like a butterfly emerging from a cocoon,

into a sweet and loving seven-year-old. That outcome is most improbable. Dr. Woodward's "policy of understanding" (which means "policy of permissiveness") leads directly to adolescent rebellion in strong-willed children.

Q26 You said Dr. Woodward's philosophy of child rearing was rather typical of the advice given to parents a generation ago. Apart from the specific example you cited, how do your views differ? What is the basic distinction between your perspective and those of more permissive advice-givers?

I never met the man, but I would think from his writings that Woodward and I perceive human nature very differently. He apparently believed in the "innate goodness" of children, which means they will turn out fine if adults will simply leave them alone. Most of Woodward's contemporaries believed just that. It is my conviction, by contrast, that boys and girls learn (and become) what they are *taught*. Thus, it is our task as parents to "civilize" them—to introduce them to manners and morals and proper behavior. If it is desirable for children to be kind, appreciative, and pleasant, those qualities should be instilled in them—not simply hoped for. If we want to see honesty, truthfulness, and unselfishness in our offspring, then these characteristics should be the conscious objectives of our early instructional process. If it is important to produce respectful, responsible young citizens, then we should teach them first to respect us as their parents. In short, heredity does not equip a child with proper attitudes; we must build the foundations of character ourselves. If that assumption is doubted, take a good look at adults whose parents did not do their homework—those who were raised on the streets with very little parental instruction. A large percentage of them have prison records today.

Q27 If you had to choose between a very authoritarian style of parenting versus one that is permissive and lax, which would you prefer? Which is healthier for kids?

Both extremes leave their characteristic scars on children, and I would be hard pressed to say which is more damaging. At the oppressive end of the continuum, a child suffers the humiliation of total domination. The atmosphere is icy and rigid, and he lives in constant fear. He is unable to make his own decisions, and his personality is squelched beneath the hobnailed boot of parental authority. Lasting characteristics of dependency, deep abiding anger, and serious adolescent rebellion often result from this domination.

But the opposite extreme is also damaging to kids. In the absence of adult leadership the child is her own master from her earliest babyhood. She thinks the world revolves around her heady empire, and she often has utter contempt and disrespect for those closest to her. Anarchy and chaos reign in her home. Her mother is often the most frazzled and frustrated woman on her block. It would be worth the hardship and embarrassment she endures if her passivity produced healthy, secure children. It typically does not.

The healthiest approach to child rearing is found in the safety of the middle ground between disciplinary extremes. I attempted to illustrate that reasonable parenting style on the cover of my first book, *Dare to Discipline,* which included this little diagram:

*love*_____*control*

Children tend to thrive best in an environment where these two ingredients, love and control, are present in balanced proportions. When the scale tips in either direction, problems usually begin to develop at home.

Unfortunately, parenting styles in a culture tend to sweep back and forth like a pendulum from one extreme to the other.

Q28 I like your idea of balancing love with discipline, but I'm not sure I can do it. My parents were extremely rigid with us, and I'm determined not to make that mistake with my kids. But I don't want to be a pushover, either. Can you give me some help in finding the middle ground between extremes?

Maybe it would clarify the overall goal of your discipline to state it in the negative. It is not to produce perfect kids. Even if you implement a flawless system of discipline at home, which no one in history has done, your children will still be children. At times they will be silly, lazy, selfish, and, yes, disrespectful. Such is the nature of the human species. We as adults have the same weaknesses. Furthermore, when it comes to kids, that's how it should be. Boys and girls are like clocks; you have to let them run. My point is that the purpose of parental discipline is not to produce obedient little robots who can sit with their hands folded in the parlor thinking patriotic and noble thoughts! Even if we could pull that off, it wouldn't be wise to try.

The objective, as I see it, is to take the raw material with which our babies arrive on this earth, and then gradually mold them into mature, responsible, and God-fearing adults. It is a twenty-year process that will bring progress, setbacks, successes, and failures. When the child turns thirteen, you'll swear for a time that he's missed everything you thought you had taught—manners, kindness, grace, and style. But then maturity begins to take over, and the little green shoots from former plantings start to emerge. It is one of the richest experiences in living to watch that blossoming at the latter end of childhood.

Q29 You place great emphasis on instilling respect during the developmental years. Why is that so important? Do you just want adults to feel powerful and in control of these little people?

Certainly not. Respect is important for several very specific reasons. First, the child's relationship with his parents provides the basis for his attitude toward every other form of authority he will encounter. It becomes the cornerstone for his later outlook on school officials, law-enforcement officers, future employers, and the people with whom he will eventually live and work. Teachers, for example, can tell very quickly when a boy or girl has been al-lowed to be defiant at home—because those atti-tudes are brought straight into the classroom. Again, relationships at home are the first and most important social encounters a youngster will have, and the problems experienced there often carry over into adult life.

Second, if you want your child to accept your val-ues when she reaches her teen years, then you must be worthy of her respect during her younger days. When a child can successfully defy your authority during his first fifteen years, laughing in your face and stubbornly flouting your leadership, he develops a natural contempt for everything you stand for. *Stu-pid old Mom and Dad!* he thinks. *I've got them wound around my little finger. Sure they love me, but I really think they're afraid of me.* A child may not utter these words, but he feels them each time he wins the confrontation with his mom or dad.

Third, and related to the second, respect is critical to the transmission of faith from one generation to the next. The child who disdains his mother and father is less likely to emulate them on the things that matter most. Why? Because young children typically identify their parents—and especially their fathers—with God. Therefore, if Mom and Dad are not worthy of respect, then neither are their morals, their country, or even their most deeply held convictions.

Q30 At what age should discipline begin?

There should be no physical punishment for a child younger than fifteen to eighteen months old, regardless of the circumstance. An infant is incapable of comprehending his or her "offense" or associating it with the resulting consequences. Some parents do not agree and find themselves "swatting" a baby for wiggling while being diapered or for crying in the midnight hours. This is a terrible mistake. Other parents will shake a child violently when they are frustrated or irritated by incessant crying. Let me warn those mothers and fathers of the dangers of that punishing response. Shaking an infant can cause serious neurological damage, which can occur as the brain is slammed against the skull. Do not risk *any* kind of injury with a baby!

Especially during the first year, a youngster needs to be held, loved, and calmed by a soothing human voice. He should be fed when hungry and kept clean and dry and warm. The foundation for emotional and physical health is laid during this twelve-month period, which should be characterized by security, affection, and warmth.

Q31 If punishment is never recommended for an infant, what form of discipline *is* appropriate at that age?

The answer is loving leadership. Parents should have the courage to do what is right for their babies, even if they protest vigorously. Dr. Bill Slonecker, a Nashville pediatrician and a good friend, has stressed the importance of parents taking charge right from the day of birth. Too often he has seen mothers in his private practice who were afraid of their infants. They would call his office and frantically huff, "My six-month-old baby is crying and seems very hot." The doctor would ask if the child had a fever, to which Mom would reply, "I don't know. He won't let me take his temperature." These mothers had already yielded their authority to their infants. Some would never regain it.

Good parenting and loving leadership go hand in hand. And it should begin on "Day One."

Q32 I believe one of the primary tasks for parents is to prepare children for the independence and responsibility of adulthood. I have an infant son, and I certainly want to teach him to be self-disciplined and responsible as the years unfold. But I don't know where to start. How can I instill these characteristics in my son, and how early should I begin?

Well, that *is* what good parenting is all about. Let me describe the task in developmental terms. A little child at birth is, of course, completely helpless. That little guy lying in his crib can do nothing for himself: He doesn't roll over or hold his bottle. He can't say please or thank you, and he doesn't apologize for getting you up six times in one night. He doesn't even have to appreciate your efforts. In other words, a child begins his life in a state of complete and total dependency, and you are in his servitude.

About twenty years later, however, some dramatic changes should have occurred in that individual. He should have developed the skills and self-discipline necessary for successful adult living. He is expected to spend his money wisely, hold a job, be loyal to one spouse (if he's married), support the needs of his family, obey the laws of the land, and be a good citizen. In other words, during the short course of childhood, an individual should progress systematically from dependency to independency— from irresponsibility to responsibility.

The question is, how does little John or Nancy or Paul get from Position A to Position B? How does that magical transformation from babyhood to maturity take place? Some parents seem to believe that it all will coalesce toward the latter end of adolescence, about fifteen minutes before the individual leaves home. I reject that notion categorically. The best preparation for adulthood comes from training in responsibility during the childhood years. This is not to say that the child should be required to work like an adult. It does mean that he can be encouraged to progress in an orderly timetable of events, carrying the level of responsibility that is appropriate for his age. Shortly after birth, for example, the mother begins transferring responsibilities from her shoulders to those of her infant. Little by little he learns to sleep through the night, hold his own bottle, and reach for what he wants. Later he is potty trained, and he learns to walk and talk. As each new skill is mastered, his mother "frees" herself that much more from his servitude.

Each year the child should make more of his own decisions as the responsibilities of living shift from his parents' shoulders to his own. A seven-year-old, for example, is usually capable of selecting his own clothing for the day (within reason). He should be keeping his room straight and making his bed each morning. A nine- or ten-year-old may be enjoying more freedom, such as choosing from approved television programs. I am not suggesting that we abdicate parental leadership during these years; rather, I believe we should give conscious thought to the reasonable, orderly transfer of freedom and responsibility so that we are preparing the child each year for that moment of full independence that must come.

Returning to your question about your infant son, let me cite two insightful phrases coined by Marguerite and Willard Beecher that will guide the instructional process I have described. They are (1) the parent needs to gain his or her freedom from the child, so that the child can obtain his or her freedom from the parent; and (2) a parent should do nothing for a child that the child can profit from doing for himself or herself.[7] If you apply those two recommendations, you'll get that boy or girl ready to be a responsible man or woman.

Q33 Please describe the best approach to the discipline of a one-year-old child.

Many children will begin to gently test the authority of their parents as they approach their first birthday. The confrontations will be minor and infrequent at first, yet the beginnings of future struggles can be seen. My own daughter, for example, challenged her mother for the first time when she was nine months old. My wife was waxing the kitchen floor when Danae crawled to the edge of the linoleum. Shirley said, "No, Danae," gesturing to the child not to enter the kitchen. Since our daughter began talking very early, she clearly understood the meaning of the word *no*. Nevertheless, she crawled straight onto the sticky wax. Shirley picked her up and set her down in the doorway while saying no even more strongly as she put her down. Seven times this process was repeated until Danae finally yielded and crawled away in tears. As far as we can recall, that was the first direct confrontation of wills between my daughter and my wife. Many more were to follow.

How does a parent discipline a one-year-old? Very carefully and gently! A child at this age is easy to distract and divert. Rather than jerking a wristwatch from his or her hands, show him or her a brightly colored alternative—and then be prepared to catch the watch when it falls. When unavoidable confrontations do occur, as with Danae on the waxy floor, win them by firm persistence but not by punishment. Have the courage to lead the child without being harsh or mean or gruff.

Compared to the months that are to follow, the period around one year of age is usually a tranquil, smooth-functioning time in a child's life.

Q34 Dear Dr. Dobson:

The reason I'm writing is this: The Lord has blessed us so much I should be full of joy. But I have been depressed for months now. I don't know whether to turn to a pastor, a doctor, a psychologist, a nutritionist, or a chiropractor!

Last year the Lord gave us a beautiful baby boy who is now fourteen months of age. He is just wonderful. He is cute, and he is smart, and he is strong. We just can't help but love him. But he has been very demanding. The thing that made it hardest for me was last month Jena was taking some college classes two nights a week, and I took care of Rolf. He cried and sobbed the whole time and eventually cried himself to sleep. Then I would either hold him because he would awaken and continue crying, or if I did get to put him down, I wouldn't make any noise because I was afraid I would wake him up. I am used to being able to pay bills, work on the budget, read and file mail, answer letters, type papers, etc., in the evening. But all this must be postponed to a time when Jena is here.

That's why it has been such a depressing time for me. I just can't handle all that crying. It was even worse when Jena was breast-feeding Rolf. That woke me up too, and I got very tired and had a great deal of trouble getting up in the morning to go to work. I was sick a lot at that time.

I love our baby a lot and wouldn't trade him for anything in the world, but I don't understand why I'm so depressed. Sure, Jena gets tired too because we can't seem to get Rolf to go down for the night before eleven or twelve midnight, and he wakes up twice every night.

Another thing that has been a constant struggle is leaving Rolf in the nursery at church. He isn't content to be away from us very long, so the workers end up having to track Jena down almost every week. We hardly ever get to be together for the worship service. And this has been going on for several months!

We have all the things we would ever dream of at our age—our own neat little house in a good neighborhood, a good job that I enjoy, and not least of all, our life in Christ.

I have no reason to be depressed and to be so tired all the time. I come home from work so exhausted that I'm in no frame of mind to take Rolf out of his mother's hair so she can fix dinner. He hangs on her all the time. I just don't know how she stands it. She must have a higher tolerance for frustration than I do.

If you have any insights as to what we should do, please let me know. Thanks, and God bless you!

Chuck

It might be difficult for parents of "easy babies" to believe that a fourteen-month-old child could take charge of two mature adults, but your description of Rolf has a familiar ring to it. What is occurring is an interaction between his touchy temperament and what he has learned about how to get his way. There's nothing sinister in how Rolf is behaving. The problem, in fact, is not primarily his—it is yours. In your well-intentioned zeal to make him happy and maintain a little peace and quiet in the house, you've allowed yourselves to be tyrannized by tears. It is simply not necessary for you to hold your child every moment or to be unable to leave him in the care of others. Nor should you have to tiptoe around the house to avoid disturbing his sleep. By quickly satisfying Rolf's noisy demands, you are actually reinforcing his crying and teaching him how to make you dance. It's time to pull the plug on that game.

To change the pattern, you have to be convinced first that Rolf's crying will not hurt him. As long as you're sure he doesn't have a fever and he isn't wet or in some kind of discomfort, no long-term damage will be done by a tearful session. Having made that point, I recommend that this evening you and Jena feed and diaper Rolf. Play with him and hold him close. Then when bedtime comes, place him in his crib, pat him on the back two or three times, and quietly walk away. He'll scream bloody murder, of course, but you *must not* pick him up. Even if he cries for an hour or two, you need to get across the idea that he's down for the night.

Screaming is not only unpleasant for parents to hear—it is also very hard work for the screamer. As he becomes convinced that his protest is not going to bring those big, loving people to his bed, the behavior will gradually disappear. Stay with the program for as long as necessary to change the pattern. Be sure you're giving Rolf plenty of love and attention before leaving him on each occasion. He'll get the message in time.

This probably won't be the last struggle you'll have with little Rolfie. If he is a bona fide strong-willed child, as I suspect, you and Jena can anticipate a few hundred thousand more clashes on other battlefields in the years to come. The great satisfaction in parenting, however, is to take a challenging child like Rolf and turn him into a self-disciplined, well-adjusted, and productive adult about twenty years later. You can do it!

By the way, let nothing I have said imply that you or other parents should allow newborns to "cry it out." During the first few months of life, crying is the only way the baby can alert parents that something is wrong. It is only later when they learn to "use" this technique that we must not let it succeed.

Q35 I have a two-year-old boy who is as cute as a bug's ear, and I love him dearly, but he nearly drives me crazy. He throws the most violent temper tantrums and gets into everything. Why is he like this, and are other toddlers so difficult?

Your description of your toddler comes right out of the child-development textbooks. That time of life begins with a bang (like the crash of a lamp or a porcelain vase) at about eighteen months of age and runs hot and heavy until about the third birthday. A toddler is the most hard-nosed opponent of law and order, and he honestly believes that the universe circles around him. In his cute little way, he is curious and charming and funny and lovable and exciting and selfish and demanding and rebellious and destructive. Comedian Bill Cosby, father of five, had some personal experience with toddlers. He is quoted as saying, "Give me two hundred active two-year-olds and I could conquer the world."

Children between fifteen and thirty-six months of age do not want to be restricted or inhibited in any manner, nor are they inclined to conceal their opinions. Bedtime becomes an exhausting, dreaded ordeal each night. They want to play with everything in reach, particularly fragile and expensive ornaments. They prefer using their pants rather than the potty and insist on eating with their hands. And most of what goes in their mouth is not food. When they break loose in a store, they run as fast as their little legs will carry them. They pick up the kitty by its ears and then scream bloody murder when scratched. They want Mommy within three feet of them all day, preferably in the role of their full-time playmate. Truly, the toddler is a tiger—but a precious one.

I hope you won't get too distressed by the frustrations of the toddler years. It is a very brief period of development that will be over before you know it. With all its challenges, it is also a delightful time when your little boy is at his cutest. Approach him with a smile and a hug. But don't fail to establish yourself as the boss during this period. All the years to come will be influenced by the relationship you build during this eighteen-month window.

Q36 Our twenty-four-month-old son is not yet toilet trained, although my mother-in-law feels he should be under control now. Should we spank him for using his pants instead of the potty?

No. Suggest that your mother-in-law cool down a bit. It is entirely possible that your child can't control himself at this age. The last thing you want to do is punish a child of any age for an offense that he can't comprehend. If I had to err on this matter, it would be in the direction of being too late rather than too early. Furthermore, the best approach to potty training is with rewards and encouragement rather than with punishment. Give him a sucker (or sugarless candy) for performing his duty. When you've proved that he can comply, then you can hold him responsible in the future.

Q37 If it is natural for a toddler to break all the rules, should he be disciplined for routine misbehavior?

As I've said, toddlers get into trouble most frequently because of their natural desire to touch, bite, taste, smell, and break everything within their grasp. These are normal and healthy reactions that should not be inhibited. When, then, should they be subjected to mild discipline? When they openly defy their parents' very clear commands! When he runs the other way when called, purposely slams his milk glass on the floor, dashes into the street when being told to stop, screams and throws a tantrum at bedtime, or hits his friends. These behavior patterns should be discouraged. Even in these situations, however, severe punishment is unwarranted. A firm rap on the fingers or a few minutes sitting on a chair will usually convey the same message as convincingly. Spankings should be reserved for a child's moments of greatest antagonism, usually occurring after the second, third, or fourth birthdays.

Without watering down anything I have written about discipline, it should also be understood that I am a firm believer in the judicious use of grace (and humor) in parent-child relationships. In a world in which children are often pushed to grow up too fast, their spirits can dry out like prunes beneath the constant gaze of critical eyes. It is refreshing to see parents temper their harshness with a measure of "unmerited favor." Likewise, there's nothing that buoys every member of a family quite like laughter and a lighthearted spirit in the home.

Q38 My three-year-old can be counted on to behave like a brat whenever we are in the mall or in a restaurant. He seems to know I will not punish him there in front of other people. How should I handle this tactic?

Let me answer you with an illustration from nature. They tell me that a raccoon can usually kill a dog if he gets him in a lake or river. He will simply pull the hound underwater until he drowns. Most other predatory animals prefer to do battle on the turf of their own choosing. So do children. If they're going to pick a fight with Mom or Dad, they'd rather stage it in a public place, such as a supermarket or in the church foyer. They are smart enough to know that they are "safer" in front of other people. They will grab candy or speak in disrespectful ways that would never be attempted at home. Again, the most successful military generals are those who surprise the enemy in a terrain advantageous to their troops. Public facilities represent the high ground for a rambunctious preschooler.

You may be one of the parents who has fallen into the trap of creating "sanctuaries" in which the old rules aren't enforced. It is a certainty that your strong-willed son or daughter will notice those safe zones and behave offensively and disrespectfully when there. There is something within the tougher child that almost forces him to "test the limits" in situations where the resolve of adults is in question. Therefore, I recommend that you lay out the ground rules before you enter those public arenas, making it clear that the same rules will apply. Then if he misbehaves, simply take him back to the car or around the corner and do what you would have done at home. His public behavior will improve dramatically.

Q39 I need more help understanding how to interpret childish behavior. My problem is that I don't know how to react when my son, Chris, annoys me. I'm sure there are many minor infractions that a parent should just ignore or overlook. At other times, immediate discipline is necessary. But I'm not sure I'll react in the right way on the spur of the moment.

Obviously, the first thing you have to do is determine Chris's intent, his feelings, and his thoughts. Is there evidence that Chris is challenging your authority? The more blatant his defiance, the more critical it is to respond with decisiveness. But if he has simply behaved immaturely, or perhaps he's forgotten or made a mistake, you will want to be much more tolerant. It is a very important distinction. In the first instance, the child knows he was wrong and is waiting to see what his parent will do about it; in the second, he has simply blundered into a situation he didn't plan.

Let me be specific. Suppose Chris is acting silly in the living room and falls into a table, breaking some expensive china cups and other trinkets. Or maybe he loses his books on the way home from school. These are acts of childish irresponsibility and should be handled as such. Perhaps you will want to ignore what he did, or maybe you'll require him to work to pay for whatever he lost—depending on his age and level of maturity. However, these accidents and miscalculations do not represent direct challenges to authority. Since they aren't motivated by haughty defiance, they shouldn't result in serious reprimands or punishment.

On the other hand, when a child screams obscenities at his mother or stamps his foot and tells her to
shut up, something very different is going on. He has
moved into the realm of willful defiance. As the
words imply, it is a deliberate act of disobedience
that occurs when the child knows what his parents
want but he clenches his fists, digs in his heels, and
prepares for battle. It is a refusal to accept parental
leadership, such as running when called, or disobeying and then perhaps lying about it. When this kind
of nose-to-nose confrontation occurs between generations, parental leadership is on the line. It is not
time for quiet discussions about the virtues of obedience. It is not the occasion for bribes or bargaining or
promises. Nor is it wise to wait until Dad comes
home from work to handle the misbehavior.

You have drawn a line in the dirt, and Chris has
tossed his cute little toe across it. Who is going to win?
Who has the most courage? Who is in charge here?
Those are the questions he is asking, and it is vital that
you answer them for him. If you equivocate at that
moment, he will precipitate other battles designed to
ask them again and again. That's just the way a strong-
willed child thinks. It is the ultimate paradox of childhood that youngsters want to be led but insist that
their parents earn the right to lead them.

In summary, when misbehavior occurs, your obligation is to look first at the issue of intent, and second, at the issue of respect. From your interpretation
of these two attitudes, you should know instantly
how to respond.

Q.40 Are you suggesting that I punish Mark for every
little thing he does wrong? I would be on his
back every minute of the day.

I am *not* suggesting that you be oppressive in dealing

with everyday behavior. The issues that should get
your attention are those that deal with respect for
you as Mark's mother. When he is defiant, sassy, and
disobedient, you should confidently and firmly step
in and lead. This disobedient behavior is distinctly
different, however, from that which is natural and
necessary for learning and development. Let me explain.

Toddlers most often get in trouble for simply exploring and investigating their world. That is a great
mistake. Preschoolers learn by poking their fingers
into things that adults think they should leave alone.
But this busy exploration is extremely important to
intellectual stimulation. Whereas you and I will look
at a crystal trinket and obtain whatever information
we seek from that visual inspection, a toddler will
expose that pretty object to all of her senses. She will
pick it up, taste it, smell it, wave it in the air, pound
it on the wall, throw it across the room, and listen to
the pretty sound that it makes when shattering. By
that process she learns a bit about gravity, rough versus smooth surfaces, the brittle nature of glass, and
some startling things about Mother's anger.

I am not suggesting that your child be allowed to
destroy your home and all of its contents. Neither is
it right to expect her to keep her hands to herself.
Parents should remove those items that are fragile
or dangerous, and then strew the child's path with
fascinating objects of all types. Permit her to explore everything possible, and do not ever punish
her for touching something that she did not know
was off-limits, regardless of its value. With respect
to dangerous items, such as electric plugs and
stoves, as well as a few untouchable objects, such as
the knobs on the television set, it is possible and necessary to teach and enforce the command "Don't

touch!" If the child refuses to obey even after you have made your expectations clear, a mild slap on the hands while saying no will usually discourage repeat episodes.

I would, however, recommend patience and tolerance for all those other everyday episodes that involve neither defiance nor safety.

Q41 My baby is only a year old, and she is a joy to my husband and me. But your description of toddlerhood is kind of scary. It's just around the corner. Are the "terrible twos" really so terrible?

I think the toddler years are delightful. It is a period of dynamic blossoming and unfolding. New words are being learned daily, and the cute verbal expressions of that age will be remembered for half a century. It is a time of excitement over fairy stories and Santa Claus and furry puppy dogs. And most important, it is a precious time of love and warmth that will scurry by all too quickly and will never return.

Admittedly, the toddler years can also be quite challenging to a busy mother. Not the least of her frustrations is the negativism of that period of development. It has been said that all human beings can be classified into two broad categories: Those who would vote yes to the various propositions of life, and those who would be inclined to vote no. I can tell you with confidence that each toddler around the world would definitely cast a negative vote! If there is one word that characterizes the period between fifteen and twenty-four months of age, it is no! No, he doesn't want to eat his cereal. No, he doesn't want to play with his dump truck. No, he doesn't want to take his bath. And you can be sure, no, he doesn't want to go to bed anytime at all. It is easy to see why this period of life has been called "the first adoles-

cence," because of the negatives, conflict, and independence of the age.

Perhaps the most irritating aspect of the "terrible
twos" is the tendency of kids to spill things, destroy
things, eat horrible things, fall off things, flush
things, kill things, and get into things. They also have
a knack for doing embarrassing things, like sneezing
on a nearby man at a lunch counter. During these
toddler years, any unexplained silence of more than
thirty seconds can throw an adult into a sudden state
of panic. What mother has not had the shock of
opening the bedroom door to find Tony Tornado
covered with lipstick from the top of his pink head to
the carpet on which he stands? On the wall is his own
artistic creation with a red handprint in the center,
and throughout the room is the aroma of Chanel No.
5, with which he has anointed his baby brother.
Wouldn't it be interesting to hold a national conven-
tion sometime, bringing together all the mothers
who have experienced that exact trauma?

Yes, toddlerhood is challenging, but it is also a
wonderful time of life. It will last but a brief moment
in time. There are millions of older parents today
with grown children, who would give all they possess to relive those bubbly days with their toddlers.
Enjoy these years to the full.

Q42 What would you say to my husband and me? We are doing far too much disciplining of our kids. Is there another way to encourage them to cooperate?

The best way to get children to do what you want is
to spend time with them before disciplinary problems occur, having fun together and enjoying mutual
laughter and joy. When those moments of love and
closeness happen, kids are not as tempted to chal-

lenge and test the limits. Many confrontations can be avoided by building friendships with kids and thereby making them want to cooperate at home. It sure beats anger as a motivator of little ones!

Q43 My children are still young, and they are doing fine now, but I worry a lot about the adolescent years that lie ahead. I've seen other parents go through some pretty terrible things when their teenagers began to rebel. How can I help my sons avoid that turmoil ten years from now?

The apprehension that you describe is well founded, and many parents feel something similar today. The most important suggestion I can make is for you to redouble your efforts to build good relationships with your kids while they are young. That is the key to surviving the adolescent years. If they emerge from childhood with doubts about whether you really love and care for them, anything is possible during the turbulent teens. Boundaries, restrictions, and threats will be no match for adolescent anger, frustration, and resentment. As author Josh McDowell said, "Rules without relationship lead to rebellion."[8] He is right. That's why parents can't afford to get preoccupied with business and other pursuits that interfere with the task of raising children. Kids are young for such a brief period. During that window of opportunity, they must be given priority.

Once you've done what you can to lay the proper foundation, I urge you to approach your parenting duties with confidence. Anxiety about the future is risky in itself. It can make parents tentative and insecure in dealing with their youngsters. They don't dare cross them or deny their wishes for fear of being hated in the teen years. Teenagers pick up those vibes intuitively, which often generates disrespect in return. Don't make that mistake. God has placed you in a position of authority over your young children. Lead them with confidence—and then stay on your knees for help from above.

4

CHILDREN'S HEALTH
AND WELL-BEING

Q44 I have great fear that my baby will die when I put her in her crib. What is known now about sudden infant death syndrome (SIDS)? Have researchers figured out what causes these tragic cases where seemingly healthy babies die while sleeping?

Sudden infant death syndrome is still a major concern, killing about six thousand babies each year in the United States alone. We do know more, however, about the circumstances that are often associated with this terrible event. A study was conducted by the U.S. Consumer Product Safety Commission with the collaboration of researchers at the University of Maryland and the Washington University School of Medicine in St. Louis, Missouri. The results were presented at a meeting of the Society for Pediatric Research in 1996. The epidemiologist who directed the investigation, Dr. N. J. Scheers, said, "We have not found a cause of SIDS, but our results show that specific items of bedding used in the U.S., such as comforters and pillows, were associated with an increased risk for death to prone-sleeping infants whose faces became covered, compared to infants on their sides or backs without soft bedding under them."

It was concluded that babies placed on their stomachs in soft bedding are more likely to rebreathe their own carbon dioxide that is trapped in the blankets and pillows around them. In about 30 percent of the 206 SIDS deaths in the research project, babies were found with bedding pressed against their noses and mouths. Most of them were under four months old and could not extricate themselves.[9]

The advice now being offered by doctors is that parents place their infants on their backs, not on their stomachs, and that a minimum amount of loose bedding be kept in the crib. Following this advice won't eliminate all cases of SIDS, but it could save thousands of lives every year.

Q45 My wife and I are above average in height, being six-feet-three-inches and five-feet-nine-inches tall. We both had rather tall parents, too. Nevertheless, our daughter is very tiny. She is nine years old and is only at the third percentile for height. What could be causing this, and what do you think we should do?

There are many factors that influence a child's growth, including a deficiency of growth hormones, heredity, nutrition, and the status of the boy's or girl's general health. There is only one way to know what is causing your daughter's failure to grow, and that is to take her to an endocrinologist or other physician who specializes in these problems. The right doctor can identify her condition and even predict with accuracy how tall she will eventually become. In some cases, growth hormones may be administered, although I'll leave it to your physician to make that recommendation. Since your girl is nine years old, you have no time to lose. Get her to the right medical authority quickly.

Let me ask, by the way, is your daughter an anxious child?

Q46 Yes, as a matter of fact, she is. Lannie is the most insecure of all our children. Why do you ask?

Because some recent studies have shown that persistently anxious girls tend to be shorter than their peers. This was the finding of Dr. Daniel Pine and others at Columbia University College of Physicians, New York. They found that the most insecure girls tended to be about two inches shorter as adults and were twice as likely to be under five-feet-two-inches tall than girls who were less anxious. Two specific disorders in the formative years were most predictive of less height in adults: (1) separation anxiety— seen in girls who don't have the confidence to spend the night at a friend's house or go away to summer camp; and (2) overanxiousness—not just being uneasy about a threat or problem, but a generalized worry about many things over years of time.

One study showed that anxious girls had high blood levels of the stress hormone cortisol, which can stunt growth. Interestingly, anxious boys in the investigation were not found to have higher cortisol levels, and they did not tend to be shorter than their peers. This suggests that girls may respond to stress biologically differently than boys. For whatever reasons, anxiety is linked to lesser growth in females alone.

Once again, you need to have your daughter examined and evaluated medically. There may be a more obvious and treatable reason for her growth deficiency.[10]

Q47 Should a parent try to force a child to eat?

No. In fact, the dinner table is one potential battlefield where a parent can easily get ambushed. You can't win there! A strong-willed child is like a good military general who constantly seeks an advantageous place to take on the enemy. He need look no farther than the dinner table. Of all the common points of conflict between generations—bedtime, hair, clothes, schoolwork, etc.—the advantages in a food fight are all in the child's favor! Three times a day, a very tiny youngster can simply refuse to open his mouth. No amount of coercing can make him eat what he doesn't want to eat.

I remember one three-year-old who was determined not to eat his green peas, despite the insistence of his father that the squishy little vegetables were going down. It was a classic confrontation between the irresistible force and an immovable object. Neither would yield. After an hour of haranguing, threatening, cajoling, and sweating, the father had not achieved his goal. The tearful toddler sat with a forkload of peas pointed ominously at his sealed lips.

Finally, through sheer intimidation, the dad managed to get one bite of peas in place. But the lad wouldn't swallow them. I don't know everything that went on afterward, but the mother told me they had no choice but to put the child to bed with the peas still in his mouth. They were amazed at the strength of his will.

The next morning, the mother found a little pile of mushy peas where they had been expelled at the foot of the bed! Score one for Junior, none for Dad. Tell me in what other arena a thirty-pound child could whip a grown man!

Not every toddler is this tough, of course. But many of them will gladly do battle over food. It is their ideal power game. Talk to any experienced parent or grandparent and they will tell you this is true. The sad thing is that these conflicts are unnecessary. Children will eat as much as they need if you

Food

keep them from indulging in the wrong stuff. They will not starve. I promise!

The way to deal with a poor eater is to set good food before him. If he claims to not be hungry, wrap the plate, put it in the refrigerator, and send him cheerfully on his way. He'll be back in a few hours. God has put a funny little feeling in his tummy that says, "Gimme food!" When this occurs, do not put sweets, snacks, or confectionery food in front of him. Simply retrieve the earlier meal, warm it up, and serve it again. If he protests, send him out to play again. Even if twelve hours or more go by, continue this procedure until food—all food—begins to look and smell wonderful. From that time forward, the battle over the dinner table should be history.

Q48 What causes a child to wet the bed? Our five-year-old soaks his sheets nearly every night, which drives me crazy.

There are about seven million kids in the United States who wet the bed nightly.[11] They are a misunderstood lot. Many of their parents believe that their bed-wetting is deliberate and that it can be eliminated by punishment. Others think these kids are just too lazy to go to the bathroom. These are wrong and unfortunate notions.

Bed-wetting is often caused by medical factors, such as a small bladder, physical immaturity, or other physical conditions. That's why you should begin by consulting a pediatrician or a urologist when bed-wetting starts. About 50 percent of the kids can be helped or cured by medication.

For other boys and girls, the problem is emotional in origin. Any change in the psychological environment of the home may produce midnight moisture. During summer camps conducted for young children, the directors routinely put plastic mattress covers on the beds of all the little visitors. The anxiety associated with being away from home apparently creates a high probability of bed-wetting during the first few nights, and it is particularly risky to be sleeping on the lower level of bunk beds!

There is a third factor that I feel is a frequent cause of enuresis. During children's toddler years, they wet the bed simply because they are too immature to maintain nighttime bladder control. Some parents, in an effort to head off another episode, begin getting these kids up at night to go to the potty. The youngster is still sound asleep, but he or she is told to "go tinkle," or whatever. After this conditioning has been established, the child who needs to urinate at night dreams of being told to "go." Particularly when jostled or disturbed at night, the child can believe he or she is being ushered to the bathroom. I would recommend that parents of older bed wetters stop getting them up at night, even if the behavior continues for a while.

Q49 I get so mad at my kid for wetting the bed. Every morning I have to strip and wash his bedding and pajamas. I told him last week that I would spank him if it happened again. Do you think that will help?

Most certainly not! Unless your child's bed-wetting is an act of defiance occurring after he is awake, which I doubt, his enuresis is an *involuntary* act for which he is not responsible. Punishment under those circumstances is dangerous and unfair. Your son is humiliated by waking up wet anyway, and the older he gets, the more foolish he will feel about it.

The bed wetter needs reassurance and patience from parents, and they should be there for him or her. They would be wise to try to conceal the embarrassing problem from those who would laugh at him.

Even good-natured humor within the family, associated with bed-wetting, is often very painful.

Q50 Aside from medical help, what suggestions do you have for dealing with enuresis?

There are other remedies that sometimes work, such as electronic devices that ring a bell and awaken the child when the urine completes an electrical circuit. This conditions a child to associate the feeling of needing to urinate with the bell that awakens him. I have seen some dramatic success stories where "hard-core" bed wetters were cured within a few weeks using such a device. Trying it certainly can't hurt.

Until the problem is solved, I hope you can keep your frustrations at a minimum. A smile sometimes helps. I received a letter from a mother who wrote down her three-year-old son's bedtime prayer. He said, "Now I lay me down to sleep. I close my eyes; I wet the bed."

Q51 My seven-year-old son has just recently begun demonstrating some rather cruel behavior toward animals. We've caught him doing some pretty awful things to neighborhood dogs and cats. Of course we punished him, but I wonder if there is anything to be more concerned about here?

Cruelty to animals is often a symptom of serious psychological dysfunction to be evaluated by a professional. Children who do such things are not typically just going through a phase. It should be seen as a warning sign of possible emotional problems that could be rather persistent. It also appears to be associated with sexual abuse in childhood. I don't want to alarm you or overstate the case, but adults committed to a life of violent crime were often cruel to animals in their childhood. This fact was verified in a recent study by the

American Humane Association.[12] I suggest that you take your son to a psychologist or other behavioral specialist who can evaluate his mental health. And by all means, do not tolerate unkindness to animals.

Q52 My daughter is five years old, and she has been having some very scary nightmares lately. She wakes up screaming in the middle of the night, but she can't tell us what frightened her. The next morning, she doesn't seem to recall the dream, but something is obviously troubling her. My wife and I are worried that she may be developing psychological problems that are being expressed in these terrible dreams. Is that possible?

I think your daughter is all right. She is probably having a "night terror" rather than a nightmare. Let me describe the difference between the two. Nightmares occur primarily in what is known as "stage-three" sleep and are often remembered if the dreamer awakens. They are sometimes linked to emotional distress during waking hours and may play a role in "working through" those disturbing experiences. A person can often talk about a nightmare and recount its scary story.

Night terrors, by contrast, usually occur in "stage-four" sleep, which is even deeper and further from consciousness. In this physiological state, the body mechanisms are reduced to a minimum to sustain life. Breathing, heart rate, metabolism, and every other function go into superslow motion. Some children experience strange dreams during this phase, which cause them to sit up and scream in terror. However, when adults come to the child's rescue, they find that the child is unresponsive. The eyes are open, but the boy or girl is obviously not awake. And the next morning, there is no memory of what was so deeply disturbing.

This appears to be what you are describing with reference to your daughter. You'll be encouraged to know that there seems to be no connection between night terrors and psychological stress. It is not predictive of any known health problems or emotional disruption. Nor do we know what causes them.

The good news is that your little girl is apparently fine. The bad news is that you may have to deal for a time with her midnight terrors that drag you from your own stage-four sleep.

Q53 Is there any way to prevent the child from having night terrors? It is happening in our house nearly every night, and it is really hard on my husband and me.

Yes, you can usually prevent your child from going into stage-four sleep by giving him or her a minor amount of medication. I wouldn't suggest that you do that unless the night terrors are regular and disruptive to adult sleep patterns. You should talk to your physician about this matter if that is the case.

Q54 Did either of your children experience night terrors?

No, but our daughter once had a very unusual nightmare. When she was four years old, she woke up screaming at about midnight. When I came to her bed, she told me excitedly that the wall was about to collapse on her.

"It's falling! It's falling, Daddy! The wall is falling!" she screamed.

She was obviously very frightened by the dream. I took her hand and said, "Danae, feel that wall. It has been there a long time. It isn't going to fall. You are okay. Now go back to sleep."

As she settled down in the covers, I went back to

bed and was quickly asleep again. But six hours later,
a powerful earthquake rattled the city of Los Angeles
and shook my wife and me right out of bed. I rushed
to Danae's room to bundle her up and get her out of
the way of that wall, which was jumping and shaking
like crazy.

Did our four-year-old have some kind of fore-
warning of the earthquake in the midnight hours? I
don't know, but I'll tell you this: I made up my mind
that day to believe her the next time she told me the
wall was going to fall.

Q55 How do you feel about the dangers of marijuana use? I've heard that it isn't addictive and
therefore isn't harmful; I've also heard that it is very
dangerous. What are the facts?

Let me quote Harold Voth, M.D., senior psychiatrist for the Menninger Foundation in Topeka, Kansas, and associate chief of psychiatry for education at
Topeka Veterans Administration Medical Center,
Topeka, Kansas. These are the facts he provided,
which speak for themselves:

Ninety percent of those using hard drugs such
as heroin started with marijuana.

Five marijuana cigarettes have the same
cancer-causing capacity as 112 conventional
cigarettes.

Marijuana stays in the body, lodged in the
fat cells, for three to five weeks. Mental and
physical performance is negatively affected
during this entire period of time.

A person smoking marijuana on a regular
basis suffers from a cumulative buildup and
storage of THC, a toxic chemical, in the fat
cells of the body, particularly in the brain. It

takes three to five months to effectively detoxify a regular user.

The part of the brain that allows a person to focus, concentrate, create, learn, and conceptualize at an advanced level is still growing during the teenage years. Continuous use of marijuana over a period of time will retard the normal growth of these brain cells.

A study at Columbia University revealed that female marijuana smokers suffer a sharp increase in cells that damage DNA (the chemical that carries the genetic code). It was also found that the female reproductive eggs are especially vulnerable to damage by marijuana.

A second Columbia University study found that a control group smoking a single marijuana cigarette every other day for a year had a white-blood-cell count that was 39 percent lower than normal, thus damaging the immune system and making the user far more susceptible to infection and sickness.

One marijuana cigarette causes a 41 percent decrease in driving skills. Two cigarettes cause a 63 percent decrease.[13]

Given these facts, it is unconscionable that people who should know better continue to advocate the legalization of marijuana.

Q 56 I just found out that I'm pregnant. When the doctor told me, he warned me not to drink anything with alcohol in it until the child is born. I'm used to having a few beers after work, and I like a cocktail several times a week. Is it really necessary for me to give up all alcohol until my baby arrives?

I urge you to heed the advice of your physician. That

precious baby inside of you could be severely damaged if you continue to drink in the next few months. Your child could have what is known as "fetal alcohol syndrome," which can cause heart anomalies, central nervous system dysfunction, head and facial abnormalities, and lifelong behavior problems. Fetal alcohol syndrome is also thought to be the leading cause of mental retardation.[14] It is a terrible thing to inflict on a child.

Babies can be harmed by alcohol in the blood of the mother at any time throughout gestation, but they are especially vulnerable during the first trimester. That's why you should not drink during the remaining seven months of your pregnancy, but by all means, don't swallow a drop of alcohol right now.

You may remember the Old Testament story of Samson, who terrorized his enemies, the Philistines. Before he was born, his mother was told by an angel that her child was destined for greatness and that she must not weaken him by imbibing strong drink while she was pregnant. Medical science has now verified the wisdom of that advice. That's why a similar warning to pregnant women is posted by law wherever liquor, beer, or wine is sold.

For you and for all pregnant women and those who anticipate becoming pregnant—don't take chances with your baby's future. There is no level of alcohol that is known to be safe. Abstain for the entire nine months. You and your baby will be glad you did.

Q57 Clarify the terms *anorexia* and *bulimia* for me, and indicate what causes these eating problems.

The anorexic individual is one who starves himself or herself (it's usually a woman) by refusing to eat enough to sustain his or her body's minimal requirements. Before long, a woman with a normal weight of 130 pounds may have starved herself down to 80 pounds. And though she may actually be starving to death, she may still perceive herself to be overweight.

A person with bulimia follows the opposite pattern. She gorges uncontrollably and then purges herself by vomiting or by using harsh laxatives. Like the anorexic, she can do serious damage to her health if not diagnosed and treated.

It's generally believed that both anorexia and bulimia represent an intense desire for control of one's life. The typical anorexic patient is a female in late adolescence or early adulthood. She is usually a compliant individual who was always a "good little girl." She withheld her anger and her frustration at being powerless throughout the developmental years. Then one day, her need for control began being manifested as a serious eating disorder. There, at least, was one area where she could be the boss. Such individuals also perceive fatness to be hated and ridiculed by their peer groups, which strikes terror into their hearts.

I would strongly recommend that parents of adolescent girls keep a very close eye on their daughters' weight and behavior after thirteen years of age. Seeking proper treatment for an eating disorder can mean the difference between life and death.

Q58 Our school psychologist said she thinks our son is suffering from childhood depression. My goodness! The kid is only nine years old. Is it reasonable that this could be his problem?

We used to believe that depression was exclusively an adult problem, but that understanding is changing. Now we're seeing signs of serious despondency in children as young as five years old.

Symptoms of depression in an elementary school child may include general lethargy, a lack of interest in things that used to excite him or her, sleep disturbances, chewed fingernails, loss of appetite, and violent emotional outbursts. Other common reactions are stomach complaints and low tolerance for frustration of any kind.

If depression is a problem for your child, it is only symptomatic of something else that is bothering him or her. Help him or her verbalize feelings. Try to anticipate the explanation for sadness, and lead the youngster into conversations that provide an opportunity to ventilate. Make yourself available to listen, without judging or belittling the feelings expressed. Simply being understood is soothing for children and adults alike.

If the symptoms are severe or if they last more than two weeks, I urge you to take the advice of the school psychologist or seek professional help for your son. Prolonged depression can be destructive for human beings of any age and is especially dangerous to children.

Q59 Do childhood traumas inevitably twist and warp a person in the adult years?

No. It is well known that difficult childhoods leave some people wounded and disadvantaged, but for others, they fuel great achievement and success. The difference appears to be a function of individual temperaments and resourcefulness.

In a classic study called "Cradles of Eminence," Victor and Mildred Goertzel investigated the home backgrounds of three hundred highly successful people. The researchers sought to identify the early experiences that may have contributed to remarkable achievement. All of the subjects were well known for their accomplishments; they included Einstein, Freud, Churchill, and many others.

The backgrounds of these people proved very interesting. Three-fourths of them came from troubled childhoods, enduring poverty, broken homes, or parental abuse. One-fourth had physical handicaps. Most of those who became writers and playwrights had watched their own parents embroiled in psychological dramas of one sort or another. The researchers concluded that the need to compensate for disadvantages was a major factor in the drive toward personal achievement.[15]

One of the best illustrations of this phenomenon is seen in the life of Eleanor Roosevelt, a former First Lady. Being orphaned at ten, she underwent a childhood of utter anguish. She was very homely and never felt she really belonged to anybody. According to Victor Wilson, Newhouse News Service, "She was a rather humorless introvert, a young woman unbelievably shy, unable to overcome her personal insecurity and with a conviction of her own inadequacy." The world knows, however, that Mrs. Roosevelt rose above her emotional shackles. As Wilson said, "From some inner wellspring, Mrs. Roosevelt summoned a tough, unyielding courage, tempered by remarkable self-control and self-discipline." That "inner wellspring" has another appropriate name: compensation!

Obviously, one's attitude toward a handicap determines its impact on one's life. It has become popular to blame adverse circumstances for irresponsible behavior (e.g., poverty causes crime, broken homes produce juvenile delinquents, a sick society imposes drug addiction on its youth). There is some truth in this assumption, since people in those difficult circumstances are more likely to be-

have in destructive ways. But they are not forced to
do so. To say that adverse conditions cause irresponsible behavior is to remove all responsibility from the
shoulders of the individual. The excuse is hollow.
We must each decide what we will do with inner
doubt and outer hardship.

The application to an individual family should be
obvious. If a child has gone through a traumatic experience or is physically disadvantaged, his or her
parents need not give up hope. They should identify
his or her strengths and natural abilities, which can
be used to overcome the hurdle. The problem that
seems so formidable today may become the inspiration for greatness tomorrow.

Q60 I have been teaching school for thirty years,
and I am noticing a significant change in the
health of my children. More of them are overweight, and
they just don't get enough exercise. I wonder if my observation is accurate, and if so, what is causing it.

You are absolutely correct. A recent medical study
conducted at Columbia Children's Hospital in Ohio
has confirmed that today's children are heavier and
have significantly higher cholesterol and triglyceride
levels than kids did even fifteen years ago. One of the
researchers, Dr. Hugh Allens, said, "Unless these
trends change, 30 million of the 80 million children
alive today in the United States will eventually die of
heart disease."

Dr. Allens said, "Kids need to turn off the TV, get
off the couch, and stop the nincompooping of America."[16] The problem is that high-fat junk food has replaced good nutrition. And even when healthy foods
are consumed, kids are not exercising the calories
off. Between television, car pools, computer games,

and just hanging out at the pizza parlor, kids just don't run and jump like they used to.

So Mom and Dad should find activities to do together with kids that are active. Things like walking and bicycling and playing catch or hiking. They can also get their children involved in community or school sports programs ranging from softball to soccer.

Children are busy forming habits for a lifetime, so eating right and exercising every day will contribute to greater health in the future.

Q61 Should I be concerned about my two-and-a-half-year-old son's tendency to stammer and repeat words? If he has a real stuttering problem, I don't want to wait too long before doing something about it.

Your son's stammer will probably disappear in time, but just to be safe, you should take him in *now* for an evaluation. There is a "normal stuttering" that is common between the ages of two and six, when a child's knowledge and vocabulary are expanding faster than his neurological ability to verbalize his thoughts. However, you should be aware of some secondary mannerisms which are indicative of a pathological stuttering beyond the normal disfluency found in preschoolers, including the child's struggling noticeably to get words out; obvious frustration in the child while trying to speak; increasing vocal tension resulting in rising pitch or loudness; or very long prolongation (several seconds) of syllables.

Whether these secondary mannerisms are present or not, the Speech and Hearing Divison of Childrens Hospital Los Angeles encourages parents to bring a child with speech difficulties in for an evaluation as early as two years of age.[17] The likelihood of your son's having a pathological stuttering problem is slim, but experts believe it is best to be cautious at this age—they would rather take the time to put a child through an unnecessary evaluation than to allow a potential speech problem to go unchecked.

Q62 You have recommended for many years that parents take their preteens away from home for what you called a "Preparing for Adolescence" weekend, during which they talk about the physical and emotional changes about to occur. I'm interested in your comment that kids want this information before they become teenagers, but they won't want to talk about it after puberty. Do their attitudes really change that much overnight?

As a matter of fact, they do. A study of 1,023 children between ten and thirteen showed that the number who felt uncomfortable talking to their parents about sexuality nearly doubled after puberty occurred. Prior to that, they were very open to instruction and guidance at home. Ninety-three percent of those aged ten to twelve felt loved by their parents "all the time," said Dr. Alvin Poussaint, a psychiatrist at Harvard University. He said, "I think parents may be surprised that children of this age are saying, 'We want to be close to you. We need you and we're still afraid. We need the sense of safety and security that you supply.'"[18]

The study showed, however, that attitudes changed dramatically when the children reached the eighth grade. Those who had been open to advice the year before were suddenly unwilling to talk to their parents. The window of accessibility had closed.

The moral to the story? Invest a little time in the months before puberty to get your children ready for the stresses of adolescence. The effort will pay big dividends.

Q63 Our family physician wants to examine my thirteen-year-old son without my being in the room. That's okay with me, but I expect him to tell me what my boy says and what his medical condition is. That's where we disagree. He says he must keep their conversation confidential. Am I right to expect to be informed and involved?

Teenagers are typically sensitive and modest about their bodies—especially when their parents are around—so I can understand the need for privacy during a physical exam. The larger issue here, however, is the physician's accountability to you as the mother, and at this point, I agree entirely with the position you have taken. Other parents have expressed similar concerns to me.

I'm reminded of a mother who told me that she took her fourteen-year-old daughter to their pediatrician for a routine physical exam. The mother was aware that her daughter was beginning to develop physically and might be sensitive to her being in the examining room with her. She offered to remain in the waiting room, but the girl objected.

"I don't want to go in there by myself," she said. "Please come with me." After arguing with her daughter for a moment, the mother agreed to accompany her to the examining room.

When the exam was over, the doctor turned to the mother and criticized her for intruding. He said in front of the girl, "You know, you really had no business being in the examining room. It is time I related directly to your daughter. You should not even be aware of the care that I give her or the medication I prescribe. Nor should you know the things that are said between us. My care of your daughter should now be a private matter between her and me."

The girl had been going through a period of rebel-

lion, and the mother felt her authority was weakened
by the doctor's comments. It was as though he were
saying, "Your day of supervision of your daughter has
now passed. She should now make her own decisions." Fortunately, that mother was unwilling to do
as she was told and promptly found a new doctor.
Good for her!

I have discussed this conversation with several pediatricians, and they have each agreed with the doctor in this case. They emphasized the importance of
a youngster having someone to talk with in private.
Perhaps. But I object to the autonomy demanded by
the physician. Fourteen-year-old boys and girls are
not grown, and their parents are still the best people
to care for them and oversee their development. It is
appropriate for a physician to have some private moments with a young patient, but he or she should
never forget to whom accountability is owed.

Furthermore, if greater authority is to be granted
to the doctor, the parent had better find out just
what he or she believes about contraceptives for mi-
nors, premarital sex, spiritual matters, and the like.
Be careful whom you choose to trust with the body
and the soul of your child. The pace of living is so
frantic today that we have become dangerously willing to accept surrogate parenting from a variety of
professionals who meander through our lives. Educators, youth ministers, athletic coaches, music in-
structors, psychologists, counselors, and physicians
are there to assist parents in raising their kids—but
never to replace them.

5

ATTENTION DEFICIT
DISORDER IN CHILDREN
AND ADULTS

Q64 I hear so much about children who have ADD. Can you describe this problem for me and tell me how I might recognize it in my son?

The term *ADD* stands for attention deficit disorder, which is an inherited neurological syndrome that affects approximately 5 percent of children in the United States. It refers to individuals who are easily distracted, have a low tolerance for boredom or frustration, and tend to be impulsive and flighty. Some of them are also hyperactive, and hence, they are said to have ADHD (attention deficit/hyperactivity disorder.)

Children with ADD have a pattern of behavior that sets them up for failure in school and conflict with their parents. They have difficulty finishing tasks, remembering details, focusing on a book or assignment, or even remaining seated for more than a few minutes. Some appear to be driven from within as they race wildly from one thing to another. They are often very bright and creative, yet they're seen as lazy, disruptive, and terribly disorganized. ADD children often suffer from low self-esteem because they have been berated as goof-offs and anarchists who refuse to follow the rules. They sometimes have

few friends because they can drive everyone crazy—
even those their own age.

As for how you can recognize such a child in your
home, it is unwise for a parent to attempt to do so.
There are many other problems, both psychological
and physical, that can cause similar symptoms. Disorders of the thyroid, for example, can make a child
hyperactive or sluggish; depression and anxiety can
cause the distractibility associated with ADD.
Therefore, you must have assistance from a physician, a child developmentalist, or a psychologist who
can confirm the diagnosis.

If you see in your child the symptoms I've described, I urge you to have him or her seen profes-
sionally. Again, you should not try to diagnose your
child! The sooner you can get that youngster in to
see a person who specializes in this disorder, the
better.

Q65 I understand that I can't diagnose my own son,
but it would be helpful if you would list the
kinds of behavior to look for in a child who may have ADD.
You've described the condition in general terms, but what
are the specific characteristics of someone who has this
disorder?

Hallowell and Ratey, authors of an excellent text entitled *Driven to Distraction,* list twenty symptoms that
are often evident in a person with ADD or ADHD.
They are:

Suggested Diagnostic Criteria for Attention Deficit Disorder

1. A sense of underachievement, of not meeting
   one's goals (regardless of how much one has
   accomplished)
2. Difficulty getting organized

3. Chronic procrastination or trouble getting started

4. Many projects going simultaneously; trouble with follow-through

5. Tendency to say what comes to mind without necessarily considering the timing or appropriateness of the remark

6. An ongoing search for high stimulation

7. A tendency to be easily bored

8. Easy distractibility, trouble focusing attention, tendency to tune out or drift away in the middle of a page or a conversation, often coupled with an ability to focus at times

9. Often creative, intuitive, highly intelligent

10. Trouble going through established channels, following proper procedure

11. Impatient; low tolerance for frustration

12. Impulsive, either verbally or in action, as in impulsive spending of money, changing plans, enacting new schemes or career plans, and the like

13. Tendency to worry needlessly, endlessly; tendency to scan the horizon looking for something to worry about, alternating with inattention to or disregard for actual dangers

14. Sense of impending doom, insecurity, alternating with high risk-taking

15. Depression, especially when disengaged from a project

16. Restlessness

17. Tendency toward addictive behavior

18. Chronic problems with self-esteem

19. Inaccurate self-observation

20. Family history of ADD, manic-depressive illness, depression, substance abuse, or other disorders of impulse control or mood.[19]

Q66 My daughter has some of the symptoms you described, but she is a very quiet child. Are some ADD kids withdrawn and sedate?

Yes. ADD is not always associated with hyperactivity, especially in girls. Some of them are "dreamy" and detached. Regrettably, they are sometimes called "airheads" or "space cadets." Such a child can sit looking at a book for forty-five minutes without reading a word. One teacher told me about a girl in her class who would lose every article of clothing that wasn't hooked to her body. Nearly every day, the teacher would send this child back to the playground to retrieve her sweater or coat, only to have her return fifteen minutes later without it. She had forgotten what she went after. A boy or girl with that kind of distractibility would find it extremely difficult, if not impossible, to get home night after night with books and assignments written down, and then to complete the work and turn it in the next morning.

Frankly, the "faraway" child worries me more than the one who is excessively active. She may be seen as a good little girl who just isn't very bright, while the troublemaker is more likely to get the help he needs. He's too irritating to ignore.

Those who are and are not hyperactive have one characteristic in common. It is distractibility. Even though they flit from one thing to another, the name attention deficit disorder is not quite on target. It's better than the old term ("minimal brain damage"), but there is also misinformation in the current designation. The problem is not that these children have a short attention span. At times, they can become lost in something that greatly interests them to the point that they aren't aware of anything going on around them. Instead, they have an insatiable need for mental stimulation during every waking moment. The moment they become bored with what they are doing, they dash off in search of the next exciting possibility.

One father told me about his four-year-old son with ADD. He said, "If you let that kid get bored, you deserve what he's going to do to you." That applies to millions of children.

Q67 What causes attention deficit disorder?

It is believed to be inherited. Russell Barkley of the University of Massachusetts Medical Center estimates that 40 percent of ADHD kids have a parent with similar symptoms, and 35 percent have an affected sibling. If one identical twin is affected, the chances are between 80 and 92 percent that his or her sibling will be also. ADD is two to three times as likely to be diagnosed in boys as girls.[20]

The cause of ADD is unknown, but it is probably associated with subtle differences in brain structure, its neural pathways, its chemistry, its blood supply, or its electrical system. As of this writing, some interesting hypotheses are emerging, although definitive conclusions can't yet be drawn.

Q68 I've heard that ADD is controversial and that it may not even exist. You obviously disagree.

Yes, I disagree, although the disorder has become faddish and tends to be overdiagnosed. But when a child actually has this problem, I assure you that his or her parents and teachers don't have to be convinced.

Q69 Does ADD go away as children grow up?

We used to believe the problem was eliminated with the onset of puberty. That's what I was taught in graduate school. Now it is known that ADD is a lifelong condition, usually influencing behavior from the cradle to the grave. Some ADD adults learn to be less disorganized and impulsive as they get older. They channel their energy into sports activities or professions in which they function very well. Others have trouble settling on a career or holding a job. Follow-through remains a problem as they flit from one task to another. They are particularly unsuited for desk jobs, accounting positions, or other assignments that demand attention to detail, long hours of sitting, and the ability to juggle many balls at once.

Another consequence of ADD in adolescence and adulthood is the thirst for high-risk activity. Even as children, they are accident-prone, and their parents get well acquainted with the local emergency room. As they get older, rock climbing, bungee jumping, car racing, motorcycle riding, white-water rafting, and related activities are among their favorite activities. Adults with ADD are sometimes called "adrenaline junkies" because they are hooked on the "high" produced by the adrenaline rush associated with dangerous behavior. Others are more susceptible to drug use, alcoholism, and other addictive behaviors. Approximately 40 percent will have been arrested by eighteen years of age.[21]

Some of those who have ADD are at higher risk for marital conflict, too. It can be very irritating to a compulsive, highly ordered husband or wife to be married to a "messie"—someone whose life is chaotic and one who forgets to pay the bills, fix the car, or keep records for income-tax reports. Such a couple usually need professional counseling to help them learn to work together and capitalize on each other's strengths.

Q 70 You've given us a pretty bleak picture. Is there anything good you can tell those of us who are raising an ADHD child?

There are some advantages to having attention deficit disorder. In a sense, even the word *disorder* is misleading because the syndrome has many positive features. As *Time* reported, "[ADD adults] see themselves as creative; their impulsiveness can be viewed as spontaneity; hyperactivity gives them enormous energy and drive; even their distractibility has the virtue of making them alert to changes in the environment. Kids with ADHD are wild, funny, effervescent. They have lots of life."[22]

Let's not forget, also, that ADD can be treated successfully in many cases.

Q 71 What kind of treatment is available?

Treatment involves a range of factors, beginning with education. The adult with ADD is often greatly relieved to learn that he or she has an identifiable, treatable condition. Dr. Robert Reid from the University of Nebraska calls it the "label of forgiveness." He said, "The kid's problems are not his parents' fault, not the teacher's fault, not the kid's fault."[23] That is good news to the person who has been told all his life that he's dumb, stupid, lazy, obnoxious, and disruptive.

The first step in rebuilding the self-concept of an adult, then, is to get an understanding of the forces operating within. My advice to that individual and to his or her family is to read, read, read! One helpful book for laymen is *Driven to Distraction,* by Edward Hallowell, M.D., and John Ratey, M.D. An excellent set of cassette tapes by these authors is also available. Another well-written book by a Christian psychologist is entitled *The Hyperactive Child,* by Grant Martin, Ph.D.[24]

The second step is to teach the ADD person, especially the adult, to minimize his or her distractibility and impulsivity. They can learn to use "to-do lists," daily calendars, schedules, and written plans. "It ain't easy," as they say, but it can be done.

The third step is to secure the assistance of what Hallowell and Ratey call "a coach." A knowledgeable friend is needed to stand nearby with a whistle—offering encouragement, pointing out mistakes, teaching, and modifying behavior. If a wise instructor can teach a novice to play tennis or golf, a caring coach can help a person with ADD learn to behave in more successful ways.

In regard to children, a knowledgeable professional is needed to advise and encourage parents who are often bewildered and frustrated by behavior they neither control nor understand.

Finally, there are the considerable benefits to the use of prescription drugs for both children and adults. Approximately 70 percent of ADD patients benefit from appropriate medication.[25] Surprisingly, certain stimulants are often effective in helping ADD children—including those who are hyperactive. No one knows exactly how they work, but they probably affect the electrochemical processes in frontal lobes of the brain that regulate behavior. The most commonly prescribed drug is Ritalin, although some patients do better on Dexedrine or Cylert. In some instances, these substances have a remarkably positive effect.[26]

Q72 Do you worry about Ritalin and other drugs being overprescribed? Should I be reluctant to give them to my ten-year-old?

Yes. Prescription drugs have been used as a cure-all

for various forms of misbehavior. That is unfortunate. We should never medicate kids just because their parents have failed to discipline them properly or because someone prefers to have them sedated. Every medication has undesirable side effects and should be administered only after careful evaluation and study. Ritalin, for example, can reduce the appetite and cause insomnia in some patients. It is, nevertheless, considered remarkably safe.

If your child has been evaluated and diagnosed with ADD by a professional who is experienced in treating this problem, you should not hesitate to accept a prescription for an appropriate medication. Some dramatic behavioral changes can occur when the proper substance is identified for a particular child. A boy or girl who sits and stares off into the distance or one who frantically climbs the walls is desperately in need of help. To give that individual a focused mind and internal control is a blessing. Medication often works just that way.

Q.73 We have a five-year-old son who has been diagnosed with ADD. He is really difficult to handle, and I have no idea how to manage him. I know he has a neurological problem; I don't feel right about making him obey like we do our other children. It is a big problem for us. What do you suggest?

I understand your dilemma, but I urge you to discipline your son. Every youngster needs the security of defined limits, and the ADD or ADHD boy or girl is no exception. Such a child should be held responsible for his or her behavior, although the approach may be a little different. For example, most children can be required to sit on a chair for disciplinary reasons, whereas some very hyperactive children would not be able to remain there. Similarly, corporal punishment is sometimes ineffective with a highly excitable little bundle of electricity. As with every aspect of parenthood, disciplinary measures for the ADD child must be suited to his or her unique characteristics and needs.

Q74 How, then, is such a child to be managed?

Let me share a list of eighteen suggestions that were provided in a book by Dr. Domeena Renshaw entitled *The Hyperactive Child*. Though her book is now out of print, Dr. Renshaw's advice on this problem is still valid.

1. Be consistent in rules and discipline.
2. Keep your own voice quiet and slow. Anger is normal. Anger can be controlled. Anger does not mean you do not love a child.
3. Try hard to keep your emotions cool by bracing for expected turmoil. Recognize and respond to any positive behavior, however small. If you search for good things, you will find a few.
4. Avoid a ceaselessly negative approach: "Stop"— "Don't"—"No."
5. Separate behavior, which you may not like, from the child's person, which you like, e.g., "I like you. I don't like your tracking mud through the house."
6. Have a very clear routine for this child. Construct a timetable for waking, eating, play, TV, study, chores, and bedtime. Follow it flexibly when he disrupts it. Slowly your structure will reassure him until he develops his own.
7. Demonstrate new or difficult tasks, using action accompanied by short, clear, quiet explanations. Repeat the demonstration until learned. This uses audiovisual-sensory perceptions to rein-

force the learning. The memory traces of a hyperactive child take longer to form. Be patient and repeat.

8. Designate a separate room or a part of a room that is his own special area. Avoid brilliant colors or complex patterns in decor. Simplicity, solid colors, minimal clutter, and a worktable facing a blank wall away from distractions assist concentration. A hyperactive child cannot filter out overstimulation himself yet.

9. Do one thing at a time: Give him one toy from a closed box; clear the table of everything else when coloring; turn off the radio/TV when he is doing homework. Multiple stimuli prevent his concentration from focusing on his primary task.

10. Give him responsibility, which is essential for growth. The task should be within his capacity, although the assignment may need much supervision. Acceptance and recognition of his efforts (even when imperfect) should not be forgotten.

11. Read his preexplosive warning signals. Quietly intervene to avoid explosions by distracting him or discussing the conflict calmly. Removal from the battle zone to the sanctuary of his room for a few minutes is useful.

12. Restrict playmates to one or at most two at one time, because he is so excitable. Your home is more suitable, so you can provide structure and supervision. Explain your rules to the playmate and briefly tell the other parent your reasons.

13. Do not pity, tease, be frightened by, or overindulge this child. He has a special condition of the nervous system that is manageable.

14. Know the name and dose of his medication. Give it regularly. Watch and remember the effects to report back to your physician.

15. Openly discuss with your physician any fears you have about the use of medications.
16. Lock up all medications to avoid accidental misuse.
17. Always supervise the taking of medication, even if it is routine, over a long period of years. Responsibility remains with the parents! One day's supply at a time can be put in a regular place and checked routinely as he becomes older and more self-reliant.
18. Share your successful "helps" with his teacher. The outlined ways to help your hyperactive child are as important to him as diet and insulin are to a diabetic child.[27]

6

EFFECTIVE PARENTING
TODAY

Q75 What has been your greatest challenge as a father? What did you learn from it?

Raising healthy, well-educated, self-disciplined children who love God and their fellow human beings is, I believe, the most challenging responsibility in living. Not even rocket science can approach it for complexity and unpredictability. And of course, the job is even more difficult today when the culture undermines and contradicts everything Christian parents are trying to accomplish at home. Fortunately, we are not asked to do everything perfectly as moms and dads. Our kids usually manage to survive our mistakes and failures and turn out better than we have any right to boast about.

I certainly made my share of mistakes as a father. Like millions of other men of my era, I often had a tough time balancing the pressure of my profession with the needs of my family. Not that I ever became an "absentee father," but I did struggle at times to be as accessible as I should have been. As it happened, my first book, *Dare to Discipline,* was published the same week that our second child, Ryan, arrived. A baby always turns a house upside down, but the reaction to my book added to the turmoil. I was a full-time professor at a medical school, and yet I was inundated by thousands of letters and requests of every sort. There was no mechanism to handle this sudden notoriety. I remember flying to New York one Thursday night, doing seventeen television shows and press interviews in three days, and returning to work on Monday morning. It was nothing short of overwhelming.

My father, who always served as a beacon in dark times, saw what was happening to me and wrote a letter that was to change my life. First he congratulated me on my success, but then he warned that all the success in the world would not compensate if I failed at home. He reminded me that the spiritual welfare of our children was my most important responsibility and that the only way to build their faith was to model it personally and then to stay on my knees in prayer. That couldn't be done if I invested every resource in my profession. I have never forgotten that profound advice.

It eventually led to my resignation from the university and to the development of a ministry that permitted me to stay at home. I quit accepting speaking requests, started a radio program that required no travel, and refused to do "book tours" or accept other lengthy responsibilities that would take me away from my family. As I look back on that era today, I am so grateful that I chose to preserve my relationship with my children. The closeness that we enjoy today can be traced to that decision to make time for them when they needed me most. I could easily have made the greatest mistake of my life at that time.

I'm sure many fathers will read this response and find themselves today where I was back then. If you are one of them, I urge you to give priority to your family. Those kids around your feet will be grown and gone before you know it. Don't let the opportunity of these days slip away from you. No professional accomplishment or success is worth that cost. When you stand where I am today, the relationship with those you love will outweigh every other good thing in your life.

Q76 I worry so much about my children and wonder if I'm raising them wisely. Every few days my husband and I encounter a problem we don't know how to handle. Is it common for parents to feel this way?

Yes, it has never been easy to raise healthy and productive children. After all, babies come into the world with no instructions, and you pretty much have to assemble them on your own. They are also maddeningly complex, and there are no guaranteed formulas that work in every instance. And finally, the techniques that succeed magnificently with one child can fail bewilderingly with another.

This difficulty in raising children is a recurring theme in the letters we receive at Focus on the Family. We have heard it so often, in fact, that we decided to conduct a poll to ascertain the common frustrations of parenting. The answers received from more than a thousand mothers and fathers were very revealing. Some responded with humor, especially those who were raising toddlers. They told the most delightful stories about sticky telephones, wet toilet seats, and knotted shoestrings. Their experiences reminded me of the days when Shirley and I were chasing ambitious preschoolers.

Tell me why it is that a toddler never throws up in the bathroom? Never! To do so would violate some great unwritten law of the universe. It is even more difficult to understand why he or she will gag violently at the sight of a perfectly wonderful breakfast of oatmeal, eggs, bacon, and orange juice—and then go play in the toilet. I have no idea what makes a kid do that. I only know that it drives a mother crazy!

Unfortunately, the majority of those who responded to our questionnaire did not share funny stories about cute kids. Many of them were experiencing considerable frustration in their parenting responsibilities. Rather than being critical of their children, however, most said they were troubled by their own inadequacies as mothers and fathers!

Their answers, including these actual responses, revealed the self-doubt that is prevalent among parents today:

- "I don't know how to cope with my children's problems"

- "I'm not able to make the kids feel secure and loved"

- "I've lost confidence in my ability to parent"

- "I've failed my children"

- "I'm not the example I should be"

- "Seeing my own bad habits and character traits in my children"

- "My inability to relate to my children"

- "The guilt I feel when it seems that I have failed my daughters"

- "My inability to cope"

- "Knowing it's too late to go back and do it right"

- "I'm overwhelmed by the responsibility of it all"

Isn't it incredible to observe just how tentative we have become about this task of raising children? Parenting is hardly a new technology. Since Adam and Eve graced the Garden, perhaps 15 billion people have lived on this earth, yet we've become increasingly nervous about bringing up the baby. It is a sign of the times.

Q77 Why do you think parents are so quick to criticize themselves? What is the source of the self-doubt you mentioned?

It is a cultural phenomenon. Mothers, especially, have been blamed for everything that can conceivably go wrong with children. Even when their love and commitment are incalculable, the experts accuse them of making grievous errors in toilet training, disciplining, feeding, medicating, and educating their youngsters. They are either overpossessive or undernurturing. Their approach is either harsh or permissive. One psychiatrist even wrote an entire book on the dangers of religious training, blaming parents for scaring kids with talk of the next world. Thus, no matter how diligently Mom approaches her parenting responsibilities, she is likely to be accused of twisting and warping her children.

Perhaps this explains why women are more critical of themselves than men. Eighty percent of the respondents to our poll were women, and their most frequent comment was "I'm a failure as a mother!" What nonsense! Women have been taught to think of themselves in this way, and it is time to set the record straight.

The task of procreation was never intended to be so burdensome. Of course it is demanding. And children are challenging, to be sure. But the guilt and self-doubt that often encumber the parenting responsibility are not part of the divine plan. Throughout the Scriptures, the raising of children is presented as a wonderful blessing from God——a welcome, joyful experience. And today, it remains one of the greatest privileges in living to bring a baby into the world to love and care for. What a wonderful opportunity it is to teach these little ones to revere God with all their hearts and to serve others throughout their lives. There is no higher calling than that!

Q.78 I don't believe my parents went through this kind of anxiety when my sisters and I were young. We were all relatively happy, and none of us rebelled. Am I right in assuming that a good family life was easier to achieve in those days?

I'm sure your memory is generally correct despite the exceptions we can all recall. The majority of parents in earlier years spent less energy worrying about their children. They had other things on their minds. I remember talking to my dad about this subject a few years before his death. Our children were young at the time, and I, like you, was feeling the heavy responsibility of raising them properly.

I turned to my father and asked, "Do you remember worrying about me when I was a kid? Did you think about all the things that could go wrong as I came through the adolescent years? How did you feel about these pressures associated with being a father?"

Dad was rather embarrassed by my question. He smiled sheepishly and said, "Honestly, Bo," (his pet name for me) "I never really gave that a thought."

How do we explain his lack of concern? Was it because he didn't love me or because he was an uninvolved parent? No. He prayed for me until the day he died. And as I have said on many occasions, he was a wonderful father to me. Instead, his answer reflected the time in which I grew up. People worried about the depression that was just ending, and the war with Germany and Japan, and later the cold war with Russia. They did not invest much effort in hand-wringing over their children . . . at least not until some kind of problem developed. Trouble was not anticipated.

And why not? Because there were fewer land mines for kids in that era. I attended high school during the "Happy Days" of the 1950s, and I never saw or even heard of anyone taking an illegal drug. It happened, I suppose, but it was certainly no threat to me. Some students liked to get drunk, but alcohol was not a big deal in my social environment. Others played around with sex, but the girls who did were considered "loose" and were not respected. Virginity was still in style for males and females. Occasionally a girl came up pregnant, but she was packed off in a hurry, and I never knew where she went. As for homosexuals and lesbians, I heard there were a few around, but I didn't know them personally. There were certainly no posters on our bulletin boards advertising Gay Pride Month or Condom Week. Most of my friends respected their parents, went to church on Sundays, studied hard enough to get by, and lived fairly clean lives. There were exceptions, of course, but this was the norm.

Today's kids, by contrast, are walking through the valley of the shadow! Drugs, sex, alcohol, rebellion, and deviant lifestyles are everywhere. Those dangers have never been as evident as they are now, and the worst may be yet to come.

Q79 What does behavioral research tell us about the best way to raise children? Have scientific studies spelled out what works and what doesn't, especially regarding how to discipline properly?

My answer may sound like heresy coming from a man who spent ten years of his life as a professor of pediatrics, responsible for medical and behavioral research, but I don't believe the scientific community is capable of determining the best parenting techniques. There have been some worthwhile studies, to be sure, but the subject of discipline almost defies definitive investigation.

Why? Because the only way to study this topic scientifically would be to place newborns randomly in "permissive" vs. "disciplined" families and then keep them under close observation for ten or fifteen years. Since it is impossible to do that, researchers have tried to tease out information where they could find it. But family relationships are so multidimensional and complicated that they almost defy rigorous scrutiny. Indeed, most of the studies reported in the literature are scientifically useless. For example, Dr. David Larson, psychiatrist and formerly a researcher at the National Institutes of Health, reviewed 132 articles in professional journals that purported to investigate the long-term consequences of corporal punishment. He found most of them flawed in design. Ninety percent of the studies failed to distinguish between good homes where spanking was administered by loving parents, and those bordering on (or actually inflicting) child abuse. This distinction is critical for obvious reasons. Dr. Larson concluded that the findings were invalidated by this failure to consider the overall health of family relationships.[28]

To repeat, the consequences of various approaches to parental discipline appear to be beyond the reach of social research. It is simply not possible to study this complex subject scientifically without warping families to set up the research design. Even if such studies were conducted, the researchers would be studying contrived families—not typical parent-child relationships.

Q.80 My wife and I are keenly aware of how difficult it is to be good parents, and at times, we feel very inadequate to do the job. How does a mom or dad know what's best for a child from day to day?

The most dedicated parents go through times when they fear they aren't responding properly to their children. They wonder if they're overreacting or underreacting, being too strict or too lenient. They suspect that they're making major mistakes that will haunt them later on. Fortunately, parents don't have to do everything right. We all make thousands of little mistakes—and a few big ones—that we wish we could reverse. But somehow, most kids roll with these blunders and come out just fine anyway.

Let me give you what I consider to be the key to good parenting. It is to learn how to get behind the eyes of your child, seeing what he sees and feeling what he feels. When you know his frame of mind, your response becomes obvious. For example, when he's lonely, he needs your company. When he's defiant, he needs your help in controlling impulses. When he's afraid, he needs the security of your embrace. When he's happy, he needs to share his laughter and joy with those he loves. Raising healthy children, then, is not so much a science as it is a highly developed art, and most of us have the natural intuitive faculties to learn it.

Take the time to observe those kids who live in your house. If you tune in closely to what they say and do, the feelings behind those behaviors will soon become apparent. Then your reaction to what you've seen will lead to more confident parenthood.

Q81 My husband's parents are wonderful people, and we love them very much. They have always refrained from interfering in our family; that is, until our daughter was born. Now they're arguing with us about how we're raising her and are undermining the things we're trying to teach. We want to base Amy's upbringing on biblical principles, but not being Christians, my in-laws don't really understand this. How can we deal with this situation without offending them?

It is time to have a loving but candid conversation with your in-laws about how your child will be raised. I would suggest that you take them to dinner some evening, during which this topic will be addressed. When the moment is right, tell them of your concerns. Make it clear that you love them and want them to enjoy their granddaughter. But the responsibility for how she is being managed must rest entirely with you and your husband. Remind them that they had their day—when the decisions about child rearing were theirs alone. Spell out the issues that mean the most to you, including your desire to raise your daughter according to Christian principles. Try to help them understand your reasons, but recognize that their worldview might make it impossible for them to agree. If that is the case, they'll need to honor your wishes anyway.

It is likely that sparks will fly during this conversation. If so, try to remain calm and stand your ground. If the worst occurs and the dinner ends in an emotional walkout, I suggest that you give your in-laws some space while they're cooling off. When you do come back together, let love and respect continue to be your guides—but don't back off on the issue at hand. You have the right to do what you're doing. Your in-laws are the ones who are out of line. But remember that Amy needs her grandparents, and your goal should be to harmonize your relationship. In most cases, that will occur in time.

Q 82 Should schoolchildren be required to wear clothes that they dislike?

Generally not. Children are very concerned about the threat of being laughed at by their friends and will sometimes go to great lengths to avoid that danger. Conformity is fueled by the fear of ridicule. Teens, particularly, seem to feel, *The group can't laugh at me if I am identical to them*. From this perspective, it's unwise to make a child endure unnecessary social humiliation. Children should be allowed to select their own clothes, within certain limits of budget and good taste.

Q 83 Do you think children between five and ten should be allowed to listen to rock music on the radio, TV, or CDs?

Not if it can be avoided. Today's contemporary music is an expression of an increasingly unsavory adolescent culture. The lyrics often deal with drug use, sex, and violence. This is just what you don't want your seven-year-old thinking about. Instead, his or her entertainment should consist of adventure books, children's productions, Bible stories and other Christian literature, and family activities— camping, fishing, sporting events, games, etc.

On the other hand, it is unwise to appear dictatorial and oppressive in such matters. I would suggest that you keep your preteen so involved with wholesome activities that he does not need to dream of the days to come.

Q84 It seems to me that children are far too familiar—too informal—with adults today. When I was a kid, we always addressed grown-ups as "Mr." or "Mrs.," or if they were in the family, we called them "Uncle" or "Aunt" or "Grandpa" or "Grandma." We would never have referred to an adult as Sam or Alice. But today's parents don't teach that courtesy to their children. Some of them introduce other adults to four-year-olds by their first names. Am I the only one who is concerned about this? What can I do to counteract this trend with my own son and daughter?

I've been bothered by that same observation. It's a by-product of a cultural shift within society itself. We are less respectful of one another today in many ways. Fifty years ago, for example, men didn't curse around women, and cultured women didn't curse at all. How that has changed! Both men and women used to address each other with formal titles (Mr., Mrs., Miss, etc.) unless they had become very close friends. Now, a waitress whom you've never met approaches your table and says, "Hi, I'm Stephanie, and I'm going to be serving you today."

I don't suppose today's informality is harmful, although I agree that children should be taught to speak to their elders with a certain deference. I still like to hear them respond with "Yes, ma'am" and "No, sir," instead of "yeah," "yep," and "nope." When their manners are respectful, their entire demeanor is on a higher plane.

As for how you can instill these and other courtesies in your child, you simply make up your mind to do it. You might explain that there are many things your family does differently than others: For example, "We don't use bad language, we don't attend certain kinds of movies, and we don't (fill in the blank). Why? Because we've set a higher standard for ourselves. This is what makes us unique as a family, and we believe it is what God would have us do. Someday you will understand that, too."

Q85 We are not able financially to take long car trips or get into expensive hobbies, like skiing. Could you suggest some simple traditions that will appeal to small children?

You don't have to spend huge amounts of money to have a meaningful family life. Children love the most simple, repetitive kinds of activities. They want to be read the same stories hundreds of times and to hear the same jokes long after they've heard the punch lines. These interactions with parents are often more fun than expensive toys or special events.

A friend of mine once asked his grown children what they remembered most fondly from their childhoods. Was it the vacations they took together or the trips to Disney World or the zoo? No, they told him. It was when he would get on the floor and wrestle with the four of them. They would gang-tackle the "old man" and laugh until their sides hurt. That's the way children think. The most meaningful activities within families are often those that focus on that which is spontaneous and personal.

This is why you can't buy your way out of parenting responsibilities, though many have tried. Busy and exhausted mothers and fathers, especially those who are affluent, sometimes attempt to "pay off" their deprived kids with toys, cars, and expensive experiences. It rarely works. What boys and girls want most is time spent with their parents— building things in the garage or singing in the car or hiking to an old fishing pond.

I would also recommend reserving at least one night a week for reading out loud with the family.

That can be difficult to accomplish with children of varying ages. If your sons and daughters are clustered in age, I think it's a great activity. You can read *Tom Sawyer, Little House on the Prairie, Stuart Little,* and other books that have been so popular down through the years. The idea is to read together as a family.

In short, many families have forgotten how to have fun in everyday experiences. The things they do together can become hallmarks of their years together. No toy to be played with alone can ever compete with the enjoyment of such moments. And they will be remembered for a lifetime.

Q86 We have an adopted girl who came to us when she was four years old. She is very difficult to handle and does pretty much what she pleases. For us to make her obey would be very unpleasant for her, and frankly, we don't feel we have the right to do that. She has been through a lot in her short life. Besides, we're not her real parents. Do you think she'll be okay if we just give her a lot of love and attention?

I'm afraid you have a formula for serious problems with this girl later on. The danger is in seeing yourselves as substitute or stand-in parents who don't have the right to lead her. That is a mistake. Since you have legally adopted this child, you *are* her "real" parents, and your failure to see it that way may be setting up the defiant behavior you mentioned. It is a common error made by parents of older adopted children. They pity their youngsters too much to confront them. They feel that life has already been too hard on them, and they must not make things worse by discipline and occasional punishment. As a result, they are tentative and permissive with a child who is crying out for leadership.

Transplanted children have the same needs for

guidance and discipline as those remaining with their biological parents. One of the surest ways to make them feel insecure is to treat them as though they are different, unusual, or brittle. If the parents view such a child as an unfortunate waif to be shielded, he will tend to see himself that way too.

Parents of sick and disabled children often make this same mistake. They find discipline harder to implement because of the tenderness they feel for that child. Thus, a boy or girl with a heart condition or some terminal illness can become a little terror, simply because the usual behavioral boundaries are not established and defended. It must be remembered that the need to be led and governed is almost universal in childhood, and it isn't lessened by other problems and difficulties in life. In some cases, the desire for boundaries is actually increased by other troubles, for it is through loving control that parents build security and a sense of personal worth in a child.

Returning to the question, I advise you to love that little girl like crazy—and hold her to the same standards of behavior that you would your own flesh and blood. Remember, you *are* her parents!

Q87 Are adopted children more likely to be rebellious than children raised by biological parents? If so, are there any steps I can take to prevent or ease the conflict? My husband and I are thinking about adopting a toddler, and the question has me worried.

Every child is different, and adopted kids are no exception. They come in all sorts of packages. Some boys and girls who were abused or unloved prior to the adoption will react to those painful experiences in some way . . . usually negatively. Others, even those who were not mistreated, will struggle with identity problems and wonder why their "real" mothers and fathers didn't want them. They may be driven to find their biological parents during or after adolescence to learn more about their heritage and family of origin. I must emphasize, however, that many adopted kids do not go through any of these personal crises. They take root where they are replanted and never give a thought to the questions that trouble some of their peers. As with so many other behavioral issues, the critical factors are the particular temperament of the child and how he or she is handled by the parents.

I hope you won't be reluctant to adopt that child because some special problems might—but probably won't—develop. *Every* child has his or her own particular challenges. *Every* child can be difficult to raise. *Every* child requires all the creative energy and talent a parent can muster. But *every* child is also worth the effort, and there is no higher calling than to do that job excellently.

Let me add one more thought. I knew a man and woman who had waited for years to adopt a baby. When a female infant was finally made available to them, they were anxious to know if she was healthy and of good heritage. They asked if her biological parents had used drugs, how tall they were, whether or not they had attended college, etc. Then, the father told me later, he realized what he and his wife were doing. They were approaching the adoption of this baby much like they would have bought a used car. They were "kicking tires" and "testing the engine." But then they thought, *What in the world are we doing? That little girl is a human being with an eternal soul. We have been given the opportunity to mold and shape her as a child of God, and here we are demanding that she be a high-quality product.* They repented of their inappropriate attitudes and embraced that child in love.

Adopted children, like all children, are a blessing from God, and we are privileged indeed to be granted the honor of raising one of His precious kids.

Q88 How would you go about telling a child he or she is adopted, and when should that disclosure occur?

First, begin talking to your toddlers about their adoption before they can understand the meaning of the words. That way there will never be a moment when disclosure is necessary. To learn of adoption from a neighbor or other family member can be an awful shock to an individual. Don't risk the devastation of a later discovery by failing to take the sting out of the issue in babyhood.

Second, celebrate two birthdays with equal gusto each year: the anniversary of her birth, and the anniversary of the day she became your daughter. That is a handy mechanism by which the fact of adoption can be introduced. It also provides a way to equalize the status of siblings. Biological children have a psychological advantage that they sometimes lord over their adopted brother or sister. That one-upmanship is neutralized somewhat when the adopted child gets a second birthday.

Third, present the adoptive event as a tremendous blessing (as implied above) that brought great excitement to the household. Tell about praying for a child and waiting patiently for God's answer. Then describe how the news came that the Lord had answered those prayers and how the whole family thanked Him for His gift of love. Let your child know your delight when you first saw him lying in a crib, and how cute he looked in his blue blanket, etc. Tell him that his adoption was one of the happiest days of your life, and how you raced to the telephone to call all your friends and family members to share the fantastic news. (Again, I'm assuming that these details are true.)

Tell him the story of Moses' adoption by Pharaoh's daughter, and how God chose him for a great work with the children of Israel. Look for similar situations that convey respect and dignity to the adoptee. You see, the child's interpretation of the adoptive event is almost totally dependent on the manner in which it is conveyed during the early years. Most certainly, one does not want to approach the subject sadly, admitting reluctantly that a dark and troublesome secret must now be confessed.

Fourth, when the foundation has been laid and the issue defused, then forget it. Don't constantly remind the child of his uniqueness to the point of foolishness. Mention the matter when it is appropriate, but don't reveal anxiety or tension by constantly throwing adoption in the child's face. Youngsters are amazingly perceptive at reading these thinly disguised attitudes.

I believe it is possible, by following these commonsense suggestions, to raise an adopted child without psychological trauma or personal insult.

Q89 What should you tell an adopted child about his or her biological parents in "closed" adoption situations? How do you answer his tough questions about why he wasn't wanted, etc.?

I'll give you an answer written by Dr. Milton Levine in a vintage parenting book entitled *Your Child from Two to Five,* then I'll comment on his recommendation. Dr. Levine was associate professor of pediatrics, New York Hospital, at the time. He listed three possible ways to tell an adopted child about his origin, as follows:

1. Tell the child his biological parents are dead.
2. State plainly that the biological parents were unable to care for their baby themselves.
3. Tell the child nothing is known about the biological parents but that he was secured from an agency dedicated to finding good homes for babies.

Dr. Levine preferred the first approach because "the child who is told that his biological parents are dead is free to love the mother and father he lives with. He won't be tormented by a haunting obligation to search for his biological parents when he's grown."

He continued, "Since the possibility of losing one's parents is one of childhood's greatest fears, it is true that the youngster who is told that his biological parents are dead may feel that all parents, including his second set, are pretty impermanent. Nevertheless, I feel that in the long run the child will find it easier to adjust to death than to abandonment. To tell a youngster that his parents gave him up because they were unable to take care of him is to present him with a complete rejection. He cannot comprehend the circumstances which might lead to such an act. But an unwholesome view of himself as an unwanted object, not worth fighting to keep, might be established."[29]

I disagree with Dr. Levine at this point. I am unwilling to lie to my child about anything and would not tell him that his natural parents were dead if that were not true. Sooner or later, he will learn that he has been misled, which could undermine our relationship and bring the entire adoption story under suspicion.

Instead, I would be inclined to tell the child that very little is known about his biological parents. Several inoffensive and vague possibilities could be offered to him, such as, "We can only guess at the reasons the man and woman could not raise you. They may have been extremely poor and were unable to give you the care you needed, or maybe the woman was sick, or she may not have had a home. We just don't know. But there is one thing we *do* know. She must have loved you very, very much—enough to give you life and to make sure you were raised in a loving home where you would be taken care of. We're so thankful that the Lord led her to let us raise you."

Q90 Are there times when good, loving parents don't like their own kids very much?

Yes, just as there are times in a good marriage when husbands and wives don't like each other for a while. What you should do in both situations is hang tough. Look for ways to make the relationship better, but never give up your commitment to one another. That is especially true during the teen years, when the person we see will be very different in a few years. Wait patiently for him or her to grow up. You'll be glad you did.

Q91 Don't you think most of the differences between the sexes result from cultural conditioning? If we would raise boys and girls the same way, these differences would disappear.

I couldn't disagree more. God created two sexes, not one. He built genetic characteristics in males and females that no amount of training in childhood will eliminate. Let me quote Christina Hoff Sommers, author of *Who Stole Feminism?* She wrote:

The feminist fight against the facts of life is unceasing. Last year, Hasbro Toys tested a doll house they were considering marketing to both boys and girls. The Hasbro researchers found that girls and boys did not interact with the doll house in the same way. The girls dressed the dolls and played house; the boys catapulted the baby carriage from the roof. Sharon Hartley, a Hasbro general manager, explained what in prior times would have been considered obvious: "Boys and girls have different play patterns."

Despite the overwhelming evidence that males' and females' brains are wired differently, feminists still cling to the mistaken belief that cultural influences are all that separate them. They are wrong. Nevertheless, Gloria Steinem still believes "We badly need to raise our boys more like girls."[30]

There used to be an old proverb that proclaimed "Boys will be boys." Guess what? It's true. And girls will be girls. That's the way they're made.

Q92 Is there a way I as a father can influence my daughter's attitude toward boys? If she chooses to marry, she will need to understand men and know how to relate to them. Is that something I should be thinking about?

You bet it is. Long before a girl finds her first real boyfriend or falls in love, her attitude toward men has been shaped quietly by her father. Why? Because the father-daughter relationship sets the stage for all future romantic involvements.

If a young woman's father rejects her, she'll spend her life trying to find a man who can meet the needs he never fulfilled in her heart. If he's warm and nurturing, she'll look for a lover to equal him. If he thinks she's beautiful and feminine, she'll be inclined to see herself that way. But if he rejects her as unattractive and uninteresting, she's likely to carry self-image problems into her adult years.

It's also true that a woman's relationship with her husband is significantly influenced by the way she perceived her father's authority. If he was overbearing or capricious during her earlier years, she may precipitate power struggles with her husband throughout married life. But if Dad blended love and discipline in a way that conveyed strength, she may be more comfortable with a give-and-take marriage characterized by mutual respect.

So much of what goes into marriage starts with the bride's father. That's why it behooves those of us with daughters to give our best effort to raising them properly. You are right to be thinking about that vital relationship.

Q93 When do children begin to develop a sexual nature? Does this occur suddenly during puberty?

No, it occurs long before puberty. Perhaps the most important concept suggested by Freud was his observation that children are not asexual. He stated that sexual gratification begins in the cradle and is first associated with feeding.[31] Behavior during childhood is influenced considerably by sexual curiosity and interest, although the happy hormones do not take full charge until early adolescence. Thus, it is not uncommon for a four-year-old to be interested in nudity and the sexual apparatus of the opposite sex.

The elementary school years are an important time in the forming of sexual attitudes. Parents should be careful not to express shock and disgust over this kind of curiosity, even though they have to disapprove of exploratory behavior. It is believed that many sexual problems begin as a result of inappropriate training during early childhood.

Q.94 My four-year-old has recently "discovered" his penis and seems rather preoccupied with it. Do you think it's unusual or sinful for him to fondle himself so much?

The answer to both of your questions is an emphatic no! Unintentional (or even intentional) self-arousal in young children, specifically boys, is neither unusual nor sinful. Your little guy is simply showing that he is "properly wired." There are no long-term consequences to this kind of innocent childish behavior, and it will soon resolve itself.

The only significance to early fondling activity is in how you as a parent deal with it. I've received letters from mothers who say they have spanked their preschoolers for touching themselves. Some have described great concerns about this behavior, seeing it as evidence of an immoral nature that had to be crushed. That is a very dangerous posture to take. I suggest that you not make a big deal over it.

Q.95 That's easy for you to say. My four-year-old daughter doesn't just fondle herself at home, where we ignore it. She rubs herself whenever we are in public, such as at church or at a restaurant. How should I deal with that?

You should respond as a teacher, not a disciplinarian. Take your daughter aside and talk about your concern. Explain that there are some things that we don't do in public—not because they are wrong, but because they are impolite. Just as you wouldn't urinate in front of other people, you should not be touching yourself when others can see you. If she continues to fondle herself, other people will think she is strange and some may laugh at her——something you're sure she wouldn't like. Your purpose in speaking this way is to sensitize her to the social implications involved in what she's doing. Show yourself to be firm and confident, not shocked or embarrassed.

The key to your approach is the avoidance of any suggestion that her body is dirty or "wrong" or evil. Such an implication might raise a whole host of other problems for your child that could carry over into adolescence and even adulthood.

Q96 I am concerned about the impact of television in our home. How can we control it without resorting to dictatorial rules and regulations?

It seems that we have three objectives as parents: First, we want to monitor the quality of the programs our children watch. Second, we want to regulate the quantity of television they see. Even good programs may have an undesirable influence on the rest of children's activities if they spend too much time watching them. Third, we should include the entire family in establishing a TV policy.

I read about a system recently that is very effective in accomplishing all three of these purposes. First, it was suggested that parents sit down with the children and agree upon a list of approved programs that are appropriate for each age level. Then type that list (or at least write it clearly) and enclose it in clear plastic so it can be referred to throughout the week.

Second, either purchase or make a roll of tickets. Issue each child ten tickets per week, and let him or her use them to "buy" the privilege of watching the programs on the approved list. When the tickets are gone, television viewing is over for that week. This teaches a child to be discriminating about what is watched. A maximum of ten hours of viewing per week might be an appropriate place to start, compared with the national average of forty to fifty hours per week. That's far too much, especially for an elementary school child.

This system can be modified to fit individual home situations or circumstances. If there's a special program that all the children want to see, such as a feature broadcast or a holiday program during Christmas and Thanksgiving, you can issue more tickets. You might also give extra tickets as rewards for achievement or some other laudable behavior.

The real test will occur when parents reveal whether or not they have the courage to put themselves on that limited system, too. We often need the same regulations in our viewing habits!

Q97 I am very irritated by all the sex and violence on television night after night. The movies are bad enough, but now the sitcoms are just as bad. Is there any way we can influence the networks to be more responsible in their programming?

We have more power to influence television programming than we think. I'm told that every letter received is estimated to represent forty thousand viewers who didn't take time to write. It's important to know, however, where those letters should be sent. In earlier days, I wrote directors, producers, and other executives at the television networks. My complaints either received rude replies or were largely ignored. I've since learned it's more beneficial to write the sponsors—the people who pay the bills. They have better reason to care what I think.

Witness the success of Fort Worth dentist Dr. Richard Neill, who became upset with the kind of filthy programming aired regularly on the *Phil*

Donahue show during hours when children could have been watching. He began writing the commercial sponsors and informing them of what their money was supporting. One after another, more than one hundred of these advertisers began dropping the show. By 1996, the Donahue program was no longer viable, and it went off the air. Almost single-handedly, Dr. Neill took on a media giant—an icon—and put an end to the junk he was producing.[32] This kind of effort can and should be duplicated all over the country. It is the only way we will clean up the tube.

Advertisers are very responsive to the opinions of viewers because they are spending millions of dollars to promote their products. We can bring pressure on them by letting them know how we feel—positively and negatively. And indeed, we must do this.

Q 98 The children who play with my kids in the neighborhood are familiar with terrible programs on television and cable. I can't believe that their parents let them watch such violent and sexualized stuff. What is the long-term consequence of this programming on children?

It is sad and very difficult to understand why so many parents fail to supervise what their kids watch. To those who let them watch anything they wish, I would pose this proposition: Suppose a complete stranger came to your door and said, "You look tired. Why don't you let me take care of your children for a day or two?" I doubt if many of you would say, "Great idea. Come on in."[33]

That's a story Peggy Charren, president of Action for Children's Television, likes to tell. Her point is well taken. When we sit our children in front of the television set, we're giving control over them to complete strangers; and more and more, that's a risky thing to do. An increasing number of studies have found that violence on television frequently leads to later aggressive behavior by children and teenagers.

One of the most conclusive studies was conducted by Dr. Leonard D. Aaron. He examined a group of children at age eight and then again at nineteen and finally at thirty. Children in the United States, Australia, Finland, Israel, and Poland were studied. The outcome was the same; the more frequently the participants watched violent television at age eight, the more likely they were to be convicted of crimes by age thirty, and the more aggressive was their behavior when drinking.[34]

It's time for parents to control the amount and the content of television that their children are watching. The consequences of not doing so can be catastrophic.

Q99 What is your opinion of Nintendo and other kinds of video games? They've been claiming a big portion of our son's time over the past few months, and I'm getting uneasy about it.

Depending on the particular games in question, you may have a valid cause for concern. Dr. Vince Hammond, head of the National Coalition on Television Violence, has described the potentially harmful nature of video games, especially those with violent themes.[35] Some observers have come to the conclusion that these games can become obsessive and encourage aggressive behavior. There's even evidence to suggest that children between the ages of eight and ten are 80 percent more likely to fight with one another after playing with them.[36]

I'd advise you to put clear limits on the amount of

time your son will be allowed to spend with video games or the Internet so that he won't become obsessed with them. Insist that he avoid the violent ones altogether. With realistic guidelines I think it's possible to keep this kind of activity under control rather than let it control your son and your family.

Q. 100 What's the appeal of all this human suffering and violence on television and in movies? Why do people want more of it?

I'm sure it has something to do with our desire for excitement and our need to escape from the boring existence many people experience. But I have to admit I don't fully understand it. It is difficult to comprehend why people enjoy watching such bloody events. A number of years ago, the number-one television program of the entire year, watched by more people than all the sporting events or any other single program in the course of the twelve-month period, was *Helter Skelter,* the story of the Charles Manson family.[37] One incident in that TV special was the murder of a woman, eight months pregnant, who was brutally stabbed in the abdomen. Why would anyone want to see such brutality? The popularity of that program and others like it speaks dramatically about the depravity of the American people and our lust for violence.

Q. 101 What do you think it will do to us to continue watching extreme violence night after night?

Walter Lippman once wrote that a saturation of this kind of sensationalism can actually destroy a people and a culture. I agree with him completely. We've already come to the point where decent people are afraid to go outdoors at night. We live in terror. No one is safe, not even old people who have so little that criminals really want. Television *does* have the power to destroy us as a nation. I fear it may already have damaged us beyond repair.

Q 102 I have a friend who guards her kids as if they were in mortal danger. I feel like I should let my daughters spread their wings a little, even though they're only nine and eleven years of age. Who do you think is right?

Two decades ago I would have suggested that you give them space, because overprotection of children creates some characteristic problems. Today, however, I have to agree with your friend. The environment in which children are being raised has changed dramatically in recent years. Unspeakable dangers that were almost unheard of a generation ago haunt our schools and streets. Yesterday's families didn't worry much about drive-by shootings, illegal drugs, sexual molesters, and kidnappers. When I was a kid in the early 1950s, my folks were more concerned about a disease called polio than all sources of violence combined. As a ten-year-old, I moved freely around my hometown. If I was a half hour late coming home for dinner, the Dobson household was not seized by panic. But now we worry about our kids playing in the front yard. Indeed, little Polly Klaas was abducted in 1993 from her bedroom, where she was surrounded by friends, and then was brutally murdered for the perverse pleasure of her killer. When that horrible news broke, a collective shudder was felt by every loving parent in the nation. Three years later, beautiful little six-year-old JonBenét Ramsey was sexually assaulted and beaten to death in the basement of her own home on Christmas night 1996. Between these two tragedies and in the years since, tens of thousands of other children were mur-

dered and abducted. During my term of service on
the Attorney General's Board on Missing and Exploited Children, I was dismayed by what I saw happening to innocent boys and girls.

There was a time when the culture interceded on
behalf of kids to protect them from anything harmful
or immoral. Movies were censored, music was mon-
itored, and young couples were chaperoned. But this
generation is exposed to every kind of evil and violence. Some boys and girls live in a combat zone. Indeed, a child in the United States is fifteen times
more likely to be killed by gunfire than one growing
up in Northern Ireland! More American children are
shot per year than are police officers![38] Parents in
some inner-city neighborhoods make their kids sleep
in bathtubs to protect them from stray bullets crash-
ing through the walls. Some mothers keep short
leashes on their little ones when walking through
malls to protect them from potential molesters. Instruction is given to wide-eyed preschoolers on how
to scream when approached by a stranger and how to
report unwelcome touches. Many children spend
their after-school hours behind bolted doors and
barred windows. That is the way it is in most Western nations today, and especially in the United
States.

How can you as a parent protect your precious
children? By watching them every moment! Never
leave them in the care of those whom you don't
know personally and aren't sure you can trust. Do
not let teenage boys baby-sit your girls. I know that
is a controversial recommendation, but I've seen too
many tragic cases of abuse resulting from masculine
adolescence and the sexual curiosity that is typical of
that age. Walk your kids to and from school or the
school bus. Pick them up on time. Watch for any un-

usual behavior that may signal sexual abuse or molestation from neighbors or child-care workers. Protect
them at every turn.

Does that sound unnecessarily cautious? Just remember this: The average pedophile abuses 150
children in the course of a lifetime.[39] Each sexual exploitation lasts for seven years, typically, before the
truth comes to light.[40] Boys and girls are often too intimidated to call for help. Don't give a child abuser a
shot at your kids.

As for your own anxieties, I suggest that you take
them to the Lord in prayer. He loves your girls even
more than you do, and I believe He will help you
take care of them. Hold their names before Him
every day in prayer. Commit to intercede not only
for their physical safety but also for their spiritual
welfare. Then when you've done everything you can
to be a good parent, put your children in God's
hands and let Him help you carry the burden.

7

DISCIPLINING THE
ELEMENTARY SCHOOL CHILD

Q103 Philosophically, I recognize the need to take charge of my kids, but I need more specifics. Give me a step-by-step approach to discipline that will help me do the job correctly.

All right, let me outline six broad guidelines that I think you'll be able to apply. These principles represent the essence of my philosophy of discipline.

First: Define the boundaries before they are enforced. The most important step in any disciplinary procedure is to establish reasonable expectations and boundaries in advance. The child should know what is and what is not acceptable behavior before he is held responsible for those rules. This precondition will eliminate the sense of injustice that a youngster feels when he is slapped or punished for his accidents, mistakes, and blunders. If you haven't defined it—don't enforce it!

Second: When defiantly challenged, respond with confident decisiveness. Once a child understands what is expected, she should then be held accountable for behaving accordingly. That sounds easy, but as we have seen, most children will assault the authority of their elders and challenge their right to lead. In a moment of rebellion, a little child will consider her parents' instructions and defiantly choose to disobey. Like a military general before a battle, she will calculate the potential risk, marshal her forces, and attack the enemy with guns blazing. When that nose-to-nose confrontation occurs between generations, it is extremely important for the adult to win decisively and confidently. The child has made it clear that she's looking for a fight, and her parents would be wise not to disappoint her! Nothing is more destructive to parental leadership than for a mother or father to disintegrate during that struggle. When parents consistently lose those battles, resorting to tears and screaming and other evidence of frustration, some dramatic changes take place in the way they are seen by their children. Instead of being secure and confident leaders, they become spineless jellyfish who are unworthy of respect or allegiance.

Third: Distinguish between willful defiance and childish irresponsibility. A child should not be punished for behavior that is not willfully defiant. When he forgets to feed the dog or make his bed or take out the trash—when he leaves your tennis racket outside in the rain or loses his bicycle—remember that these behaviors are typical of childhood. It is the mechanism by which an immature mind is protected from adult anxieties and pressures. Be gentle as you teach him to do better. If he fails to respond to your patient instruction, it then becomes appropriate to administer some well-deserved consequences (he may have to work to pay for the item he abused or be deprived of its use, etc.). Just remember that childish irresponsibility is very different from willful defiance and should be handled more patiently.

Fourth: Reassure and teach as soon as the confrontation is over. After a time of conflict during which the parent has demonstrated his or her right to lead (particularly if it resulted in tears for the child), the young-ster between two and seven (or older) may want to be loved and reassured. By all means, open your arms and let her come! Hold her close and tell her of your love. Rock her gently and let her know, again, why she was punished and how she can avoid the trouble next time. This moment of communication builds love, fidelity, and family unity. And for the Christian family, it is extremely important to pray with the child at that time, admitting to God that we have all sinned and no one is perfect. Divine forgiveness is a marvelous experience even for a very young child.

Fifth: Avoid impossible demands. Be absolutely sure that your child is capable of delivering what you require. Never punish him for wetting the bed invol-untarily or for not becoming potty trained by one year of age or for doing poorly in school when he is incapable of academic success. These impossible de-mands put the child in an unresolvable conflict: There is no way out. That condition brings inevitable damage to the human emotional apparatus.

Sixth: Let love be your guide! A relationship that is characterized by genuine love and affection is likely to be a healthy one, even though some parental mistakes and errors are inevitable.

Q 104 I want to manage and lead my strong-willed child properly, but I'm afraid I'll break his spirit and damage him in some way. How can I deal with his misbehavior without hurting his self-concept?

I sense that you do not have a clear understanding of the difference between breaking the spirit and shap-ing the will of a child. The human spirit, as I have de-fined it, relates to the self-esteem or the personal worth that a child feels. As such, it is exceedingly fragile at all ages and must be handled with care. You as a parent correctly assume that you can damage your child's spirit quite easily—by ridicule, disrespect, threats to withdraw love, and by verbal rejection. Anything that depreciates his self-worth can be costly to his spirit.

However, while the spirit is brittle and must be treated gently, the will is made of steel. It is one of the few intellectual components that arrives full strength at the moment of birth. In a past issue of *Psychology Today,* this heading described the research findings from a study of infancy: "A baby knows who he is before he has language to tell us so. He reaches deliberately for control of his environment, especially his parents."[41] This scientific disclosure would be no surprise to the parents of a strong-willed infant. They have walked the floor with him in the wee small hours, listening to this tiny dictator as he made his wants and wishes abundantly clear.

Later, some defiant toddlers can become so angry that they are capable of holding their breath until they lose consciousness. Anyone who has ever witnessed this full measure of willful defiance has been shocked by its power. One headstrong three-year-old recently refused to obey a direct command from her mother, saying, "You're just my mommy, you know!" Another mere mommy wrote me that she found herself in a similar confrontation with her three-year-old son over something that she wanted him to eat. He was so enraged by her insistence that he refused to eat or drink anything for two full days. He became weak and lethargic but steadfastly held his ground. The mother was worried and guilt-ridden, as might be expected. Finally, in desperation, the father looked the child in the eyes and convinced him that he was going to receive a well-deserved spanking if he didn't eat his dinner. With that maneuver, the contest was over. The toddler surrendered. He began to consume everything he could get his hands on and virtually emptied the refrigerator.

Now tell me, please, why have so few child-development authorities recognized this willful defiance? Why have they written so little about it? My guess is that the acknowledgment of childish imperfection would not fit neatly with the humanistic notion that little people are infused with sunshine and goodness and merely learn the meaning of selfishness and disobedience. To those who hold that rosy view I can only say, "Take another look!"

Returning to your question, your objective as a parent is to shape the will of your child while leaving his spirit intact.

Q105 How early in life is a child capable of making a stand like that?

Depending on the temperament of the individual, defiant behavior can be displayed by very young children. A father once told me of taking his three-year-old daughter to a basketball game. The child was, of course, interested in everything in the gym except the athletic contest. The father permitted her to roam freely and climb on the bleachers, but he set up definite limits regarding how far she could stray. He took her by the hand and walked with her to a stripe painted on the gym floor.

"You can play all around the building, Janie, but don't go past this line," he instructed her.

Dad had no sooner returned to his seat than the toddler scurried in the direction of the forbidden territory. She stopped at the border for a moment, then flashed a grin over her shoulder to her father and deliberately placed one foot over the line as if to say, "Whacha gonna do about it?" Virtually every parent the world over has been asked the same question at one time or another. That's the way some kids are made.

Q 106 Are we all rather like that little girl, or is the inclination toward disobedience something people grow out of when they get older?

The entire human race is afflicted with the same rebellious nature, although it takes different forms when we get older. Think about it. The behavior of that child in the gym is not so different from the disobedience of the first family, Adam and Eve. The Creator had told them they could eat anything in the Garden of Eden except the forbidden fruit (i.e., "do not go past this line"). Yet they foolishly disobeyed God and thereby introduced a character flaw into the human race. Perhaps our willful behavior is the essence of original sin, which has infected our species. It certainly explains why I place such stress on the proper response to disobedience during childhood. Rebellion is dangerous, whether it responds to parental leadership or to the authority of God Himself.

Q 107 My little boy always wants to know just how far I will let him go. Once he has tested me and found I'm serious about what I say, he'll usually cooperate at that point. What is going on in his mind?

Your child, like most other kids, has a great need to know where behavioral boundaries are and who has the courage to enforce them. Let me illustrate how that works.

Years ago, during the early days of the progressive-education movement, an enthusiastic theorist decided to take down the chain-link fence that surrounded the nursery-school yard. He thought the children would feel more freedom of movement without that visible barrier surrounding them. When the fence was removed, however, the boys and girls huddled near the center of the play yard. Not only did they not wander away, they didn't even venture to the edge of the grounds. Clearly, there is a security for all of us in defined boundaries. That's why a child will push a parent to the point of exasperation at times. She's testing the resolve of the mother or father and exploring the limits of her world.

Do you want further evidence of this motivation? Consider the relationships within a family where the dad is a firm but loving disciplinarian, the mother is indecisive and weak, and the child is a strong-willed spitfire. Notice how the mother is pushed, challenged, sassed, disobeyed, and insulted—but the father can bring order with a word or two. What is going on here? The child simply understands and accepts Dad's strength. The limits are clear. There is no reason to test him again. But Mom has established no rules, and she is fair game for a fight—every day, if necessary.

The very fact that your child accepts the boundaries you have set tells you that he or she respects you. That youngster will still test the outer limits occasionally to see if the "fence" is still there.

Q 108 I think you are right about the motivation of a strong-willed child. My five-year-old is one of those rambunctious kids who gives us fits. There are times when I think he's trying to take over the entire family. I've never really understood him before, but I guess he just doesn't want anyone telling him what to do.

That is precisely how he feels. It is surprising how commonly this basic impulse of children is overlooked. Indeed, I think the really tough kids understand the struggle for control even better than their parents, who are bogged down with adult responsibilities and worries. Children devote their primary effort to the power game while we grown-ups play only when we must. Sometime you might ask a group of children about the adults who lead them. They will instantly tell you, with one voice, which grown-ups are skilled in handling them and which aren't. Every schoolchild can name the teachers who are in control and those who are intimidated by kids.

One father overheard his five-year-old daughter, Laura, say to her little sister, who was doing something wrong, "Mmmm, I'm going to tell Mommy on you. No! I'll tell Daddy. He's worse!" Laura had evaluated the authority of her two parents and concluded that one was more effective than the other.

This same child was observed by her father to have become especially disobedient and defiant. She was irritating other family members and looking for ways to avoid minding her parents. Her dad decided not to confront her directly but to punish her consistently for every offense until she settled down. Thus, for three or four days, he let Laura get away with nothing. She was spanked, stood in the corner, and sent to her bedroom. Near the end of the fourth day, she was sitting on the bed with her father and younger sister. Without provocation, Laura pulled the hair of the toddler, who was looking at a book. Her dad promptly thumped her on the head with his large hand. Laura did not cry but sat in silence for a moment or two and then said, "Harrumph! All my tricks are not working!"

This is the conclusion you want your strong-willed son to draw: "It's too risky to take on Mom or Dad, so let's get with the program."

Q 109 Are children *really* that calculating about their misbehavior? If so, I've not understood them at all.

Some are; some aren't. We're talking here about the child who is driven to be his own boss—to take orders from no one. That kid can be very deliberate about his purposes. I had a friend when I was a child who best typified this calculating spirit. Earl was like a military general who had deciphered the enemy code, permitting him to outmaneuver his opponents at every turn. He seemed to know every move his parents were going to make. I once spent the night with him, and after we were tucked into our own twin beds, he gave me an astounding description of his father's temper.

Earl said, "When my dad gets very angry, he uses some really bad words that will amaze you." He gave me three or four startling examples of things his dad would say.

I replied, "I don't believe it!"

Mr. Walker was a very tall, reserved man who seemed to have it all together. I just couldn't conceive of his saying the words Earl had quoted.

"Want me to prove it to you?" said Earl mischievously. "All we have to do is keep on laughing and talking instead of going to sleep. My dad will come and tell us to be quiet over and over, and he'll get madder and madder every time he has to settle us down. Then you'll hear his cuss words. Just wait and see."

I was a bit dubious about this plan, but I did want to see the dignified Mr. Walker at his profane best. So Earl and I kept his poor father running back and forth like a yo-yo for over an hour. And as predicted, he became more intense and angry each time he returned to our bedroom. I was getting very nervous and would have called off the project, but Earl had been through it all before. He kept telling me, "It won't be long now."

Finally, about midnight, it happened. Mr. Walker ran out of patience. He came thundering down the hall toward our room, shaking the entire house as his feet pounded the floor. He burst through the bedroom door and leaped on Earl's bed, flailing at the boy who was safely buried beneath three or four layers of blankets. Then from his lips came a stream of words that had seldom reached my tender ears. I was shocked, but Earl was delighted.

Even while his father was whacking the covers with his hand and screaming his profanity, Earl shouted to me from beneath the blankets, "Did ya hear 'em? Huh? Didn't I tell ya? I told ya he would say it!" It's a wonder that Mr. Walker didn't kill his son that night!

I lay awake in the dark thinking about what had happened and made up my mind never to let a child manipulate me like that when I grew up. Don't you see how important disciplinary techniques are to a boy's or girl's respect for parents? When a forty-five-pound bundle of trouble can deliberately reduce his or her powerful mother or father to a trembling, snarling mass of frustrations, something changes in their relationship. Something precious is lost. The child develops an attitude of contempt that is certain to erupt during the stormy adolescent years to come. I sincerely wish every adult understood that simple characteristic of human nature.

Q 110 I understand your emphasis on a child's being taught to respect the authority of his or her parents. But doesn't that coin have two sides? Don't parents have an equal responsibility to show respect for their children?

They certainly do! The self-concept of a child is extremely fragile, and it must be handled with great care. A youngster should live in complete safety at home, never belittled or embarrassed deliberately, never punished in front of friends, never ridiculed in a way that is hurtful. His strong feelings and requests, even if foolish, should be considered and responded to politely. He should feel that his parents "really do care about me." My point is that respect is *the* critical ingredient in all human relationships, and just as parents should insist on receiving it from their children, they are obligated to model it in return.

Q 111 Sometimes my husband and I disagree on our discipline and argue in front of our children about what is best. Do you think this is damaging?

Yes, I do. You and your husband should present a united front, especially when children are watching. If you disagree on an issue, it can be discussed later in private. Unless the two of you can come to a consensus, your children will begin to perceive that standards of right and wrong are arbitrary. They will also make an "end run" around the tougher parent to get the answers they want. There are even more serious consequences for boys and girls when parents are radically different in their approach.

Here's the point of danger: Some of the most hostile, aggressive teenagers I've seen have come from family constellations where the parents have leaned in opposite directions in their discipline. Suppose the father is unloving and disinterested in the welfare of his kids. His approach is harsh and physical. He comes home tired and may knock them around if they get in his way. The mother is permissive by nature. She worries every day about the lack of love in the father-child relationship. Eventually she sets out to compen-

sate for it. When Dad sends their son to bed without
his dinner, Mom slips him milk and cookies. When
he says no to a particular request, she finds a way to
say yes. She lets the kids get away with murder because it is not in her spirit to confront them.

What happens under these circumstances is that
the authority figures in the family contradict and can-
cel out each other. Consequently, the child is caught
in the middle and often grows up hating both. It
doesn't always work that way, but the probability
for trouble is high. The middle ground between extremes of love and control must be sought if we are
to produce healthy, responsible children.

Q112 Isn't it our goal to produce children with self-discipline and self-reliance? If so, how does your approach to *external* discipline imposed by parents get translated into *internal* control?

There are many authorities who suggest that parents
take a passive approach to their children for the reason implied by your question: They want their kids
to discipline themselves. But since young people lack
the maturity to generate that self-control, they
stumble through childhood without experiencing either internal *or* external discipline. Thus, they enter
adult life having never completed an unpleasant assignment or accepted an order that they disliked or
yielded to the leadership of their elders. Can we expect such a person to exercise self-discipline in
young adulthood? I think not. That individual
doesn't even know the meaning of the word.

My belief is that parents should introduce their
children to discipline and self-control by any reasonable means available, including the use of external influences, when they are young. By being required to
behave responsibly, he gains valuable experience in

controlling his own impulses and resources. Then as he grows into the teen years, responsibility is transferred year by year from the shoulders of the parent directly to the child. He is no longer required to do what he has learned during earlier years in hopes that he will want to function on his own initiative. To illustrate, a child should be required to keep his room relatively neat when he is young. Then somewhere during the midteens, his own self-discipline should take over and provide the motivation to continue the task. If it does not, the parent should close the door and let him live in a dump, if that is his choice.

In short, self-discipline does not come automatically to those who have never experienced it. Self-control must be learned, and it must be taught.

Q 113 You have described the nature of willfully defiant behavior and how parents should handle it. But does all unpleasant behavior result from rebellion and disobedience?

No. Defiance can be very different in origin from the "challenging" response I've been describing. A child's negativism may be caused by frustration, disappointment, fatigue, illness, or rejection and therefore must be interpreted as a warning signal to be heeded. Perhaps the toughest task in parenthood is to recognize the difference between these behavioral messages. A child's resistant behavior always contains a message to his parents, which they must decode before responding.

For example, a disobedient youngster may be saying, "I feel unloved now that I'm stuck with that screaming baby brother. Mom used to care for me; now nobody wants me. I hate everybody." When this kind of message underlies the defiance, the parents should move quickly to pacify its cause. The art

of good parenthood, then, revolves around the interpretation of behavior.

Q114 My six-year-old has suddenly become sassy
and disrespectful in her manner at home. She
told me to "buzz off" when I asked her to take out the
trash, and she calls me names when she gets angry. I feel
it is important to permit this emotional outlet, so I haven't
tried to suppress it. Do you agree?

I'm afraid I don't. Your daughter is aware of her sudden defiance, and she's waiting to see how far you
will let her go. If you don't discourage disrespectful
behavior now, you can expect some wild experiences during the adolescent years to come.

With regard to your concern about emotional
ventilation, you are right in saying your daughter
needs to express her anger. She should be free to say
anything to you provided it is said in a respectful
manner. It is acceptable to say, "I think you love my
brother more than me," or "You weren't fair with
me, Mommy." There is a thin line between what is
acceptable and unacceptable behavior at this point.
The child's expression of strong frustration, even resentment and anger, should be encouraged if it exists. You certainly don't want her to bottle it inside.
On the other hand, you should not permit your
daughter to resort to name-calling and open rebellion. "Mom, you hurt my feelings in front of my
friends" is an acceptable statement. "You stupid id-
iot, why didn't you shut up when my friends were
here?!" is obviously unacceptable.

If approached rationally, as described in the first
statement, it would be wise for the mother to sit
down and try to understand the child's viewpoint.
She should be big enough to apologize to the child if
she was wrong. If she feels she was right, however,

she should calmly explain why she reacted as she did and tell the child how he or she can avoid a collision next time. It is possible to ventilate feelings without sacrificing parental respect, and the child should be taught how to do it. This communicative tool will be very useful later in life, especially in a possible future marriage.

Q.115 What is the most common error made by parents in disciplining their children?

I would have to say it is the inappropriate use of anger in attempting to manage boys and girls. It is one of the most ineffective methods of attempting to influence human beings (of all ages). Unfortunately, most adults rely primarily on their own emotional response to secure the cooperation of children. One teacher said on a national television program, "I like being a professional educator, but I hate the daily task of teaching. My children are so unruly that I have to stay mad at them all the time just to control the classroom." How utterly frustrating to be required to be mean and angry to do a job year after year. Yet many teachers (and parents) know of no other way to manage children. Believe me, it is exhausting and it doesn't work!

Consider your own motivational system and your own response to the anger of others. Suppose you are driving your automobile home from work this evening and you exceed the speed limit by forty miles per hour. Standing on the street corner is a lone police officer who has not been given the means to arrest you. He has no squad car or motorcycle; he wears no badge, carries no gun, and can write no tickets. All he is commissioned to do is stand on the curb and scream insults as you speed past. Would you slow down just because he turns red in the face and shakes his fist in protest? Of course not! You might wave to him as you streak by. But his anger would achieve little except to make him appear comical and foolish.

On the other hand, nothing influences the way you drive quite like seeing a black-and-white vehicle in hot pursuit with nineteen red and blue lights flashing in the rearview mirror. When you pull your car over to the curb, a dignified, courteous officer approaches the window. He is six-foot-nine, has a voice like the Lone Ranger, and carries a gun on his right hip.

"Sir," he says firmly but politely, "our radar unit indicates that you were traveling sixty-five miles per hour in a twenty-five-miles-per-hour zone. May I see your driver's license, please?" He opens his leather-bound book of citations and leans toward you. He has revealed no hostility and offers no criticism, yet you immediately go to pieces. You fumble nervously to locate the license with that ugly picture on it. Why are your hands moist and your mouth dry? Why is your heart thumping in your throat? Because the course of action that John Law is about to take is notoriously unpleasant. It is that action that dramatically affects your future driving habits. Alas, children think and respond in much the same way you do.

Disciplinary action influences behavior; anger does not. When it comes to boys and girls, in fact, I am convinced that adult anger incites a malignant kind of disrespect in their minds. They perceive that our frustration is caused by our inability to control the situation. We represent justice to them, yet we're on the verge of tears as we flail the air with our hands and shout empty threats and warnings. Let me ask: Would you respect a superior court judge who behaved that way in administering legal justice? Certainly not. This is why the judicial system is carefully designed to appear objective, rational, and dignified.

I am not recommending that parents and teachers conceal their legitimate emotions from their children. I am not suggesting that we be like bland and unresponsive robots who hold everything inside. There are times when our kids become insulting or disobedient and our irritation is entirely appropriate. In fact, it should be revealed, or else we appear artificial and insincere. My point is merely that anger often becomes a tool used for the purpose of influencing behavior. It is ineffective and can be damaging to the relationship between generations. Instead, try taking action that your children will care about. Then administer it with cool.

Q116 I see now that I've been doing many things wrong with my children. Can I undo the harm?

I doubt if it is too late to do things right, although your ability to influence your children lessens with the passage of time. Fortunately we are permitted to make many mistakes with our kids. They are resilient, and they usually survive most of our errors in judgment. It's a good thing they do, because none of us can be a perfect parent. Besides, it's not the occasional mistakes that hurt a child—it is the consistent influence of destructive conditions throughout childhood that does the damage.

Q117 What place should fear occupy in a child's attitude toward his mother or father?

There is a narrow difference between acceptable, healthy respect and destructive fear. A child should have a general apprehension about the consequences of defying his or her parent. But he or she should not lie awake at night worrying about parental harshness or threats of punishment. Perhaps a crude example will illustrate the difference between these aspects of fear. A busy highway can be a dangerous place to take a walk. In fact, it would be suicidal to stroll down the fast lane of a freeway at 6:00 P.M. on any Friday. I would not be so foolish as to get my exercise in that manner because I have a healthy fear of fast-moving automobiles. However, as long as I don't behave stupidly, I have no cause for alarm. I am not threatened by this source of danger because it only reacts to my willful defiance. Without stretching the analogy too far, I want my child to view me with the same healthy regard. As long as she does not choose to challenge me, openly and willfully, she lives in total safety. She need not duck and flinch when I suddenly scratch my eyebrow. She should have no fear that I will ridicule her or treat her unkindly. She can enjoy complete security and safety—until she defies me. Then she'll have to face the consequences. This concept of fear, which is better labeled "awe" or "respect," is modeled after God's relationship with man. "Fear of God is the beginning of wisdom," we are taught. He is a God of justice, and at the same time, a God of infinite love and mercy. These attributes are complementary and should be represented in our homes.

Q118 I find I'm more likely to say no to my children than to say yes, even when I don't feel strongly about the permission they are seeking. I wonder why I automatically respond so negatively.

It is easy to fall into the habit of saying no to our kids.

"No, you can't go outside."

"No, you can't have a cookie."

"No, you can't use the telephone."

"No, you can't spend the night with a friend."

We could have answered affirmatively to all of these requests, but we chose almost automatically to respond in the negative. Why? Because we didn't take time to stop and think about the consequences; because the activity could cause us more work or strain; because there could be danger in the request; because our children ask for a thousand favors a day and we find it convenient to refuse them all.

While every child needs to be acquainted with denial of some of his or her more extravagant wishes, there is also a need for parents to consider each request on its own merit. There are so many necessary "no's" in life that we should say yes whenever we can.

Q.119 The children in our neighborhood are bratty with one another and disrespectful with adults. This upsets me, but I don't know what to do about it. I don't have a right to discipline the children of my neighbors, so they get away with murder. How can I deal with this?

Parents in a neighborhood need to learn to talk to each other about their kids—although that is difficult to do! There is no quicker way to anger one mother than for another woman to criticize her precious cub. It is a delicate subject, indeed. That's why the typical neighborhood is like yours, providing little feedback to parents in regard to the behavior of their children. The kids know there are no lines of communication between adults, and they take advantage of the barrier. What each block needs is a mother who has the courage to say to her neighbors, "I want to be told what my child does when she is beyond her own yard. If she is a brat with other children, I would like to know it. If she is disrespectful with adults, please mention it to me. I will not consider it tattling, and I won't resent your coming to me. I hope I can share my insights regarding your children, too. None of our kids is perfect, and we'll know better how to teach them if we can talk openly to each other as adults."

Until this openness exists between parents living nearby, the children will create and live by their own rules in the neighborhood.

Q120 My husband and I are divorced, so I have to handle all the discipline of the children myself. How does this change the recommendations you've made about discipline in the home?

Not at all. The principles of good discipline remain the same, regardless of the family setting. The procedures do become somewhat harder for one parent to implement since they have no one to support them when the children become testy. Single mothers and fathers have to play both roles, which is not easily done. Nevertheless, children do not make allowances for difficult circumstances. Parents must earn their respect, or they will not receive it.

Q121 My little girl, Tara, is sometimes sugar sweet, and other times she is unbearably irritating. How can I get her out of a bad mood when she has not really done anything to deserve punishment?

I would suggest that you take her in your arms and talk to her in this manner: "I don't know whether you've noticed it or not, Tara, but you have two 'personalities.' A personality is a way of acting and talking and behaving. One of your personalities is sweet and loving. No one could possibly be more lovable and happy when this personality is in control. It likes to work and looks for ways to make the rest of the family happy. But all you have to do is press a little red button, *ding,* and out comes another personality. It is cranky and noisy and silly. It wants to fight with your brother and disobey your mom. It gets up grouchy in the morning and complains all day.

"Now, Tara, I know that you can press the button for the neat personality or you can call up the unpleasant one. Sometimes you need help to make you want to press the right button. That's where I come in. If you keep on pressing the wrong button, like you have been today, then I'm going to make you uncomfortable one way or the other. I'm tired of the cranky character, and I want to see the grinny one. Can we make a deal?"

When discipline becomes a game, as in a conversation such as this, then you've achieved your purpose without conflict and animosity.

Q122 Our six-year-old is extremely negative and disagreeable. He makes the entire family miserable, and our attempts to discipline him have been ineffective. He just happens to have a sour disposition. How should we deal with him?

The objective with such a child is to define the needed changes and then reinforce those improvements when they occur. Unfortunately, attitudes are abstractions that a six-year-old may not fully understand, and you need a system that will clarify the "target" in his or her mind. To help accomplish this, I have developed an Attitude Chart (see illustration on page 140), which translates these subtle mannerisms into concrete mathematical terms. Please note: The system that follows would not be appropriate for the child who merely has a bad day, or one whose unpleasantness is associated with illness, fatigue, or environmental circumstances. Rather, it is a remedial tool to help change persistently negative and disrespectful attitudes by making the child conscious of his problem.

The Attitude Chart should be prepared and then

MY ATTITUDE CHART   Date _____

	EXCELLENT 1	GOOD 2	OKAY 3	BAD 4	TERRIBLE 5
My Attitude toward Mother					
My Attitude toward Dad					
My Attitude toward Sister					
My Attitude toward Friends					
My Attitude toward Work					
My Attitude at Bedtime					

TOTAL POINTS   _____

- -

CONSEQUENCES

6–9 POINTS
The family will do something fun together

10–18 POINTS
Nothing happens, good or bad

19–20 POINTS
I have to stay in my room for one hour

21–22 POINTS
I get one swat with paddle

23+ POINTS
I get two swats with paddle

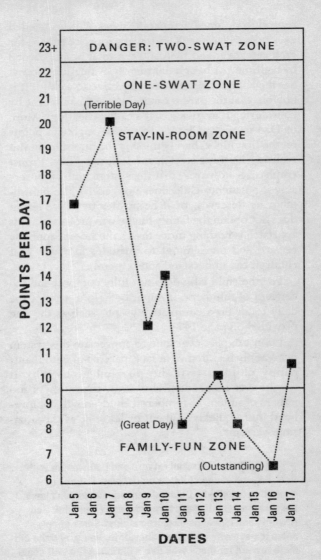

reproduced, since a separate sheet will be needed every day. Place an X in the appropriate square for each category, and then add the total points earned by bedtime. Although this nightly evaluation process has the appearance of being objective to a child, it is obvious that the parent can influence the outcome by considering it in advance (it's called cheating). Mom or Dad may want Junior to receive eighteen points on the first night, barely missing the punishment but realizing he must stretch the following day. I must emphasize, however, that the system will fail miserably if a naughty child does not receive the punishment he deserves, or if he hustles to improve but does not obtain the family fun he was promised. This approach is nothing more than a method of applying reward and punishment to attitudes in a way that children can understand and remember.

For the child who does not fully comprehend the concept of numbers, it might be helpful to plot the daily totals on a cumulative graph, such as the one provided on page 141.

I don't expect everyone to appreciate this system or to apply it at home. In fact, parents of compliant, happy children will be puzzled as to why it would ever be needed. However, the mothers and fathers of sullen, ill-tempered children will comprehend more quickly. Take it or leave it, as the situation warrants.

Q123 I understand reward and punishment with young children work better if they are applied very quickly. Delayed consequences don't have the same impact. If that's true, why don't you think God rewards and punishes us more quickly? Some people seem to get away with bad behavior for years, and the ultimate reward for those who live a Christian life will come

only after death. Surely the Lord knows about the importance of immediate reinforcement.

He certainly does. He created the characteristics we only observe and try to understand. So why does He not reinforce the behavior He desires more quickly? I don't know, although the principle of immediate response is acknowledged in Scripture: Solomon, one of the wisest men to ever live, wrote: "When the sentence for a crime is not quickly carried out, the hearts of the people are filled with schemes to do wrong. Although a wicked man commits a hundred crimes and still lives a long time, I know that it will go better with God-fearing men, who are reverent before God" (Ecclesiastes 8:11-12).

The thirty-seventh psalm also deals with the issue of evil people seeming to prosper despite their wrongdoing. Although they appear to be succeeding, the psalmist assured us that justice will eventually prevail. It is written, "Do not fret when men succeed in their ways, when they carry out their wicked schemes" (37:7). "A little while, and the wicked will be no more; though you look for them, they will not be found. But the meek will inherit the land and enjoy great peace" (37:10-11). Whether the consequences of evil arrive on time or not, the warnings and promises in Scripture are more reliable than anything else in the universe. He will have the last word!

Q.124 **I could use some advice about a minor problem we're having. Tim, my six-year-old son, loves to use silly names whenever he speaks to my husband and me. This past week it's been "You big hot dog." Nearly every time he sees me now he says, "Hi, Hot Dog." Before that it was "Dummy," then "Moose" (after he studied *M* for *moose* in school). I know it's silly and it's not a huge problem, but it gets so annoying after such a long**

time. He's been doing this for a year now. How can we get him to talk to us with more respect, calling us Mom or Dad instead of Hot Dog and Moose?

Ordinarily, it would not be a big deal for a child to use a playful name for his parent. But that isn't what appears to be happening with Tim. It sounds more like a classic power game to me. And contrary to what you said, it is not so insignificant. Your son is continuing to do something that he knows is irritating to you and your husband, yet you are unable to stop him. That is the issue. He has been using humor as a tactic of defiance for a full year.

It is time for you to sit down and have a quiet little talk with young Timothy. Tell him that he is being disrespectful and that the next time he calls either you or his father a name of any kind, he will be punished. You must then be prepared to deliver on the promise, because he will continue to challenge you until it ceases to be fun. That's the way he is made. If that response never comes, his insults will probably become more pronounced. Appeasement for a strong-willed child is an invitation to warfare. This is the time to deal with it.

Q125 **How can I acquaint my twelve-year-old with the need for responsible behavior throughout his life? He is desperately in need of this understanding.**

One important objective during the preadolescent period is to teach the child that actions have inevitable consequences. One of the most serious casualties in a permissive society is the failure to connect those two factors, behavior and consequences. A three-year-old child screams insults at his mother, but Mom stands blinking her eyes in confusion. A first grader defies his teacher, but the school makes allowances for his age and takes no action. A ten-year-old is caught stealing candy in a store but is released to the recognizance of her parents. A fifteen-year-old sneaks the keys to the family car, but her father pays the fine when she is arrested. A seventeen-year-old drives his Chevy like a maniac, and his parents pay for the repairs when he wraps it around a telephone pole. All through childhood, loving parents seem determined to intervene between behavior and consequences, breaking the connection and preventing the valuable learning that could and should have occurred.

Thus, it is possible for a young man or woman to enter adult life not really knowing that life bites— that every move we make directly affects our future—and that irresponsible behavior eventually produces sorrow and pain. Such a person secures his first job and arrives late for work three times during the first week. Later, when he is fired in a flurry of hot words, he becomes bitter and frustrated. It was the first time in his life that Mom and Dad couldn't come running to rescue him from the unpleasant consequences. (Unfortunately, many American parents still try to bail out the grown children even when they are in their twenties and live away from home.) What is the result? This overprotection produces emotional cripples who often develop lasting characteristics of dependency and a kind of perpetual adolescence.

How does one connect behavior with consequences? By being willing to let the child experience a reasonable amount of pain or inconvenience when he behaves irresponsibly. When Jack misses the school bus through his own dawdling, let him walk a mile or two and enter school in midmorning (unless safety factors prevent this). If Janie carelessly loses her lunch money, let her skip a meal. Obviously, it is possible to carry this principle too far, being harsh and inflexible with an immature child. But the best approach is to expect boys and girls to carry the responsibility that is appropriate for their age and occasionally to taste the bitter fruit that irresponsibility bears. In so doing, behavior is wedded to consequences, just like in real life.

Q 126 I have a horrible time getting my ten-year-old daughter ready to catch the school bus each morning. She will get up when I insist, but she dawdles and plays as soon as I leave the room. I have to goad and push and warn her every few minutes or else she will be late. So I get more and more angry and usually end up screaming insults at her. I know this is not the best way to handle the situation, but I declare, she makes me want to clobber her. Is there a way I can get her moving without a fight every day?

In a sense, you are perpetuating your daughter's folly by assuming the responsibility for getting her ready each morning. A ten-year-old should definitely be able to handle that task on her own initiative, but your anger is not likely to bring it about. We had a very similar problem with our own daughter when she was ten. Perhaps the solution we worked out will be helpful to you.

Danae's morning time problem related primarily to her compulsivity about her room. She would not leave for school each day unless her bed was made perfectly and every trinket was in its proper place. This was not something we taught her; she has always been very meticulous about her possessions. Danae could easily finish these tasks on time if she was motivated to do so, but she was never in a particular hurry. Therefore, my wife began to fall into the same habit you described, warning, threatening, punishing, and ultimately becoming angry as the clock moved toward the deadline.

Shirley and I discussed the problem and agreed that there had to be a better method of getting through the morning. I subsequently created a system that we called "Checkpoints." It worked like this: Danae was instructed to be out of bed and standing upright before six-thirty each morning. It was her responsibility to set her own clock radio and get herself out of bed. If she succeeded in getting up on time (even one minute later was considered a missed item), she immediately went to the kitchen, where a chart was taped to the refrigerator door. She then circled yes or no, with regard to the first checkpoint for that date. It couldn't have been more simple. She either did or did not get up by six-thirty.

The second checkpoint occurred forty minutes later, at seven-ten. By that time, she was required to have her room straightened to her own satisfaction, be dressed and have her teeth brushed, hair combed, etc., and be ready to begin practicing the piano. Forty minutes was ample time for these tasks, which could actually be done in ten or fifteen minutes if she wanted to hurry. Thus, the only way she could miss the second checkpoint was to ignore it deliberately.

Now, what meaning did the checkpoints have? Did failure to meet them bring anger and wrath and gnashing of teeth? Of course not. The consequences were straightforward and fair. If Danae missed one checkpoint, she was required to go to bed thirty minutes earlier than usual that evening. If she missed two, she hit the "lily whites" an hour before her assigned hour. She was permitted to read during that time in bed, but she could not watch television or talk on the telephone.

This little game took all the morning pressure off

Shirley and placed it on our daughter's shoulders, where it belonged. There were occasions when my wife got up just in time to fix breakfast, only to find Danae sitting soberly at the piano, clothed and in her right mind.

This system of discipline can serve as a model for parents who have similar behavioral problems with their children. It was not oppressive; in fact, Danae seemed to enjoy having a target to shoot at. The limits of acceptable performance were defined beyond question. The responsibility was clearly placed on the child. And it required no adult anger or foot stamping.

Adaptations of this concept are available to resolve other problems in your home, too. The only limit lies in the creativity and imagination that you bring to the situation.

Q 127 I am uncomfortable using rewards to influence my kids. It seems too much like bribery to me. I'd like to hear your views on the subject.

Many parents feel as you do, and in response I say, don't use them if you are philosophically opposed to the concept. It is unfortunate, however, that one of our most effective teaching tools is often rejected because of what I would consider to be a misunderstanding of terms. Our entire society is established on a system of rewards, yet we don't want to apply them where they are needed most: with young children. As adults, we go to work each day and receive a paycheck every other Friday. Getting out of bed each morning and meeting the requirements of a job are thereby rewarded. Medals are given to brave soldiers, plaques are awarded to successful businesspeople, and watches are presented to retiring employees. Rewards make responsible effort worthwhile.

The main reason for the overwhelming success of

capitalism is that hard work and personal discipline are rewarded materially. The great weakness of socialism is the absence of reinforcement; why should a person struggle to achieve if there is nothing special to be gained? This system is a destroyer of motivation, yet some parents seem to feel it is the only way to approach children. They expect little Marvin to carry responsibility simply because it is noble for him to do so. They want him to work and learn and sweat for the sheer joy of personal accomplishment. He isn't going to buy it!

Consider the alternative approach to the "bribery" I've recommended. How are you going to get your five-year-old son to behave more responsibly? The most frequently used substitutes are nagging, complaining, begging, screaming, threatening, and punishing. The mother who objects to the use of rewards may also go to bed each evening with a headache, vowing to have no more children. She doesn't like anything resembling a bribe, yet later she will give money to her child when some opportunity comes along. Since her youngster never earns his own cash, he doesn't learn how to save it or spend it wisely or pay tithe on it. The toys she buys him are purchased with her money, and he values them less. But most important, he is not learning the self-discipline and personal responsibility that are possible through the careful reinforcement of that behavior.

Yes, I do believe the judicious use of rewards can be very helpful to parents. But—they're not for everyone.

Q128 Isn't a mother manipulating the child by using rewards and punishment to get him to do what she wants?

No more than a factory supervisor manipulates his

employees by docking their pay if they arrive late. No more than a policeman manipulates a speeding driver by giving him a traffic ticket. No more than an insurance company manipulates that same driver by increasing his premium. No more than the IRS manipulates a taxpayer who files his return one day late by charging a penalty for his tardiness. The word *manipulation* implies a sinister or selfish motive of the one in charge. I don't agree.

Q.129 When would you *not* recommend the use of rewards?

Rewards should never be used as a payoff to a child for not disobeying. That becomes a bribe—a substitute for authority. For example, Mom is having trouble controlling her three-year-old in a supermarket. "Come here, Pamela," she says, but the youngster screams, "No!" and runs the other way. Then in exasperation Mom offers Pam a sucker if she'll come quickly. Rather than rewarding obedience, Mom has actually reinforced the child's defiance.

Another misuse of rewards is to pay a child for doing the routine jobs that are his responsibility as a member of the family. Taking out the trash and making his bed might be included in those regular duties. But when he is asked to spend half his Saturday cleaning the garage or weeding the garden, it seems very appropriate to make it worth his time.

Q.130 I worry about putting undue emphasis on materialism with my kids. Do rewards have to be in the form of money or toys?

Certainly not. A word of praise is a great enticement to some children. An interesting snack can also get their attention, although that has its downside. When my daughter was three years of age, I began to teach her some prereading skills, including how to recognize the letters of the alphabet. By planning the training sessions to occur after dinner each evening, bits of chocolate candy provided the chief source of motivation. (I was less concerned about the effects of excess sugar consumption in those days than I am now.) Late one afternoon I was sitting on the floor drilling her on several new letters when a tremendous crash shook the neighborhood. The whole family rushed outside to see what had happened. A teenager had overturned his car on our quiet residential street. He was not badly hurt, but his automobile was a mess. We sprayed the smoldering car with water and called the police. It was not until the excitement passed that we realized our daughter had not followed us out of the house. I returned to the den where I found her elbow-deep in the large bag of candy I had left behind. She must have put a half-pound of chocolate in her mouth, and most of the remainder was distributed around her chin, nose, and forehead. When she saw me coming, she managed to jam another handful into her chipmunk cheeks. From this experience, I learned one of the limitations of using material, or at least edible, rewards.

Anything the child wants can be used as a reinforcer, from praise to pizza to playtime.

Q 131 My four-year-old daughter, Karen, is a whiner. She rarely speaks in a normal voice anymore. How can I break her of this habit?

There is a process called "extinction" that is very useful in situations like this. Here is how it works: Any behavior that has been learned by reinforcement (i.e., by rewards) can be unlearned by withholding those rewards. It sounds complex, but the technique is simple and very applicable to Karen's problem.

Why do you think she whines instead of speaking in a normal voice? Because you have rewarded that sound by letting it get your attention! As long as Karen is speaking in her usual voice you are too busy to listen to her. Like most toddlers, she probably babbles all day long, so you have often tuned out most of her verbiage. But when she speaks in a grating, irritating, obnoxious tone, you turn to see what is wrong. Therefore, Karen's whining brings results; her normal voice does not, and she becomes a whiner.

In order to break the habit of whining, you must simply reverse the process. You should begin by saying, "I can't hear you because you're whining, Karen. I have funny ears; they just can't hear whining." After this message has been passed along for a day or two, you should show no indication of having heard a moan-tone. You should then offer immediate attention to anything she says in a normal voice. If this control of reward is applied properly, I guarantee it to achieve the desired results. Most human learning is based on this principle, and the consequences are certain and definite. Of course, Grandma and Uncle Albert may continue to reinforce the behavior you are trying to eliminate, and they can keep it alive.

Q 132 I have to fight with my nine-year-old daughter to get her to do *anything* she doesn't want to do. It's so unpleasant that I've about decided not to take her on. Why should I try to force her to work and help around the house? What's the downside of my just going with the flow and letting her off the hook?

It is typical for nine-year-olds not to want to work, of course, but they still need to become acquainted with it. If you permit a pattern of irresponsibility to prevail in your child's formative years, she may fall behind her developmental timetable leading toward the full responsibilities of adult living. As a ten-year-old, she won't be able to do anything unpleasant since she has never been required to stay with a task until it is completed. She won't know how to give to anyone else because she's only thought of herself. She'll find it hard to make decisions or control her own impulses. A few years from now, she will steamroll into adolescence and then adulthood completely unprepared for the freedom and obligations she will find there. Your daughter will have had precious little training for those pressing responsibilities of maturity.

Obviously, I've painted a worst-case scenario with regard to your daughter. You still have plenty of opportunity to help her avoid it. I just hope your desire for harmony doesn't lead you to do what will be harmful to her in later years.

Q133 You have said that your philosophy of discipline (and of family advice in general) was drawn from the Scriptures. On what specific verses do you base your views?

Since God is the Creator of children, He must certainly know how our kids ought to be raised and how our families should function. Indeed, He does! We find in His Word a very consistent and easily understood prescription for parents who want to do things His way. Let me quote a few verses that illustrate this divine wisdom. Note three concepts within them that I have emphasized: (1) The authority of parents is endorsed; (2) discipline is in the best interest of children; (3) discipline must not be harsh and destructive to the child's spirit. Here they are:

> He [the father] must manage his own family well and see that his children obey him with proper re-

spect. (If anyone does not know how to manage his own family, how can he take care of God's church?)

1 TIMOTHY 3:4-5

Children, obey your parents in the Lord, for this is right. "Honor your father and mother"—which is the first commandment with a promise—"that it may go well with you and that you may enjoy long life on the earth."

EPHESIANS 6:1-3

Fathers, do not exasperate your children; instead, bring them up in the training and instruction of the Lord.

EPHESIANS 6:4

Children, obey your parents in everything, for this pleases the Lord. Fathers, do not embitter your children, or they will become discouraged.

COLOSSIANS 3:20-21

"My son, do not make light of the Lord's discipline, and do not lose heart when he rebukes you, because the Lord disciplines those he loves, and he punishes everyone he accepts as a son." Endure hardship as discipline; God is treating you as sons. For what son is not disciplined by his father? If you are not disciplined (and everyone undergoes discipline), then you are illegitimate children and not true sons. Moreover, we have all had human fathers who disciplined us and we respected them for it. [Note the linkage between discipline and respect.] How much more should we submit to the Father of our spirits and live! Our fathers disciplined us for a little while as they thought best; but God disciplines us for our good, that we may share in his holiness. No discipline seems pleasant at the time, but painful. Later on,

*however, it produces a harvest of righteousness and
peace for those who have been trained by it.*

HEBREWS 12:5-11

*Correct thy son, and he shall give thee rest; yea, he
shall give delight unto thy soul.*

PROVERBS 29:17, KJV

These Scriptures and related verses contain more
wisdom than all the child-development textbooks
ever written. They came from the heart of One who
flung the stars in space and created Adam from a handful of dust. He makes no mistakes! To summarize the
primary theme from all the related biblical passages, it
is for parents to shape the will without breaking the
spirit. That's the formula. That's the prescription.

Q134 What do you think of the phrase "Children should be seen and not heard"?

That statement reveals a profound ignorance of children and their needs. I can't imagine how any loving
adult could raise a vulnerable little boy or girl by that
philosophy.

Q135 I really believe in giving children the freedom to do wrong as long as there isn't any danger involved. For example, I let my kids curse and use swear-words and don't see any harm in it. Do you agree?

No. I would hope that parents wouldn't use that kind
of language and certainly don't believe they should
permit their kids to do so. It is disrespectful, crude,
and unnecessary to talk like that.

Q136 Why is it that children are often the most obnoxious and irritating on vacations and at other times when parents specifically try to please them?

On those special days, you'd think the kids would say to themselves, *Wow! Mom and Dad are doing something really nice for us, taking us on this great vacation. We're going to give them a break and be really good kids today.* Isn't that reasonable?

Sure it's reasonable, but children just don't think that way. In fact, many boys and girls misbehave even more at these times. Why is this? One reason, I think, is because children often feel compelled to re-examine the boundaries whenever they think they may have moved. In other words, whenever the normal routine changes, the tougher kids often push the limits to see if the old rules still apply.

Q 137 So how can parents preserve their own peace of mind and maintain harmony during car trips and family holidays?

Sometimes it helps to redefine the boundaries at the beginning of your time together. Let the children know exactly what you're doing and what's expected of them. If they still misbehave, respond with good, loving discipline right from the start.

No parent wants to be an ogre on vacation, but it helps to show a little firmness at the outset that can make the rest of the time together fun for the entire family.

Q 138 Would you go so far as to apologize to a child if you felt you had been in the wrong?

I certainly would—and indeed, I have. A number of years ago I was burdened with pressing responsibilities that fatigued me and made me irritable. One particular evening I was especially grouchy and short-tempered with my ten-year-old daughter. I knew I was not being fair but was simply too tired to correct my manner. Through the course of the evening, I blamed Danae for things that were not her fault and upset her needlessly several times. After going to bed, I felt bad about the way I had behaved, and I decided to apologize the next morning. After a good night of sleep and a tasty breakfast, I felt much more optimistic about life. I approached my daughter before she left for school and said, "Danae, I'm sure you know that daddies are not perfect human beings. We get tired and irritable just like other people, and there are times when we are not proud of the way we behave. I know I wasn't fair with you last night. I was terribly grouchy, and I want you to forgive me."

Danae put her arms around me and shocked me down to my toes. She said, "I knew you were going to have to apologize, Daddy, and it's okay; I forgive you."

Can there be any doubt that children are often more aware of the struggles between generations than are their busy, harassed parents?

Q 139 My children are still in elementary school, and I want to avoid adolescent rebellion in the future if I can. What can you tell me to help me get ready for this scary time?

I can understand why you look toward the adolescent years with some apprehension. This is a tough time to raise kids. Many youngsters sail right through that period with no unusual stresses and problems, but others get caught in a pattern of rebellion that disrupts families and scares their moms and dads to death. I've spent several decades trying to understand that phenomenon and how to prevent it. The encouraging thing is that the most rebellious teens usually grow up to be responsible and stable adults who can't remember why they were so angry in earlier days.

I once devoted a radio program to a panel of formerly rebellious teens that included three successful ministers, Rev. Raul Ries, Pastor Mike MacIntosh, and Rev. Franklin Graham, son of Dr. Billy and Ruth Graham. Each of them had been a difficult adolescent who gave his parents fits. With the exception of Raul, who had been abused at home, the other two couldn't recall what motivated their misbehavior or why they didn't just go along and get along.[42] That is often the way with adolescence. It's like a tornado that drops unexpectedly out of a dark sky, tyrannizes a family, shakes up the community, and then blows on by. Then the sun comes out and spreads its warmth again.

Even though the teen years can be challenging, they're also filled with excitement and growth. Rather than fearing that experience, therefore, I think you ought to anticipate it as a dynamic time when your kids transition from childhood to full-fledged adulthood.

Q140 One more time, could you summarize your philosophy of child rearing in a single paragraph? What's the bottom line?

Let me emphasize my approach by stating its opposite. I am not recommending that your home be harsh and oppressive. I am not suggesting that you give your children a spanking every morning with their ham and eggs or that you make your boys sit in the living room with their hands folded and their legs crossed. I am not proposing that you try to make adults out of your kids so you can impress your adult friends with your parental skill, or that you punish your children whimsically, swinging and screaming when they didn't know they were wrong. I am not suggesting that you insulate your dignity and authority by being cold and unapproachable. These parental tactics do not produce healthy, responsible children. By contrast, I am recommending a simple principle: When you are defiantly challenged, win decisively. When the child asks, "Who's in charge?" tell him. When he mutters, "Who loves me?" take him in your arms and surround him with affection. Treat him with respect and dignity, and expect the same in return. Then begin to enjoy the sweet benefits of competent parenthood.

Q 141 My wife and I have a strong-willed child who is incredibly difficult to handle. I honestly believe we are doing our job about as well as any parents would do under the circumstances, yet she still breaks the rules and challenges our authority. I guess I need some encouragement. First, tell me if an especially strong-willed kid can be made to smile and give and work and cooperate. If so, how is that accomplished? And second, what is my daughter's future? I see trouble ahead but don't know if that gloomy forecast is justified.

There is no question about it, an especially willful child such as yours can be difficult to manage even when her parents handle her with great skill and dedication. It may take several years to bring her to a point of relative obedience and cooperation within the family unit, but it will happen. While this training program is in progress, it is important not to panic. Don't try to complete the transformation overnight. Treat your child with sincere love and dignity, but require her to follow your leadership. Choose carefully the matters that are worthy of confrontation; then accept her challenge on those issues and win decisively. Reward every positive, cooperative gesture she makes by offering your attention, affection, and verbal praise. Then take two aspirin and call me in the morning.

8

TO SPANK OR
NOT TO SPANK

Q.142 I have never spanked my three-year-old because I am afraid it will teach her to hit others and be a violent person. Do you think I am wrong?

You have asked an important question that reflects a common misunderstanding about child management. First, let me emphasize that it *is* possible—even easy—to create a violent and aggressive child who has observed this behavior at home. If he is routinely beaten by hostile, volatile parents or if he witnesses physical violence between angry adults or if he feels unloved and unappreciated within his family, that child will not fail to notice how the game is played. Thus, corporal punishment that is not administered according to very carefully thought-out guidelines is a risky thing. Being a parent carries no right to slap and intimidate a child because you had a bad day or are in a lousy mood. It is this kind of unjust discipline that causes some well-meaning authorities to reject corporal punishment as a method of discipline.

Just because a technique is used wrongly, however, is no reason to reject it altogether. Many children desperately need this resolution to their disobedience. In those situations when the child, aged two to ten, fully understands what he is being asked to do but refuses to yield to adult leadership, an appropriate spanking is the shortest and most effective route to an attitude adjustment. When he lowers his head, clenches his fists, and makes it clear he is going for broke, justice must speak swiftly and eloquently. Not only does this response not create aggression in children, it helps them control their impulses and live in harmony with various forms of benevolent authority throughout life. Many people disagree, of course. I can only tell you that there is not a single well-designed scientific study that confirms the hypothesis that spanking by a loving parent breeds violence in children.

Q 143 It just seems barbaric to cause pain to a defenseless child. Tell me why you think it is healthy to spank him or her.

Corporal punishment, when used lovingly and properly, is beneficial to a child because it is in harmony with nature itself. Consider the purpose of minor pain in a child's life and how he learns from it. Suppose two-year-old Peter pulls on a tablecloth and with it comes a vase of roses that cracks him between the eyes. From this pain, he learns that it is dangerous to pull on the tablecloth unless he knows what sits on it. When he touches a hot stove, he quickly learns that heat must be respected. If he lives to be a hundred years old, he will never again reach out and touch the red-hot coils of a stove. The same lesson is learned when he pulls the doggy's tail and promptly gets a neat row of teeth marks across the back of his hand, or when he climbs out of his high chair when Mom isn't looking and discovers all about gravity.

During the childhood years, he typically accumulates minor bumps, bruises, scratches, and burns, each one teaching him about life's boundaries. Do these experiences make him a violent person? No! The pain associated with these events teaches him to avoid making the same mistakes again. God created this mechanism as a valuable vehicle for instruction.

When a parent administers a reasonable spanking in response to willful disobedience, a similar nonverbal message is being given to the child. He must understand that there are not only dangers in the physical world to be avoided. He should also be wary of dangers in his social world, such as defiance, sassiness, selfishness, temper tantrums, behavior that puts his life in danger, that which hurts others, etc. The minor pain associated with this deliberate misbehavior tends to inhibit it, just as discomfort works to shape behavior in the physical world. Neither conveys hatred. Neither results in rejection. Neither makes the child more violent.

In fact, children who have experienced corporal punishment from loving parents do not have trouble understanding its meaning. I recall my good friends Art and Ginger Shingler, who had four beautiful children whom I loved. One of them went through a testy period where he was just "asking for it." The conflict came to a head in a restaurant, when the boy continued doing everything he could to be bratty. Finally, Art took him to the parking lot for an overdue spanking. A woman passerby observed the event and became irate. She chided the father for "abusing" his son and said she intended to call the police. With that, the child stopped crying and said to his father, "What's wrong with that woman, Dad?" He understood the discipline even if his rescuer did not. A boy or girl who knows that love abounds at home will not resent a well-deserved spanking. One who is unloved or ignored will hate any form of discipline!

Q144 As an advocate of spankings as a disciplinary tool, don't you worry about the possibility that you might be contributing to the incidence of child abuse in this country?

Yes, I do worry about that. One of my frustrations in teaching parents has been the difficulty in achieving a balance between permissiveness and oppression. The tendency is to drift toward one extreme or another. Let it never be said that I favor harshness of any kind with children. It can wound the spirit and inflict permanent scars on the psyche.

No subject distresses me more than the phenomenon of child abuse, which is so prevalent in North America today. There are millions of families out there in which crimes against children are being committed day after day. It is hard to believe just how cruel some mothers and fathers can be to defenseless, wide-eyed kids who don't understand why they are hated. I remember the terrible father who regularly wrapped his small son's head in the sheet that the boy had wet the night before. Then he crammed the tot upside down into the toilet bowl for punishment. I also think of the disturbed mother who cut out her child's eyes with a razor blade. That little girl will be blind throughout her life, knowing that her own mother deprived her of sight!

Unthinkable acts like these are occurring every day in cities and towns around us. In fact, it is highly probable that a youngster living within a mile or two of your house is experiencing abuse in one manner or another. Brian G. Fraser, attorney for the National Center for Prevention and Treatment of Child Abuse and Neglect, has written: "Child abuse . . . once thought to be primarily a problem of the poor and downtrodden . . . occurs in every segment of society and may be the country's leading cause of death in children."[43]

Let me say with the strongest emphasis that aggressive, hard-nosed, "Mommy Dearest" kinds of discipline are destructive to kids and must not be tolerated. Given the scope of the tragedy we are facing, the last thing I want to do is to provide a rationalization and justification for it. I don't believe in harsh discipline, even when it is well-intentioned. Children must be given room to breathe and grow and love. But there are also harmful circumstances at the permissive end of the spectrum, and many parents fall into one trap in an earnest attempt to avoid the other.

Q145 Are all forms of child abuse illegal?

Not in any practical sense. Within certain limits it is not illegal to ignore a child or raise him or her without love. Nor is it against the law to ridicule and humiliate a boy or girl. Those forms of rejection may be more harmful even than some forms of physical abuse, but they are tougher to prove and are usually not prosecutable.

Q146 You have described two extremes that are both harmful to kids, being too permissive and being too harsh. Which is the most common error in Western cultures today?

Permissiveness is still more common and has been since the 1950s. But harshness and severity still occur frequently as well. These dual dangers are equally harmful to children and were described by Marguerite and Willard Beecher in their book *Parents on the Run*. This is how they saw the two extremes:

The adult-centered home of yesteryear made parents the masters and children their slaves. The child-centered home of today has made parents the slaves and children the masters. There is no true cooperation in any master-slave relationship, and therefore no democracy. Neither the restrictive-authoritative technique of rearing children nor the newer "anything goes" technique develop the genius within the individual, because neither trains him to be self-reliant.[44]

The way to raise healthy children is to find the safety of the middle ground between disciplinary extremes.

Q 147 What advice would you give parents who recognize a tendency within themselves to abuse their kids? Maybe they're afraid they'll get carried away when spanking a disobedient child. Do you think they should avoid corporal punishment as a form of discipline?

That's exactly what I think. Anyone who has ever abused a child—or has ever felt himself or herself losing control during a spanking—should not expose the child to that tragedy. Anyone who has a violent temper that at times becomes unmanageable should not use that approach. Anyone who secretly enjoys the administration of corporal punishment should not be the one to implement it. And grandparents probably should not spank their grandkids unless the parents have given them permission to do so.

Q 148 Do you think you should spank a child for every act of disobedience or defiance?

No. Corporal punishment should be a rather infrequent occurrence. There is an appropriate time for a child to sit on a chair to think about his misbehavior, or he might be deprived of a privilege or sent to his room for a "time-out" or made to work when he had planned to play. In other words, you should vary your response to misbehavior, always hoping to stay one step ahead of the child. Your goal is to react continually in the way that benefits the child and is in accordance with his "crime." In this regard, there is no substitute for wisdom and tact in the parenting role.

Q149 On what part of the body would you administer a spanking?

It should be confined to the buttocks area, where permanent damage is very unlikely. I don't believe in slapping a child on the face or in jerking him around by the arms. A common form of injury seen in the emergency room at Children's Hospital when I was on the attending staff involved children with shoulder separations. Parents had pulled tiny arms angrily and dislocated the shoulder or elbow. If you spank a child only on the behind, you will be less likely to inflict any physical injury on him.

Q150 After I spank my child, she usually wants to hug me and make up. I don't feel good about that because I need to show her my displeasure at what she's done. That's why I continue to be cool to her for a few hours. Do you think that is right?

No, I think it is very important after punishment to embrace the child in love. That is the time to assure her that it was the misbehavior that brought your disapproval, rather than your dislike for her personally. It is also the best time to talk about why she got in trouble and how she can avoid your displeasure in the future. It is the "teachable moment," when the object of your discipline can be explained. Such a conversation is difficult or impossible to achieve when a rebellious, stiff-necked little child is clenching her fist and taking you on. But after a confrontation has occurred—especially if it involved tears—the child usually wants to hug you and get reassurance that you really care for her.

Many parents, like you, say they feel awkward showing affection after punishment because they've been upset with the child. I think that is wrong. It's best to open your arms and let that youngster come.

Q.151 How long do you think a child should be allowed to cry after being punished or spanked? Is there a limit?

Yes, I believe there should be a limit. As long as the tears represent a genuine release of emotion, they should be permitted to fall. But crying quickly changes from inner sobbing to an expression of protest aimed at punishing the enemy. Real crying usually lasts two minutes or less but may continue for five. After that point, the child is merely complaining, and the change can be recognized in the tone and intensity of his voice. I would require him to stop the protest crying, usually by offering him a little more of whatever caused the original tears. In younger children, crying can easily be stopped by getting them interested in something else.

Q.152 There is some controversy over whether a parent should spank with his or her hand or with some other object, such as a belt or paddle. What do you recommend?

I recommend a neutral object of some type. To those who disagree on this point, I'd encourage them to do what seems right. It is not a critical issue to me. The reason I suggest a switch or paddle is because the hand should be seen as an object of love—to hold, hug, pat, and caress. However, if you're used to suddenly disciplining with the hand, your child may not know when she's about to be swatted and can develop a pattern of flinching when you make an unexpected move. This is not a problem if you take the time to use a neutral object.

My mother always used a small switch, which could not do any permanent damage. But it stung enough to send a very clear message. One day when I had pushed her to the limit, she actually sent me to the backyard to cut my own instrument of punishment. I brought back a tiny little twig about seven inches long. She could not have generated anything more than a tickle with it. She never sent me on that fool's errand again.

As I conceded above, some people (particularly those who are opposed to spanking in the first place) believe that the use of a neutral object in discipline is tantamount to child abuse. I understand their concern, especially in cases when a parent believes "might makes right" or loses her temper and harms the child. That is why adults must always maintain a balance between love and control, regardless of the method by which they administer disciplinary action.

Q.153 Is there an age when you begin to spank?

There is no excuse for spanking babies or children younger than fifteen to eighteen months of age. Even shaking an infant can cause brain damage and death at that delicate age! But midway through the second year (eighteen months), boys and girls become capable of knowing what you're telling them to do or not do. They can then very gently be held responsible for how they behave. Suppose a child is reaching for an electric socket or something that will hurt him. You say, "No!" but he just looks at you and continues reaching toward it. You can see the mischievous smile on his face as he thinks, *I'm going to do it anyway!* I'd encourage you to speak firmly so that he knows he is pushing past the limits. If he persists, slap his fingers just enough to sting. A small amount of pain goes a long way at that age and begins to introduce children to realities of the physical world and the importance of listening to what you say.

Through the next eighteen months, you gradually establish yourself as the benevolent boss who means what you say and says what you mean. Contrary to what you have read in popular literature, this firm but loving approach to child rearing will not harm a toddler or make him violent. To the contrary, it is most likely to produce a healthy, confident child.

Q154 I have spanked my children for their disobedience, and it didn't seem to help. Does this approach fail with some children?

Children are so tremendously variable that it is sometimes hard to believe that they are all members of the same human family. Some kids can be crushed with nothing more than a stern look; others seem to require strong and even painful disciplinary measures to make a vivid impression. This difference usually results from the degree to which a child needs adult approval and acceptance. The primary parental task is to see things as the child perceives them, thereby tailoring the discipline to his or her unique needs. Accordingly, a boy or girl should never be so likely to be punished as when he or she knows it is deserved.

In a direct answer to your question, disciplinary measures usually fail because of fundamental errors in their application. It is possible for twice the amount of punishment to yield half the results. I have made a study of situations in which parents have told me that their children disregard the threat of punishment and continue to misbehave. There are four basic reasons for this lack of success:

1. The most common error is whimsical discipline. When the rules change every day and when punishment for misbehavior is capricious and inconsistent, the effort to change behavior is undermined. There is no inevitable consequence to be anticipated. This entices children to see if they can beat the system. In society at large, it also encourages criminal behavior among those who believe they will not face the bar of justice.

2. Sometimes a child is more strong-willed than his parent—and they both know it. He just might be tough enough to realize that a confrontation with his mom or dad is really a struggle of wills. If he can withstand the pressure and not buckle during a major battle, he can eliminate that form of punishment as a tool in the parent's repertoire. Does he think through this process on a conscious level? Usually not, but he understands it intuitively. He realizes that a spanking *must not* be allowed to succeed. Thus, he stiffens his little neck and guts it out. He may even refuse to cry and may say, "That didn't hurt." The parent concludes in exasperation, "Spanking doesn't work for my child."

3. The spanking may be too gentle. If it doesn't hurt, it doesn't motivate a child to avoid the consequence next time. A slap with the hand on the bottom of a multidiapered thirty-month-old is not a deterrent to anything. Be sure the child gets the message—while being careful not to go too far.

4. For a few children, spankings are simply not effective. The child who has attention deficit/hyperactivity disorder (ADHD), for example, may be even more wild and unmanageable after corporal punishment. Also, the child who has been abused may identify loving discipline with the hatred of the past. Finally, the very sensitive child might need a different approach. Let me emphasize once more that children are unique. The only way to raise them correctly is to understand each boy or girl as an individual and design parenting techniques to fit the needs and characteristics of that particular child.

Q.155 Do you think corporal punishment will eventually be outlawed?

I don't doubt that an effort will be made to end it. The tragedy of child abuse has made it difficult for people to understand the difference between viciousness to kids and constructive, positive forms of punishment. Also, there are many "children's rights advocates" in the Western world who will not rest until they have obtained the legal right to tell parents how to raise their children. That has already happened in Sweden, where corporal punishment and other forms of discipline are prohibited by law.[45] Canadian courts are flirting with the same decision.[46] The American media has worked to convince the public that all spanking is tantamount to child abuse, and therefore, should be outlawed. If that occurs, it will be a sad day for families . . . and especially for children!

9

WHAT'S A
MOTHER TO DO?

Q 156 My husband and I just moved to Arizona from Pennsylvania, and I haven't established a network of friends yet. My family is back East, and I have no one but my husband to talk to about problems the kids are having. He is very busy, so all the "homework" is left to me. How can I deal with the feelings of loneliness and isolation as a mother?

It is vital that you build relationships with other women that can help satisfy the needs for friendship and emotional support. Failure to do that places too great a strain on the marital relationship, which can lead to serious interpersonal problems. I'm not saying that your husband has no responsibility to help you get through this period of loneliness, but unless he is a very unusual man, he will not be able to "carry" you emotionally while earning a living and handling the other responsibilities of living. Therefore, I recommend that you seek out women's groups that are designed to meet the needs you described. Many churches offer Bible study groups and classes called Mothers of Preschoolers (MOPS), which is an outstanding program that puts women in touch with one another. Other possibilities are out there, such as Mom's Day Out, Mothers on the

Move, etc. For mothers of school-age children, there is a Christian ministry called Moms in Touch International, designed to bring women together to pray for their local school, its teachers, principal, school board, etc. It "bonds" them together in a common cause. What I'm saying is that you are not alone, even in a new city. There are other women out there who need you as much as you need them. You can find each other with a little effort. It is dangerous under the circumstances you described to sit and wait for the world to come to your front door.

Q 157 What do you think of placing children in child-care centers so mothers can work?

Safe, clean, loving child-care facilities are a necessity in today's culture. They are especially needed by the millions of mothers who are forced to work for financial reasons. They are particularly vital to the many single parents who are the sole breadwinners in their families. Thus, we need not question the wisdom of providing well-supervised centers for children whose mothers and fathers require assistance in raising them. That debate is over.

What can be argued is whether children fare better in a child-care facility or at home with a full-time mom. Personally (and others will disagree), I don't believe any arrangement for children can compete with an intact family where the mother raises her kids and the father is also very involved in their lives. There are at least four reasons that is true.

First, children thrive and learn better when they enjoy one-on-one relationships with adults rather than as members of a group. Second, you can't pay an employee in a child-care center enough to care for children like their own mothers will do. Children are a mother's passion, and it shows. Third, research verifies that kids at home are healthier than those who are regularly exposed to diseases, coughs, and sneezes from other boys and girls.[47] Fourth, a bonding is more likely to occur between parents and children when the developmental milestones are experienced firsthand. Families should be there when the first step is taken and the first word is spoken and when fears and anxieties arise. Certainly, others can substitute for Mom in those special moments, but something precious is lost if a surrogate witnesses them.

In short, I recognize the need for healthy child-care facilities in situations that demand them, but group living is not in the best interests of kids.

Q158 If parents have to use child-care support, what kind of help do you think is best?

State-run facilities rank at the bottom of my list because Christian teaching is not permissible in public facilities. Children are not led in prayer before meals, and no reference can be made to Jesus as our friend and Lord. I also worry more about the possibility of child molestation in state centers, even though it is rare. For these and other reasons, I prefer church-run programs that are clean and safe. Even better, if available, is placement of children with relatives, such as grandparents or aunts, or supervision provided by other mothers. Children need to develop relationships with those who care for them. They should be left with adults they know and love, if possible, rather than being forced to relate to different employees from day to day in public facilities.

Q159 I'm a full-time mother with three children in the preschool years. I love them like crazy, but I am exhausted from just trying to keep up with them. I also feel emotionally isolated by being here in the house

every day of the week. What do you suggest for mothers like me?

I talk to many women like you who feel that they're on the edge of burnout. They feel like they will explode if they have to do one more load of laundry or tie one more shoe. In today's mobile, highly energized society, young mothers are much more isolated than in years past. Many of them hardly know the women next door, and their sisters and mothers may live a thousand miles away. That's why it is so important for those with small children to stay in touch with the outside world. Though it may seem safer and less taxing to remain cloistered within the four walls of a home, it is a mistake to do so. Loneliness does bad things to the mind. Furthermore, there are many ways to network with other women today, including church activities, Bible study groups, and supportive programs such as Moms in Touch and Mothers of Preschoolers.

Husbands of stay-at-home mothers need to recognize the importance of their support, too. It is a wise man who plans a romantic date at least once a week and offers to take care of the children so Mom can get a much-needed break.

Burnout isn't inevitable in a busy household. It can be avoided in families that recognize its symptoms and take steps to head it off.

Q160 You've talked about being a full-time mother versus having a full-time career. Give us your view of a woman handling both responsibilities simultaneously. Is it doable, and is it smart?

Some women are able to maintain a busy career and a bustling family at the same time, and they do it beautifully. I admire them for their discipline and dedication. It has been my observation, however, that this dual responsibility is a formula for exhaustion and frustration for many others. It can be a never-ending struggle for survival. Why? Because there is only so much energy within the human body, and when it is invested in one place it is not available for use in another. Consider what it is like to be a mother of young children who must rise early in the morning, get her kids dressed, fed, and situated for the day, then drive to work, labor from nine to five, go by the grocery store and pick up some stuff for dinner, retrieve the kids at the child-care center, and then drive home. She is dog tired by that point and needs to put her feet up for a few minutes. But she can't rest. The kids are hungry, and they've been waiting to see her all day.

"Read me a story, Mom," says the most needy.

This beleaguered woman then begins another four to six hours of very demanding "mothering" that will extend into the evening. She must fix dinner, wash the dishes, bathe the baby, help with homework, and give each child some "quality time." Then comes the task of getting the tribe in bed, saying prayers, and bringing six glasses of water to giggling kids who want to stall. I get tired just thinking of a schedule like this.

You might ask the married woman, "Where is your husband and father in all this exertion? Why isn't he carrying his share of the homework?" Well, he may be working a fifteen-hour day at his own job. Getting started in a business or a profession often demands that kind of commitment. Or he may simply choose not to help his wife. That is a common complaint among working mothers.

"Not fair," you say.

I agree, but that's the way the system often works.

The most difficult aspect of this lifestyle is the constancy of the load. Most of us could maintain such a schedule for a week or two, but the working mother must do it month after month for years on end. On weekends there's housecleaning to do and clothes to be ironed and pants to be mended. And this is the pace she maintains when things are going right. She has no reserve of time or energy when a member of the family gets sick or the car breaks down or marital problems develop. A little push in any direction and she could go over the edge.

Admittedly, I have painted a more stressful scenario than most families have to endure. But not by much. Overcommitted and frazzled families are commonplace in our culture. Husbands and wives have no time for each other. Life is nothing but work, work, work. They are continually frustrated, irritable, and harried. They don't take walks, read the Scriptures together, or do anything that is fun. Their sex life suffers because exhausted people don't even make love meaningfully. They begin to drift apart and eventually find themselves with "irreconcilable differences." It is a tragic pattern I have been observing for the past twenty-five years.

The issue, then, is not whether a woman should choose a career and be a mother, too. Of course she has that right, and it is nobody's business but hers and her husband's. I would simply plead that you not allow your family to get sucked into that black hole of exhaustion. However you choose to divide the responsibilities of working and family management, reserve some time and energy for yourselves—and for each other. Your children deserve the best that you can give them, too.

Q 161 What would you and your wife do if the resources permitted her to stay at home after the kids were in school?

I don't have to speculate about the answer to that question. Shirley and I *did* have that option (although we sold and "ate" a Volkswagen initially to make it possible), and she stayed at home as a full-time mom. Neither she nor I have ever regretted that decision. Now that our kids are grown, we would not trade the time we invested in them for anything on earth. Looking back today, we feel it was *especially* important for Shirley to be at home during our kids' teen years.

Q162 We need a little more income to make it in my family, but I have preschool children and don't want to seek employment outside the home. Is there an alternative for me to pursue?

You might want to consider building a home-based business that can be done while taking care of your children and keeping your sanity. Among the possibilities are catering, desktop publishing, pet grooming, sewing, consulting, transcribing legal documents, or even mail-order sales. Choosing which business is right for you is the first of three practical steps suggested by Donna Partow. She's the author of a book called *Homemade Business*. You can start your own enterprise by taking a personal-skills-and-interest inventory to identify your particular abilities and what you might like doing the best. The second step is to do your homework. Begin by asking your librarian to help you research your chosen field. Look up books, magazines, and newspaper articles. Talk to other people who have done what you'd like to do. Join an industry organization and a network. Subscribe to industry publications.

According to Mrs. Partow, the third step is to marshal as much support as you can. Get your children, your spouse, and your friends on your side. Setting up a small business can be stressful, and you'll need as much encouragement as you can get.[48]

If you've been torn between family and finances, having a home-based business may turn out to be the best of both worlds.

Q163 What answer do you have for those who say being a mother of small children and a homemaker is boring and monotonous?

Some women see the responsibility that way—but we should recognize that most other occupations are boring, too. How exciting is the work of a waiter who serves food to customers every day—or a medical pathologist who examines microscopic slides and bacterial cultures from morning to night—or a dentist who spends his lifetime drilling and filling, drilling and filling—or an attorney who reads dusty books in a secluded library—or an author who writes page after page after page? Few of us enjoy heart-thumping excitement each moment of our professional lives. Even the high-profile jobs have their boring dimensions.

On a trip to Washington, D.C., a few years ago, my hotel room was located next to the room of a famous cellist who was in the city to give a classical concert that evening. I could hear him through the walls as he practiced hour after hour. He did not play beautiful symphonic renditions; he repeated scales and runs and exercises, over and over and over. This practice began early in the morning (believe me!) and continued until the time of his concert. As he strolled on stage that evening, I'm sure many individuals in the audience thought to themselves, *What a glamorous life!* Some glamour! I happen to know that he had spent the entire day in his lonely hotel room in the company of his cello. Musical instruments, as you know, are terrible conversationalists.

No, I doubt if the job of a homemaker and mother

is much more boring than most other jobs, particularly if the woman refuses to be isolated from adult contact. But as far as the importance of the assignment is concerned, no job can compete with the responsibility of shaping and molding a human being in the morning of his or her life.

Q. 164 My child is afraid of the dark. How can I lessen this fear?

I consulted with another mother who was also worried about her three-year-old daughter's fear of the dark. Maybe her story will be helpful to you. Despite the use of a night-light and leaving the bedroom door open, Marla was afraid to stay in her room alone. She insisted that her mother sit with her until she went to sleep each evening, which became very time-consuming and inconvenient. If Marla happened to awaken in the night, she would call for help. It was apparent that the child was not bluffing; she was genuinely frightened.

Fears such as this are not innate characteristics in the child; they have been learned. Parents must be very careful in expressing their own fears because their youngsters are inclined to adopt those same anxieties. For that matter, good-natured teasing can also produce problems for a child. If a youngster walks into a dark room and is pounced upon from behind the door, he has learned something from the joke: The dark is not always empty! In Marla's case, it is unclear where she learned to fear the dark, but I believe her mother inadvertently magnified the problem. In her concern for Marla, she conveyed her anxiety, and the child began to think that her fears must be justified: *Even Mother is worried about it.* The fright became so great that Marla could not walk through a dimly lit room without an escort. It was at this point that the child was referred to me.

I suggested that the mother use a process known as "extinction" to change Marla's pattern of fear. She needed to help her see that there was nothing to be afraid of. (It is usually unfruitful to try to talk a child out of fears, but it helps to show that you are confident and unthreatened in response to them.) The mother bought a package of stars and created a chart that showed how a new CD player could be earned. Then she placed her chair just outside Marla's bedroom door. Marla was offered a star if she could spend a short time (ten seconds) in her bedroom with the light on and the door open.

This first step was not very threatening, and Marla enjoyed the game. It was repeated several times; then she was asked to walk a few feet into a slightly darkened room with the door still open while Mother (clearly visible in the hall) counted to ten. She knew she could come out immediately if she wished. Mother talked confidently and quietly. The length of time in the dark was gradually lengthened, and instead of producing fear, it produced stars and eventually a CD player—a source of pleasure for a small child. Courage was being reinforced; fear was being extinguished. The cycle of fright was thereby broken, being replaced by a more healthy attitude.

Extinction may be useful in helping your own child overcome her fear of the dark. In summary, the best method of changing a learned behavior is to withhold its reinforcement while rewarding its replacement.

10

EDUCATION: PUBLIC, PRIVATE AND HOMESCHOOLING

Q.165 I majored in education at a state university, and I was taught that children will provide their own motivation to learn if we give them an opportunity to do so. My professors favored a "student-led" classroom instead of one that depends on strong leadership from the teacher. The children will then want to learn rather than being forced to learn. Do you see it that way?

I certainly agree that we should try to motivate kids to work and study and learn. They'll enjoy the process more and retain the information longer if their motivation comes from within. So I think your professors are right in saying that we should capitalize on students' natural interest whenever we can. But it is naive to believe that any educational program can generate that kind of interest in every subject and sustain it for a majority of students day in and day out. That is not going to happen. Kids need to learn some things that may be boring to them, such as math or grammar, whether they choose to or not.

A former superintendent of public instruction in the state of California reacted to the notion that children have a natural interest in everything adults think they should know. He said, "To say that children have an innate love of learning is as muddle-headed as to say that children have an innate love of baseball. Some do. Some don't. Left to themselves, a large percentage of the small fry will go fishing, pick a fight, tease the girls, or watch Superman on the boob tube. Even as you and I."[49]

This educator was right. Many students will not invest one more ounce of effort in their studies than is required, and that fact has frustrated teachers for hundreds of years. Our schools, therefore, must have enough structure and discipline to require certain behavior from children whether or not they have a natural interest in the subject being taught.

Q166 Then you must favor a very structured, teacher-led program, where student behavior is rather tightly controlled. Why?

One of the purposes of education is to prepare a young person for later life. To survive as an adult in this society, one needs to know how to work, how to get there on time, how to get along with others, how to stay with a task until it's completed, and, yes, how to submit to authority. In short, it takes a good measure of self-discipline and control to cope with the demands of modern living. Maybe one of the greatest gifts a loving teacher can contribute to an immature child, therefore, is to help her learn to sit when she feels like running, to raise her hand when she feels like talking, to be polite to her neighbor, to stand in line without smacking the kid in front, and to do English when she feels like doing soccer. I would also like to see our schools readopt reasonable dress codes, eliminating suggestive clothing, T-shirts with profanity or those promoting heavy-metal bands, etc. Guidelines concerning good grooming and cleanliness should also be enforced.

I know! I know! These notions are so alien to us now that we can hardly imagine such a thing. But the benefits would be apparent immediately. Admittedly, hairstyles and matters of momentary fashion are of no particular significance, but adherence to a standard is an important element of discipline. The military has understood that for five thousand years! If one examines the secret behind a championship football team, a magnificent orchestra, or a successful business, the principal ingredient is invariably discipline. Preparation for this disciplinary lifestyle should begin in childhood. That's why I think it's a mistake to require nothing of children—to place no demands on their behavior—to allow them to giggle, fight, talk, and play in the classroom. We all need to adhere to reasonable rules, and school is a good place to get acquainted with how that is done.

Q 167 You've been somewhat critical of America's public schools in recent years. Whom do you hold accountable for what has gone wrong?

I share the concern of many others about falling test scores, increasing violence on campuses, and the high illiteracy rate, among other serious problems with today's schools. But I am not quick to blame educators for everything that has gone wrong. The teachers and school administrators who guide our children have been among the most maligned and underappreciated people in our society. They are an easy target for abuse. They are asked to do a terribly difficult job, and yet they are criticized almost daily for circumstances beyond their control. Some of their critics act as though educators are deliberately failing our kids. I strongly disagree. We would still be having serious difficulties in our schools if the professionals did everything right. Why? Because what goes on in the classroom cannot be separated from the problems occurring in the culture at large.

Educators are not responsible for the condition our kids are in when they arrive at school each day. It's not the teachers' fault that families are unraveling and that large numbers of their students have been sexually and/or physically abused, neglected, and undernourished. They can't keep kids from watching mindless television or R-rated videos until midnight, or from using illegal substances or alcohol. In essence, when the culture begins to crumble, the schools will also look bad. That's why even though I disagree with many of the trends in modern education, I sympathize with the dedicated teachers and principals out there who are doing their best on behalf of our youngsters. They are discouraged today, and they need our support.

Q 168 What immediate changes would you make in junior and senior high schools to improve the learning environment there?

Most important, we must make schools safer for students and teachers. Guns, drugs, and adolescence make a deadly cocktail. It is unbelievable what we have permitted to happen on our campuses. No wonder some kids can't think about their studies. Their lives are in danger! Yes, we can reduce the violence if we're committed to the task. Armed guards? Maybe. Metal detectors? If necessary. More expulsions? Probably. No-nonsense administrators? Definitely. When schools are blessed by strong leadership, like the legendary Joe Clark at Eastside High School in Paterson, New Jersey, they make dramatic progress academically. Above all, we must do what is required to pacify the combat zones in junior and senior high schools.

We will not solve our pervasive problems, however, with the present generation of secondary school students. Our best hope for the future is to start over with the youngsters just coming into elementary school. We can rewrite the rules with these wide-eyed kids. Let's redesign the primary grades to include a greater measure of discipline. I'm not talking merely about more difficult assignments and additional homework. I'm recommending more structure and control in the classroom.

As the first official voice of the school, the primary teacher is in a position to construct positive attitudinal foundations on which future educators can build. Conversely, she can fill her young pupils with contempt and disrespect. A child's teachers during the first six years will largely determine the nature of his attitude toward authority and the educational climate in junior and senior high school (and beyond).

Q169 What can we as parents do to improve public schools in our area?

Most educators know that parental involvement is absolutely critical to what public schools are trying to do. Others (fortunately not the majority) see themselves as the professionals and resent parental interference. We should never accede to that idea. Parents are ultimately responsible for the education of their kids, and they should not surrender that authority. Educators are their employees, paid with tax dollars, and are accountable to the school-board members whom parents elect. The best schools are those with the greatest parental involvement and support.

With that understanding, let me urge you to visit your child's school to answer questions of interest to you. Does the staff understand the necessity for structure, respect, and discipline in the classroom? If so, why don't you call your child's teacher and the principal and express your appreciation to them? They could use a pat on the back. Tell them you stand ready to assist in carrying out their important mission. If your school system is not so oriented, get involved to help turn the tide. Meet with parent groups. Join the PTA. Review the textbooks. Work for the election of school-board members who believe in traditional values and academic excellence. Let me say it again: Schools function best when the time-honored principle of local control—by parents—prevails. I believe it is making a comeback!

Q170 How do you feel about corporal punishment as a deterrent to school misbehavior? Do you believe in spanking our students?

Corporal punishment is not effective at the junior and senior high school levels, and I do not recommend its application. It can be useful for elementary students, especially with amateur clowns (as opposed to hard-core troublemakers). For this reason, I am opposed to abolishing spanking in elementary schools because we have systematically eliminated the tools with which teachers have traditionally backed up their word. We're down now to a precious few. Let's not go any further in that direction.

Q171 I have observed that elementary and junior high school students—even high schoolers—tend to admire the more strict teachers. Common sense would tell us that they would like those who are easier on them. Why do you think they are drawn to the disciplinarians?

You are right; teachers who maintain order and demand the most from their students are often the most respected members of the faculty, provided they aren't mean and grouchy. One who can control a class without being unpleasant is almost always esteemed by her students. That is true, first of all, because there is safety in order. When a class is out of control, particularly at the elementary school level, the children are afraid of each other. If the teacher can't make the class behave, how can she prevent a bully from doing his thing? How can she keep the students from laughing at one of the less-able members? Children can be vicious to each other, and they feel good about having a teacher who is strong but kind.

Second, children love justice. When someone has violated a rule, they want immediate retribution. They admire the teacher who can enforce an equitable legal system, and they find great comfort in reasonable social expectations. By contrast, the teacher who does not control her class inevitably allows crime to pay, violating something basic in the value system of children.

Third, children admire strict teachers because chaos is nerve-racking. Screaming and hitting and wiggling are fun for about ten minutes; then the confusion begins to get tiresome and irritating.

I have smiled in amusement many times as second- and third-grade children astutely evaluated the relative disciplinary skills of their teachers. They know how a class should be conducted. I only wish all of their teachers were equally aware of this important attribute.

Q.172 Can you give us a guideline for how much work children should be given to do?

There should be a healthy balance between work and play. Many farm children of the past had daily chores that made life pretty difficult. Early in the morning and again after school they would feed the pigs, gather the eggs, milk the cows, and bring in the wood. Little time was left for fun, and childhood became a pretty drab experience. That was an extreme position, and I certainly don't favor its return.

Contrast that workaday responsibility with some families today that require nothing of children—not even asking them to take out the trash, water the lawn, or feed the cat. Both extremes, as usual, are harmful to the child. The logical middle ground can be found by giving a boy or girl an exposure to responsibility and work but preserving time for play and fun. The amount of time devoted to each activity should vary with the age of the child, gradually requiring more work as he or she grows older.

Q173 Schools are asked to accomplish many things on behalf of our kids today. They are even expected to teach them how to have sex without spreading disease. What part of the curriculum would you give the greatest priority?

Schools that try to do everything may wind up doing very little. That's why I believe we should give priority to the academic fundamentals—what used to be called "readin', writin', and 'rithmetic." Of those three, the most important is basic literacy. An appalling number of students graduating from high school can't even read the employment page of the newspaper or comprehend an elementary book. Every one of those young men and women will suffer years of pain and embarrassment because of our failure. That misery starts at a very young age.

A tenth-grade boy was once referred to me because he was dropping out of school. I asked why he was quitting, and he said with great passion, "I've been miserable since first grade. I've felt embarrassed and stupid every year. I've had to stand up and read, but I can't even understand a second-grade book. You people have had your last laugh at me. I'm getting out." I told him I didn't blame him for the way he felt; his suffering was our responsibility.

Teaching children to read should be "Job One" for educators. Giving boys and girls that basic skill is the foundation on which other learning is built. Unfortunately, millions of young people are still functionally illiterate after completing twelve years of schooling and receiving high school diplomas. There is no excuse for this failure. Research shows that every student, with very few exceptions, can be taught to read if the task is approached creatively and individually. Admittedly, some can't learn in group settings because their minds wander and they don't ask questions as readily. They require one-on-one instruction from trained reading specialists. It is expensive for schools to support these remedial teachers, but no expenditure would be more helpful. Special techniques, teaching machines, and behavior-modification techniques can work in individual cases. Whatever is required, we must provide it. Furthermore, the sooner this help can be given, the better for the emotional and academic well-being of the child. By the fourth or fifth grade, he or she has already suffered the humiliation of reading failure.

Q174 What causes a child to be a "slow learner"—one who just doesn't learn like other children in the classroom?

There are many hereditary, environmental, and physical factors that contribute to one's intellect, and it is difficult to isolate the particular influences. For many children who have difficulty in school, we will never know precisely why their ability to learn is limited. Let me tell you what is now known about intellectual development that may explain some— but not all—cases of learning deficits.

Accumulating evidence seems to indicate that some children who are slow learners and even those who have borderline retardation may not have received proper intellectual stimulation in their very early years. There appears to be a critical period during the first three to four years when the potential for intellectual growth must be seized. There are enzyme systems in the brain that must be activated during this brief window. If the opportunity is missed, the child may never reach his capacity.

Children who grow up in deprived circumstances are more likely to be slow learners. They may not have heard adult language regularly. They have not been provided with interesting books and puzzles to occupy their sensory apparatus. They have not been taken to the zoo, the airport, or other exciting places. They have not received daily training and guidance from adults. This lack of stimulation may inhibit the brain from developing properly.

The effect of early stimulation on living brains has been studied in several fascinating animal experiments. In one study, researchers divided littermate rats into two identical groups. The first was given maximum stimulation during the first few months of life. These rats were kept in well-lit cages, surrounded by interesting paddle wheels and other toys. They were handled regularly and allowed to explore outside their cages. They were subjected to learning experiences and then rewarded for remembering. The second group lived the opposite kind of existence. These rats crouched in dimly lit, drab, uninteresting cages. They were not handled or stimulated in any way and were not permitted outside their cages. Both groups were fed identical food.

At 105 days of age, all the rats were sacrificed to permit examination of their neurological apparatus. The researchers were surprised to find that the high-stimulation rats had brains that differed in several important ways: (1) the cortex (the thinking part of the brain) was thicker and wider; (2) the blood supply was much more abundant; (3) the enzymes necessary for learning were more sophisticated. The researchers concluded that the stimulation experienced during the first group's early lives had resulted in more advanced and complex brains.[50]

It is always risky to apply conclusions from animal research directly to humans, but the same kinds of changes probably occur in the brains of highly stimulated children. If parents want their children to be capable, they should begin by talking to them at length while they are still babies. Interesting mobiles and winking-blinking toys should be arranged around the crib. From then on through the toddler years, learning activities should be programmed regularly.

Of course, parents must understand the difference between stimulation and pressure. Providing books for a three-year-old is stimulating. Ridiculing and threatening him because he can't read them is pressuring. Imposing unreachable expectations can have a damaging effect on children.

If early stimulation is as important as it now appears, then the lack thereof may be a leading cause of learning impairment among schoolchildren. It is imperative that parents take the time to invest their resources in their children. The necessity for providing rich, edifying experiences for young children has never been as obvious as it is today.

Q175 You have told us what kinds of homes produce children with the greatest intellectual potential. Are there other studies that would tell us how to raise kids with the healthiest attitudes toward themselves and others?

A study designed to answer that precise question was conducted some years ago by Dr. Stanley Coopersmith, associate professor of psychology, University of California. He evaluated 1,738 normal middle-class boys and their families, beginning in the preadolescent period and following them through to young manhood. After identifying those boys having the highest self-esteem, he compared their homes and childhood influences with those having a lower sense of self-worth. He found three important characteristics that distinguished them:

1. The high-esteem children were clearly more loved and appreciated at home than were the low-esteem boys.

2. The high-esteem group came from homes where parents had been significantly more strict in their approach to discipline. By contrast, the parents of the low-esteem group had created insecurity and dependence by their permissiveness. Their children were more likely to feel that the rules were not enforced because no one cared enough to get involved. Furthermore, the most successful and independent young men during the latter period of the study were found to have come from homes that demanded the strictest accountability and responsibility. And as could have been predicted, the family ties remained the strongest not in the wishy-washy homes but in the homes where discipline and self-control had been a way of life.

3. The homes of the high-esteem group were also

characterized by democracy and openness. Once the boundaries for behavior were established, there was freedom for individual personalities to grow and develop. The boys could express themselves without fear of ridicule, and the overall atmosphere was marked by acceptance and emotional safety.[51]

Q176 My six-year-old son has always been an energetic child with some of the symptoms of hyperactivity. He has a short attention span and flits from one activity to another. I took him to his pediatrician, who said he did not have attention deficit disorder. However, he's beginning to have learning problems in school because he can't stay in his seat and concentrate on his lessons. What should I do?

It sounds like your son is immature in comparison with his age-mates and could profit from being retained in the first grade next year. If his birthday is between December 1 and July 1, I would ask the school psychologist to evaluate his readiness to learn. Retaining an immature boy during his early school career (kindergarten or first grade) can give him a social and academic advantage throughout the remaining years of elementary school. However, it is very important to help him "save face" with his peers. If possible, he should change schools for at least a year to avoid embarrassing questions and ridicule from his former classmates. You have very little to lose by holding back an immature boy, since males tend to be about six months behind females in development at that time. The age of a child is the worst criterion on which to base a decision regarding when to begin a school career. That determination should be made according to specific neurological, psychosocial, and pediatric variables.

Let me add one other suggestion that you might consider. Your son appears to be a good candidate for homeschooling. Keep him in the safety of your care until he matures a bit, and then if you choose, place him in school one year behind where he would have been otherwise. He will not suffer academically and will be more secure for the experience.

Homeschooling is especially helpful for the immature child—usually a boy—who is just not ready for the social competition and rejection often experienced within large groups. It is also beneficial to children who do not have this problem, if the parent is committed to it. That's why homeschooling is the fastest growing educational movement in the United States today.[52]

Q177 If age is such a poor factor to use in determining the start of the first grade, why is it applied so universally in our country?

Because it is so convenient. Parents can plan for the definite beginning of school when their child turns six. School officials can survey their districts and know how many first graders they will have the following year. If an eight-year-old moves into the district in October, the administrator knows the child belongs in second grade, and so on. The use of chronological age as a criterion for school entrance is great for everybody—except the late bloomer who is developmentally unprepared for formal education.

Q178 We have a six-year-old son who is also a late bloomer and is having trouble learning to read. Even though he is immature, I don't understand why this would keep him from reading.

It is likely that your late-maturing youngster has not yet completed a vital neurological process involving an organic substance called myelin. At birth, the nervous system of the body is not insulated. That is why an infant is unable to reach out and grasp an object; the electrical command or impulse is lost on its journey from the brain to the hand. Gradually, a whitish substance (myelin) begins to coat the nerve fibers, allowing controlled muscular action to occur.

Myelinization typically proceeds from the head downward and from the center of the body outward. In other words, a child can control the movement of his head and neck before the rest of his body. Control of the shoulder precedes the elbow, which precedes the wrist, which precedes the large muscles in the hands, which precedes small-muscle coordination of the fingers. This explains why elementary school children are taught block-letter printing before they learn cursive writing; the broad strokes and lines are less dependent on minute finger control than the flowing curves of mature penmanship.

Since visual apparatus in humans is usually the last neural mechanism to be myelinated, your immature child may not have undergone this necessary developmental process by his present age of six years. Therefore, such a child who is extremely immature and uncoordinated may be neurologically unprepared for the intellectual tasks of reading and writing. Reading, particularly, is a highly complex neurological process. The visual stimulus must be relayed to the brain without distortion, where it should be interpreted and retained in the memory. Not all six-year-old children are equipped to perform this task. Unfortunately, however, our culture permits few exceptions or deviations from the established timetable. A child of that age must learn to read or he will face the emotional consequences of failure. This is why I favor either holding an immature child out of school for a year or homeschooling him or her for several years.

Q179 Is retention in the same grade ever advisable for a child who is not a late bloomer? How about the slow learner?

There are some students who can profit from a second year at the same grade level and many who will not. The best guideline is this: Retain only the child for whom something will be different next year. A youngster who is sick for seven months in an academic year might profit from another run-through when he or she is healthy. And as I've indicated, a late-developing child should be held back in kindergarten (or the first grade at the latest) to place him or her with youngsters of comparable development. For the slow learner, however—the child who has below-average ability—a second journey through the same grade will not help. If he was failing the fourth grade in June, he will continue to fail the fourth grade in September. The findings from research on this issue are crystal clear.

It is not often realized that the curricular content of each grade level is very similar to the year before and the year after. There is considerable redundancy in the concepts taught; the students in each grade are taken a little further, but much of the time is spent in review. The arithmetical methods of addition and subtraction, for example, are taught in the primary years, but considerable work is done on these tasks in the sixth grade, too. Nouns and verbs are taught repeatedly for several years.

Thus, the most unjustifiable reason for retention is to give the slow learner another year of exposure to easier concepts. He will not do better the second time around! Nor is there much magic in summer school. Some parents hope that a six-week program in July and August will accomplish what was impossible in the ten months between September and June. They are often disappointed.

Q 180 I've heard that we forget more than 80 percent of what we learn. When you consider the cost of getting an education, I wonder why we put all that effort into examinations, textbooks, homework, and years spent in boring classrooms. Is education really worth what we invest in it?

In fact, it is. There are many valid reasons for learning, even if forgetting will take its usual toll. First, one of the important functions of the learning process is the self-discipline and self-control that it fosters. Good students learn to follow directions, carry out assignments, and channel their mental faculties. Second, even if the facts and concepts can't be recalled, the individual knows they exist and where to find them. He or she can retrieve the information if needed. Third, old learning makes new learning easier. Each mental exercise gives us more associative cues with which to link future ideas and concepts, and we are changed for having been through the process of learning. Fourth, we don't really forget everything that is beyond the reach of our memories. The information is stored in the brain and will return to consciousness when properly stimulated. And fifth, we are shaped by the influence of intelligent and charismatic people who teach us.

I wish there were an easier, more efficient process for shaping human minds than the slow and painful experience of education. But until a "learning pill" is developed, the old-fashioned approach will have to do.

Q.181 Our junior higher is the most disorganized kid I've ever seen. His life is a jumble of forgotten assignments and missed deadlines. What can I do to help him?

You'll have no trouble believing what educational consultant Cheri Fuller considers to be the most common cause of school failure. She says it is not laziness or poor study skills. The primary problem is what you see in your son—massive disorganization. Show me a student's notebook, Fuller says, and I'll tell you whether that individual is a B student or a D student. An achieving student's notebook is arranged neatly with dividers and folders for handouts and assignments. A failing student's notebook is usually a jumbled mess and may not even be used at all.

Some children are naturally sloppy, but most of them can learn to be better organized. Fuller says this skill should be taught in the elementary school years. Once they enter junior high, students may have as many as five teachers, each assigning different textbooks, workbooks, handouts, and requirements from various classroom subjects. It is foolish to assume that kids who have never had any organizational training will be able to keep such detail straight and accessible. If we want them to function in this system, we need to give them the tools that are critical to success.[53]

You might consider having your child evaluated to see if he has attention deficit disorder or some temperamental characteristic that makes it difficult for him to organize. When you've determined what he is capable of doing, work with an educational consultant or a school psychologist to design a system that will teach him how to live a more structured life.

Q 182 I've always had an interest in creative writing, primarily because I had a teacher who encouraged me to express myself and gave me the skills to do it. My kids, however, have not had that exposure. The school system just doesn't teach writing skills anymore. How did you come to be a writer, and how might I give my children a nudge in that direction?

It is true that writing skills are seldom taught today. That was evident a while back when I was considering hiring a Ph.D. candidate from a large university. I called her major professor for a recommendation. He spoke highly of this woman and said he was sure she would do a good job for me. I then asked if she was an adequate writer. He said, "Are you kidding? None of my students have strong writing skills. Young people don't learn to put their thoughts on paper these days." He was right!

It hasn't always been that way. I remember diagramming sentences and learning parts of speech when I was in elementary school. It was a major part of the curriculum. Also, my parents encouraged me and helped me grow in this area. I wrote a letter to a friend when I was nine years old. My mother then suggested that we read it together. I had written, "Dear Tom, how are you? I am just fine." My mom asked me if I thought that sounded a little boring. She said, "You haven't said anything. You used a few words, but they have no meaning." I never wrote that phrase again, although that is the typical way a child begins a letter.

Looking back, I can see how, even at an early age, my mother was teaching me to write. In addition, I was also fortunate to have a few English teachers who were determined to teach me the fundamentals of composition. I had one in high school and another in college who insisted that I learn grammar and composition. They nearly beat me to death, but I'm glad they did. I earn a living today, at least in part, with the skills they gave to me. Especially, I would like to say thanks to Dr. Ed Harwood. His classes were like marine boot camp, but what I learned there was priceless.

It's not terribly difficult or time-consuming to encourage and teach kids some of the basics of grammar and composition. One approach is to ask a family member to correspond with your child and encourage him or her to write back. Then when the reply is written, sprinkle a few corrections, such as the one my mother offered, with a generous portion of praise. Finally, entice that youngster to engage in a little creative expression. As for what you can do to compensate for the de-emphasis on writing in school, I really don't know—except to seek instruction outside the classroom.

The ability to write has gone out of style—much like the old "homemaking" classes for girls. But it is an incredibly valuable craft that your child can use in a wide variety of settings. Don't let him or her grow up without developing it.

Q.183 I'm a teacher, and I love my students. There is one kid in my sixth-grade class, however, who drives me nuts. He works overtime trying to make everybody laugh. What drives this impish child? Why does he want to make life miserable for me?

We all remember the kid you're talking about. He's called "the class clown" and some other things that are less flattering. He is a trial to his teachers, an embarrassment to his parents, and an utter delight to every child who wants to escape the boredom of school. There are millions of class clowns on the job today. It's my belief that boards of education assign at least one such kid to every class just to make sure that schoolteachers earn every dollar of their salaries.

These skilled little disrupters are usually boys. They often have reading or other academic problems. They may be small in stature, although not always, and they'll do anything for a laugh. Their parents and teachers may not recognize that behind the boisterous behavior is often the pain of inferiority.

You see, humor is a classic response to feelings of low self-esteem. That's why within many successful comedians is the memory of a hurting little boy or girl. Jonathan Winters's parents were divorced when he was seven years old, and he said he used to cry when he was alone because other children teased him about not having a father. Joan Rivers frequently jokes about her unattractiveness as a girl. She said she was such a dog, her father had to throw a bone down the aisle to get her married. And so it goes.

These and other comedians got their training during childhood, using humor as a defense against childhood hurts. That's usually the inspiration for the class clown. By making an enormous joke out of everything, he conceals the self-doubt that churns inside.

That understanding should help us meet his needs and manage such a child more effectively.

Q184 A great deal is being made about something called "school choice" these days. Could you explain this concept and tell me whether or not you are in favor of it?

School choice is an idea whose time has come. It would give parents the right to decide whether to send their children to a public, private, or religious institution and even to select a specific school to which they would be sent.

I favor this idea for several reasons. First, giving

parents a choice would improve the quality of education because it would force school personnel to compete for students. That would make them more responsive to parents. Competition always improves the performance of human beings, whether one is selling hamburgers or automobiles. It encourages people to serve more willingly, to operate more efficiently, and to do a good job.

That is the heart of the free-enterprise system. It provides incentives to those who work hard and think creatively. Monopolies, by contrast, become unresponsive and stilted. We've seen that lethargy in the U.S. Post Office, in the various departments of motor vehicles, in Amtrak—and in the present educational system. I believe test scores will rise and parents will be more satisfied when schools that do a great job are allowed to grow. Their budgets will expand and their teachers will be proud, while disorganized and unresponsive schools with poor teachers and halfhearted administrators will wither on the vine. That prospect of competition makes educators nervous—but it makes many of us excited.

The second reason I favor school choice is related to the first: It would put power in the hands of parents. If Dad or Mom became dissatisfied with a particular school, he or she could take the child to a nearby school that better serves their needs. With that youngster would go the voucher and the money it represents. As a bad school began to dwindle under this system, you can bet there would be new motivation among administrators to listen to parents and accommodate their concerns. As it stands today, parents are virtually powerless unless they organize and storm a school-board meeting. There has to be a better way to encourage cooperation between the home and professional educators.

The third benefit of school choice is that it would grant poor people the same options now held by the affluent. Today, if an upper-class family is dissatisfied with their local public schools—or if they prefer Christian education or a first-class prep school—they have the resources to send their children where they wish. An underprivileged family has no such alternative. They are stuck with the school in their neighborhood, even if it is rife with violence and rebellion. Former president Bill Clinton, who campaigned against school choice in California, sent his daughter to an excellent private school in Washington, D.C. I would like to see everyone have the opportunity he had.

Recently, statistics released by the U.S. Department of Education itself indicated that nearly half of our nation's adult population is functionally illiterate. The future looks even dimmer. The Department of Education has forecast that three out of every five of our current school-age population will either drop out or graduate with an education below the seventh-grade level![54] Given that dismal track record, small wonder the movement to place accountability squarely in the hands of the people to whom it belongs—the staff, parents, and students at each individual school—is gaining ground. Families that care about their children's education are crucial to classroom success. School choice ensures their involvement. It is, I believe, the wave of the future.

Q 185 I've read that it is possible to teach four-year-old children to read. Should I be working on this with my child?

If a youngster is particularly sharp and if he or she can learn to read without feeling undue adult pressure, it would be advantageous to teach this skill. But that's a much bigger "if" than most people realize. There are some parents who find it difficult to work with their children without showing frustration over immaturity and disinterest.

Furthermore, new skills should be taught at the age when they are most needed. Why invest unnecessary effort trying to teach a child to read when he has not yet learned to cross the street, tie his shoes, count to ten, or answer the telephone? It seems foolish to get panicky over preschool reading. The best policy is to provide your children with many interesting books and materials, read to them every day, and answer their questions. You can then introduce them to phonics and watch the lights go on. It's fun if you don't push too hard.

Q 186 Some educators have said we should eliminate report cards and academic marks. Do you think this is a good idea?

No, I believe academic marks are valuable for students in the third grade or higher. They reinforce and reward the child who has achieved in school and act as a nudge to the youngster who hasn't. It is important, though, that grades be used properly. They have the power to create or to destroy motivation.

Through the elementary years, I've always felt that a child's grades should be based on what he does with what he has. In other words, I think we should grade according to ability. A slow child should be able to succeed in school just as certainly as a gifted youngster. If he struggles and sweats to achieve, he should somehow be rewarded—even if his work falls short of an absolute standard. By the same token, gifted children should not be given A's just because they are smart enough to excel without working.

Again, the primary purpose of grading in the elementary school years should be to reward academic effort.

However, as the student goes into high school, the purpose of grading shifts. Those who take college preparatory courses must be graded on an absolute standard. An A in chemistry or calculus is accepted by college admission boards as a symbol of excellence, and secondary teachers must preserve that meaning. Students with lesser academic skill need not take those difficult courses.

To repeat, marks for children can be the teacher's most important motivational tool, provided they are used correctly. Therefore, the recommendation that schools eliminate grading is a move away from discipline in the classroom.

Q187 What would you do if you had an elementary school child in a chaotic classroom with a disorganized teacher?

I would do everything I could to get my child reassigned to a different classroom. Some very bad habits and attitudes can develop in ten months with an incompetent teacher. Homeschooling or private education might also be considered, if resources permitted.

Q188 How do you feel about year-round schools in areas where overcrowding makes them advantageous?

I know there are administrative advantages to year-round schools, especially since the facilities are not standing idle two months a year as they are under the current system. Nevertheless, many parents say year-round schools are very hard on them. Siblings attending different schools may have their vacations at different times, making it impossible for families to take trips together. It is also more difficult to co-ordinate children's time off with parents' schedules. In short, year-round schools represent just one more hardship on families seeking to do fun and recre-ational things together each year.

Q.189 How do you feel about homework being given by elementary schools? Do you think it is a good idea? If so, how much and how often?

Having written several books on discipline and being on the record as an advocate of reasonable parental authority, my answer may surprise you: I believe homework for young children can be counterpro-ductive if it is not handled very carefully. Little kids are asked to sit for six or more hours a day doing for-mal classwork. Then many of them take a tiring bus ride home and guess what? They're placed at a desk and told to do more assignments. For a wiry, active, fun-loving youngster, that is asking too much. Learning for them becomes an enormous bore in-stead of the exciting panorama that it should be.

I remember a mother coming to see me because her son was struggling in a tough private school. "He has about five hours of homework per night," she said. "How can I make him want to do it?"

"Are you kidding?" I told his mother. "I wouldn't do that much homework!"

Upon investigation, I found that the elementary school he attended vigorously denied giving him that many assignments. Or rather, they didn't give the other students that much work. They did expect the slower boys and girls to complete the assign-ments they didn't get done in the classroom each day, in addition to the regularly assigned home-work. For the plodders like this youngster, that meant up to five hours of work nightly. There was no escape from books throughout their entire day. What a mistake!

Excessive homework during the elementary school years also has the potential of interfering with family life. In our home, we were trying to do many things with the limited time we had together. I wanted our kids to participate in church activities, have some family time, and still be able to kick back and waste an hour or two. Children need opportunities for unstructured play—swinging on the swings and throwing rocks and playing with basketballs. Yet by the time their homework was done, darkness had fallen and dinnertime had arrived. Then baths were taken, and off they went to bed. Something didn't feel right about that kind of pace. That's why I negotiated with our children's teachers, agreeing that they would complete no more than one hour per night of supervised homework. It was enough!

Homework also generates a considerable amount of stress for parents. Their kids either won't do the assignments or they get tired and whine about them. Tensions build and angry words fly. I'm also convinced that child abuse occurs at that point for some children. When my wife, Shirley, was teaching second grade, one little girl came to school with both eyes black and swollen. She said her father had beaten her because she couldn't learn her spelling words. That is illegal now, but it was tolerated then. The poor youngster will remember those beatings for a lifetime and will always think of herself as "stupid."

Then there are the parents who do the assignments for their kids just to get them over the hump. Have you ever been guilty of doing that? Shame on you! More specifically, have you ever worked for

two weeks on a fifth-grade geography project for
your eleven-year-old—and then learned later that
you got a C on it?! That's the ultimate humiliation.

In short, I believe homework in elementary
school should be extremely limited. It is appropriate
for learning multiplication tables, spelling words,
and test review. It is also helpful in training kids to
remember assignments, bring books home, and
complete them as required. But to load them down
night after night with monotonous book work is to
invite educational burnout.

In junior high classes, perhaps two hours of homework per night should be the maximum. In high
school, those students who are preparing for college
must handle more work. Even then, however, the
load should be reasonable. Education is a vitally important part of our children's lives, but it is only one
part. Balance between these competing objectives is
the key word.

Q190 Boy! Do I understand your perspective on
homework. The greatest power struggle in
our home is over school assignments. Our fifth grader
simply will not do them! When we try to force him to study,
he sits and stares, doodles, gets up for water, and just kills
time. Furthermore, we never know for sure what he's
supposed to be doing. Why is he like that?

Let me offer a short discourse on school achievement, based on years of interaction with parents. I
served as a teacher, a high school counselor, and a
school psychologist. As such, I became very well acquainted with children's learning patterns. The kind
of self-discipline necessary to succeed in school appears to be distributed on a continuum from one extreme to the other. Students at the positive end of
the scale (I'll call them Type I) are by nature rather

organized individuals who care about details. They take the educational process very seriously and assume full responsibility for assignments given. They also worry about grades, or at least they recognize their importance. To do poorly on a test would depress them for several days. They also like the challenge offered in the classroom. Parents of these children do not have to monitor their progress to keep them working. It is their way of life—and it is consistent with their temperaments.

At the other end of the continuum are the boys and girls who do not fit in well with the structure of the classroom (Type II). If their Type I siblings emerge from school cum laude, these kids graduate "thank you, laude!" They are sloppy, disorganized, and flighty. They have a natural aversion to work and love to play. They can't wait for success, and they hurry on without it. Like bacteria that gradually become immune to antibiotics, the classic underachievers become impervious to adult pressure. They withstand a storm of parental protest every few weeks and then, when no one is looking, they slip back into apathy. They don't even hear the assignments being given in school and seem not to be embarrassed when they fail to complete them. And, you can be sure, they drive their parents to distraction.

Some of these kids have what has become known as attention deficit disorder (ADD) or attention deficit/hyperactivity disorder (ADHD). Those are youngsters who have an unidentified neurological condition that makes them easily distractible, flighty, disorganized, and for some, unable to sit still and concentrate. Trying to make ADD or ADHD children function like other kids without treating them medically is a physical impossibility.

I don't know what is inhibiting your son's school

performance, but you should have him seen by a school psychologist or learning specialist. They can diagnose his problem and help you establish a strategy to get the most out of what he has.

Q 191 What else can you tell us about the differences between Type I and Type II kids? I have one of each and want to understand them.

First, you should know that these characteristics are not highly correlated to intelligence. By that I mean there are bright children who are at the flighty end of the scale, and there are slow-learning individuals who are highly motivated. The primary difference between them is a matter of temperament and maturity, although there are more smart kids in the Type I category.

Second, Type II children are not intrinsically inferior to Type I. Yes, it would be wonderful if every student used the talent he or she possessed to best advantage. But each child is a unique individual. Kids don't fit the same mold—nor do they need to. I know education is important today, and we want our boys and girls to go as far as they can academically. But let's keep our goals in proper perspective. It is possible that the low achiever will outperform the academic superstar in the long run. There are many examples of that occurring in the real world (Einstein, Edison, Eleanor Roosevelt, etc.). Don't write off that disorganized, apparently lazy kid as a lifelong loser. He or she may surprise you.

Third, you will never turn a Type II youngster into a Type I scholar by nagging, pushing, threatening, and punishing. It isn't in him. If you try to squeeze him into something he's not, you will only produce aggravation for yourself and anger from the child. That attempt can fill a house with conflict. I have concluded that it is simply not worth the price it extracts.

I am certainly not recommending that children be allowed to float through life, avoiding responsibility and wasting their opportunities. My approach to the underachiever can be summarized in these suggestions: (1) He lacks the discipline to structure his life. Help him generate it. Systematize his study hours. Look over his homework to see that it is neat and complete, etc. (2) Maintain as close contact with the school as possible. The more you and your child's teacher communicate, the better. Only then can you provide the needed structure. (3) Avoid anger in the relationship. It does not help. Those parents who become most frustrated and irritated often believe their child's irresponsibility is a deliberate thing. Usually it is not. Consider the problem a matter of temperament rather than defiance. (4) Seek tutorial assistance if necessary to stay on track. (5) Having done what you can to help, accept what comes in return. Go with the flow and begin looking for other areas of success for your child.

Let me say it once more: Not every individual can be squeezed into the same mold. There is room in this world for the creative souls who long to breathe freely. I'll bet some of you parents approached life from the same direction.

Q.192 I assume that you favor a highly structured curriculum that emphasizes the memorization of specific facts, which I consider to be a very low level of learning. We need to teach concepts to our kids and help them learn how to think—not just fill their heads with a bunch of details.

I agree that we want to teach concepts to students, but that does not occur in a vacuum. For example, we would like them to understand the concept of the solar system and how the planets are positioned in rotation around the sun. How is that done? One way is for them to learn the distances between the heavenly bodies, i.e., the sun is 93 million miles from Earth, but the moon is only 240,000. The concept of relative positions is then understood from the factual information. What I'm saying is that an understanding of the right factual information can and should lead to conceptual learning.

Q 193 But again, you're putting too much emphasis on the memorization process, which is a low academic goal.

The human brain is capable of storing some two billion bits of information in the course of a lifetime. There are many avenues through which that programming can occur, and memorization is one of them. Let me put it this way: If you ever have to go under a surgeon's knife, you'd better hope that the physician has memorized every muscle, every bone, every blood vessel, and every Boy Scout knot in the book. Your life will depend on his ability to access factual information during the operation. Obviously, I strongly oppose the perspective held in some academic circles that says, "There's nothing we know for certain, so why learn anything?" Those who feel that way have no business teaching. They are salesmen with nothing to sell!

Q 194 How can I help my child develop wholesome, respectful attitudes toward people of other racial and ethnic groups?

There is no substitute for parental modeling of the attitudes we wish to teach. Someone wrote, "The footsteps a child follows are most likely to be the ones his parents thought they covered up." It is true. Our children are watching us carefully, and they instinctively imitate our behavior. Therefore, we can hardly expect them to be kind to all of God's children if we are prejudiced and rejecting. Likewise, we will be unable to teach appreciativeness if we never say please or thank you at home or abroad. We will not produce honest children if we teach them to lie to the bill collector on the phone by saying, "Dad's not home." In these matters, our boys and girls instantly discern the gap between what we say and what we do. And of the two choices, they usually identify with our behavior and ignore our empty proclamations.

If you never speak derogatorily about racial minorities, and if you absolutely will not tolerate racist jokes and slurs, your children will not fail to notice. It's the best place to begin your teaching process.

Q195 Many of our friends have begun to home-school their children with seemingly positive results. My wife and I are considering this possibility as well but aren't quite sure. What are your views on this educational option? What would you do in my shoes?

This is a subject on which my mind has changed dramatically over the years. There was a time when I subscribed wholeheartedly to the notion that early formal childhood education was vital to the child's intellectual well-being. That was widely believed in the sixties and seventies. I no longer accept that idea and favor keeping kids with their parents for a longer time. Dr. Raymond Moore, author of *School Can Wait*[55] and an early leader of the homeschooling movement, had a great influence on me in this regard.

The research now validates the wisdom of keeping boys and girls in a protected environment until they have achieved a greater degree of maturity. Not only do they benefit emotionally from that delay, but they typically make better progress academically. That's why homeschooled individuals often gain entrance to the most prestigious universities and colleges in the country.[56] What parents can teach young children in informal one-on-one interactions surpasses what their little minds can absorb sitting among twenty-five age-mates in a classroom.

You asked what I would do in your shoes. If Shirley and I were raising our children again, we would homeschool them at least for the first few years!

Q196 Don't you think homeschooling might negatively impact the socialization process? I don't want my children growing up to be misfits.

This is the question homeschooling parents hear most often from curious (or critical) friends, relatives, and neighbors. "Socialization" is a vague, dark cloud hanging over their heads. What if teaching at home somehow isolates the kids and turns them into oddballs? For you and all those parents who see this issue as the great danger of home education, I would respectfully disagree—for these reasons.

First, to remove a child from the classroom is not necessarily to confine him or her to the house! And once beyond the schoolyard gate, the options are practically unlimited! Homeschool support groups are surfacing in community after community across the country. Some are highly organized and offer field trips, teaching co-ops, tutoring services, social activities, and various other assistances and resources. There are homeschooling athletic leagues and orchestras and other activities. Even if you're operating completely on your own, there are outings to museums and parks, visits to farms, factories, hospitals, and seats of local government, days with Dad at the office, trips to Grandma's house, extracurricular activities like sports and music, church youth groups, service organizations, and special-interest clubs. There are friends to be invited over and relatives to visit and parties to attend. The list is limitless. Even a trip with Mom to the market can provide youngsters with invaluable exposure to the lives and daily tasks of real adults in the real world. While they're there, a multitude of lessons can be learned about math (pricing, fractions, pints vs. gallons, addition, subtraction, etc.), reading labels, and other academic subjects. And without the strictures of schedule and formal curricula, it can all be considered part of the educational process. That's what I'd call socialization at its best! To accuse homeschoolers of creating strange little people in solitary confinement is nonsense.

The great advantage of homeschooling, in fact, is the protection it provides to vulnerable children from the wrong kind of socialization. When children interact in large groups, the strongest and most aggressive kids quickly intimidate the weak and vulnerable. I am absolutely convinced that bad things happen to immature and "different" boys and girls when they are thrown into the highly competitive world of other children. When this occurs in nursery school or in kindergarten, they learn to fear their peers. There stands this knobby-legged little girl who doesn't have a clue about life or how to cope with things that scare her. It's sink or swim, kid. Go for it! It is easy to see why such children tend to become more peer dependent because of the jostling they get at too early an age. Research shows that if these tender little boys and girls can be kept at home for a few more years and shielded from the impact of social pressure, they tend to be more confident, more independent, and often emerge as leaders three or four years later.[57]

If acquainting them with ridicule, rejection, physical threats, and the rigors of the pecking order is necessary to socialize our children, I'd recommend that we keep them unsocialized for a little longer.

Q197 Why don't you favor letting teachers and administrators pray with their classes and at school functions? That's the way it was when I was a kid.

I know. My public-school teachers were also my Sunday school teachers, and they spoke often of the Bible and Christian concepts in the classroom. But the world has changed since then. Today, if school officials of every belief system are permitted to write and recite prayers, our children will be exposed to a wide variety of theologies—from New Age nonsense to Islamic rituals. In some cities, especially Los Angeles and other large communities with culturally diverse populations, educators might have to develop a kind of "affirmative-action" plan to assure fairness for everyone. A typical week might include prayers to Gaia, the "mother of the earth," on Monday; prayers to Sophia, the feminist "goddess of wisdom," on Tuesday; prayers to Allah on Wednesday; prayers to the "Unknown God of Nature" on Thursday; and prayers to Jehovah, God of Abraham, Isaac, and Jacob, on Friday. Some would say this approach is preferable to today's creeping secularism, but there is another answer.

My vision is for a society that protects religious liberties for people of all faiths. I believe in the concept of pluralism, which acknowledges the widely differing values and beliefs among our citizens. What's needed is a constitutional amendment protecting the rights of students and other citizens to voice their religious convictions and apply their faith to everyday issues.

It would require an amendment to the Constitution of the United States to protect voluntary school prayer and religious liberty generally. The wording should clearly articulate a principle of government neutrality toward religion and should explicitly restore student religious expression in public school. Accordingly, the proposal would prevent the government from forbidding students to mention Jesus in a classroom discussion, sing a religious song at a school recital, draw a nativity scene in art class, share their faith with other students, wear religious clothing, or distribute religious literature. Legal experts on constitutional law have assured me that 80 to 90 percent of religious-liberty court cases could be won if such a measure were to gain passage.

11

SEX EDUCATION: WHERE, WHEN, AND HOW

Q198 We're told that sex-education programs reduce the incidence of teen pregnancy. Do they work?

Hardly! As the safe-sex ideology has been taught in the nation's schools, the rates of unwed pregnancy and abortion among teens have skyrocketed. A comprehensive study conducted by Stan Weed and Joseph Olson at the Institute for Research and Evaluation confirms that the Planned Parenthood approach actually worsens, rather than lessens, the problem of adolescent sexuality.

Weed and Olson compared rates of pregnancy, abortion, and live births on a state-by-state basis. They concluded that, all things being equal, for every one thousand teens between fifteen and nineteen years of age enrolled in family-planning clinics, we can expect between fifty and a hundred more pregnancies! Their study, based on Planned Parenthood's own data, also revealed significant contradictions between the organization-projected decreases in pregnancy and abortion rates, compared with actual increases in both categories. The researchers concluded that "when a program clearly should work, but apparently doesn't, it is important to find out why."[58]

Q 199 You have been critical of the philosophy and intent of Planned Parenthood and similar organizations. What is their program? What are they trying to accomplish with teenagers? What would their leaders do if given free rein in the schools?

As I understand their agenda, it can be summarized in the following four-point plan:

1. *Provide "value-free" guidance on sexuality to teenagers.* Heaven forbid any preference for morality or sexual responsibility being expressed.

2. *Provide unlimited access to contraceptives by adolescents, dispensed from clinics located on junior high and high school campuses.* In so doing, a powerful statement is made to teenagers about adult approval of premarital sexual activity.

3. *Keep parents out of the picture by every means possible.* Staff members for Planned Parenthood can then assume the parental role and communicate their libertarian philosophy to teens.

4. *Provide free abortions for young women who become pregnant, again without parental involvement or permission.*

Incredibly, millions of Americans and Canadians seem to buy this outrageous plan, which would have brought a storm of protest from yesterday's parents. Imagine how your father or grandfather would have reacted if a school official had secretly given contraceptives to you or arranged a quiet abortion when you were a teenager. The entire community would have been incensed.

Q 200 Our local school board is currently trying to decide whether or not boys and girls should

**be segregated for courses on sexuality and "family life."
What are your feelings with regard to coed sex-education
programs?**

I have severe reservations about highly explicit discussions occurring with both sexes present. To do so
breaks down the natural barriers that help to preserve virginity and makes casual sexual experimentation much more likely to occur. It also strips kids—
especially girls—of their modesty to have every detail of anatomy, physiology, intercourse, and condom usage made explicit in coed situations. Those
who have thereby become familiar and conversant
about the most intimate subjects later find themselves watching explicit sexual scenes in movies,
rock videos, and hot television programs. It doesn't
take a rocket scientist to recognize the combined impact of these influences. Whereas it was a weighty
decision to give up one's virginity in decades past, it
is but a small step for those whose conditioning began in the school classroom. Familiarity "breeds," as
we all know. I am also convinced that the incidence
of date rape rises when the barriers that help a girl
protect herself are removed.

In some cases, no doubt, school officials have
pushed for mixed sex-education classes out of a
sense of obligation. Somehow, they feel this is
what's expected of them—that parents and the
community at large want it. Let them know if you
disagree! Tell your school-board members about
the educational advantages of separated classes.
They may see your point if you present it to them
from that angle.

Q201 It seems clear that comprehensive sex-
education programs have failed miserably in

addressing the problems of teen pregnancy and sexually transmitted diseases, all of which have dramatically increased over the past twenty years. So what is the answer to curbing teenage sexual activity?

One significant study, authored by Stephen Small from the University of Wisconsin–Madison and Tom Luster of Michigan State and published in the *Journal of Marriage and the Family,* demonstrated rather conclusively that parental involvement and the transmitting of the parents' values were significant factors in preventing early sexual activity. In a direct and refreshingly sensible way, Small and Luster put parents back in the driver's seat (or the hot seat) when they said, "Permissive parental values regarding adolescent sexual behavior emerged as a strong risk factor for both males and females. Not surprisingly, adolescents who perceived their parents as accepting of premarital adolescent sexual activity were more likely to be sexually experienced."[59] The acorn never falls far from the tree.

Another important study, conducted by Drs. Sharon White and Richard DeBlassie (published in *Adolescence*), found that parents who set the most moderate and reasonable rules for their teens in the areas of dating and interaction with the opposite sex actually got the best results—in contrast to those who were overly strict (who experienced a lesser degree of success) and those who provided no guidelines whatsoever (whose position was least efficacious of all).[60]

From these studies and others, we can conclude that the people who are most effective in steering their children away from the precipice of premarital sex are those who understand that parenting adolescents is a delicate art. They are the parents who are present and involved, who communicate and exemplify their own values and attitudes, who ask questions, who carefully supervise their kids' choice of escorts and points of destination, and who insist on a reasonable curfew. But they also keep a light touch as far as it's possible to do so, because they know that the rod of iron comes with problems of its own. The bottom line? There is no sex-education program, no curriculum, no school or institution in the world that can match the power and influence of this kind of parental involvement.

It's worth adding that kids from intact, two-parent homes are less likely to engage in sexual experimentation than their counterparts from single-parent families or less stable backgrounds. And teens who have strong religious convictions and participate actively in church are, as a group, far more likely to practice abstinence than their peers. It's difficult to avoid the conclusion that faith and fidelity in the older generation are the best insurance against promiscuity in the younger.

Q.202 I disagree emphatically with what the local junior high school is teaching my daughter in sex-education class. Do I have a right to object, and how should I go about doing it?

You certainly do. I strongly support the historic American idea that parents are ultimately responsible for raising and educating their children. The school is an important ally in that effort, but the final authority lies in the home. Thus, when educational materials and content are contrary to a family's basic beliefs, parents have the right to ask school personnel to help them protect their children. Most educators are willing to accommodate the needs of individual families in this way. If they refuse, you as parents have two choices—stay and fight for what you believe, or find a new school. If you decide to oppose what is being taught, you will need the support of as many other parents as possible. Eventually you may have to take your case to the local school board. If so, be encouraged. You *can* win there. Parents in New York City became incensed over pro-homosexual materials being used in elementary schools. The superintendent and some board members refused to budge, which proved to be their undoing. Before it was over, the superintendent was fired, some board members lost their seats, and parents reestablished local control over the education of their children.[61] Some things are worth fighting to defend. Our kids are at the top of the list.

Q203 Since you disapprove of public school sex-education programs as currently designed, who do you think should tell children the facts of life, and when should that instruction begin?

For those parents who are able to handle the instructional process correctly, the responsibility for sex education should be retained in the home. There is a growing trend for all aspects of education to be taken from their hands (or the role is deliberately forfeited by them). This is unwise. Particularly in the matter of sex education, the best approach is one that begins casually and naturally in early childhood and extends through the years, according to a policy of openness, frankness, and honesty. Only parents can provide this lifetime training—being there when the questions arise and the desire for information is evidenced.

Unfortunately, moms and dads often fail to do the job. Some are too sexually inhibited to present the subject with poise, or they may lack the necessary technical knowledge of the human body. Another common mistake is to wait until puberty is knocking at the door and then try to initiate a desperate, tension-filled conversation that embarrasses the kid and exhausts the parent. If this is the way sex education is going to be handled, there has to be another alternative to consider.

Q204 When parents need help with sex education, who do you think should provide it?

It is my strong conviction that churches believing in abstinence before marriage and in lifelong marital fidelity should step in and offer their help to families sharing that commitment. Where else will moms and dads find proponents of traditional morality in this permissive day? There is no other agency or institution likely to represent the theology of the church better than the church itself. It is puzzling to me that so few have accepted this challenge, given the attack on biblical concepts of morality today.

A few parents who enroll their children in private schools are able to get the help they need with sex education. Even there, however, the subject is often ignored or handled inadequately. What has developed, unfortunately, is an informational vacuum that sets the stage for far-reaching programs in the public schools that go beyond parental wishes, beginning in some cases with kindergarten children.

Q205 I would like to teach my own child about human sexuality, but I'm not sure I know how to go about it. Talk about the matter of timing. When do I say what?

One of the most common mistakes made by parents and many overzealous educators is teaching too much too soon. One parent told me, for example, that the kindergarten children in her local district were shown films of animals in the act of copulation. That is unwise and dangerous! Available evidence indicates that there are numerous hazards involved in moving too rapidly. Children can sustain a severe emotional jolt by being exposed to realities for which they are not prepared.

Furthermore, it is unwise to place the youngster on an informational timetable that will result in full awareness too early in life. If eight-year-old children are given an understanding of mature sexual behavior, it is less likely that they will wait ten or twelve years to apply this knowledge within the confines of marriage.

Generally speaking, children should be given the information they need at a particular age. Six-year-olds, for example, don't need to understand the pleasures of adult sexuality. They are not ready to deal with that concept at their developmental stage. They should be told where babies come from and how they are born. Sometime between six and nine, depending on the maturity and interest of an individual (and what is being heard in the neighborhood), he or she ought to understand how conception occurs. The rest of the story can be told later in elementary school.

Admittedly, this ideal timetable can be turned upside down by exposure to precocious friends, racy videos, or unwise adults. When that occurs, you have to cope with the fallout as best as possible. It is regrettable that we expose our vulnerable children to far too much of the wrong kind of sexuality.

Q206 How do I get started? Is there a natural way to get into the topic?

Fortunately, most children will ask for information when they need it. You should be ready to grab those opportunities at the drop of a hat. Sometimes very little warning is given. Our daughter asked for very specific details when she was only seven years old, catching her mother off guard. My wife stalled for an hour, during which she alerted me. Then the three of us sat on the bed drinking hot chocolate and talking about matters we hadn't expected to discuss for several years. You never know when such a moment will arrive, and you need to think it through in advance.

Although those spontaneous conversations are easiest, some children never ask the right questions. Some boys and girls have "inquiring minds that want to know," while others never give the subject of sex a second thought. If your child is one of those who seems disinterested, you're still on the hook. The task must get done. Someone else will do the job if you won't—someone who may not share your values.

Q 207 In one of your early books you talked about something you gave to your daughter that symbolized the importance of moral purity. Describe it again.

Yes, many years ago Shirley and I gave our daughter a small gold key. It was attached to a chain worn around her neck and represented the key to her heart. She made a vow to give that key to one man only—the one who would share her love through the remainder of her life. You might consider a similar gift for your daughter or a special ring for your son. These go with them throughout adolescence and provide a tangible reminder of the lasting, precious gift of abstinence until marriage and then fidelity to the mate for life. I still recommend this approach enthusiastically.

Here is a letter I received from a fifteen-year-old girl describing how much this experience meant to her:

> I am writing to share with you a most blessed experience. . . . On my fifteenth birthday my parents gave me a surprise birthday party in

which my ring would be presented. When my father put the ring on my finger I stood there looking at unsaved relatives and my peers. Suddenly I realized this was the opportunity I had been waiting for. Saying a quick prayer I said the following: "It is a great honor for me to wear this ring, because it symbolizes the commitment I am making to God, myself, my family, my friends, my future husband, and my future children to remain physically and sexually abstinent from this day until the day I enter a biblical marriage relationship. I know it won't be easy, but as long as I keep my eyes on Jesus, things will be easier. Temptations may and will come, but my heart's prayer is that God will give me the courage and strength to stand my ground. And finally, may I always have the desire to serve, honor, and please the Lord today and forevermore." . . . The people's response was positively incredible . . . God had used my sincere statement to move even the most hardened of hearts. . . . The purpose of my letter is to encourage you when you are in the valley or maybe even feel like quitting (like we all do sometimes); remember me and this letter; remember that because you have been faithful to the call, God has blessed you by helping you reach millions like me around the world.

Q208 You've indicated when sex education should begin. When should it end?

You should plan to end your formal instructional program about the time your son or daughter enters puberty (the time of rapid sexual development in early adolescence). Puberty usually begins between ten and thirteen for girls and between eleven and four-teen for boys. Once they enter this developmental period, they are typically embarrassed by discussions of sex with their parents. Adolescents usually resent adult intrusion during this time—unless they raise the topic themselves. In other words, this is an area where teens should invite parents into their lives.

I feel that we should respect their wishes. We are given ten or twelve years to provide the proper understanding of human sexuality. After that foundation has been laid, we serve primarily as resources to whom our children can turn when the need exists. That is not to say parents should abdicate their responsibility to provide guidance about issues related to sexuality, dating, marriage, etc., as opportunities present themselves. Again, sensitivity to the feelings of the teen is paramount. If he or she wishes to talk, by all means, welcome the conversation. In other cases, parental guidance may be most effective if offered indirectly. Trusted youth workers at church or in a club program such as Campus Life or Young Life can often break the ice when parents can't.

I'd also suggest that you arrange a subscription for your kids to magazines that provide solid Christian advice—from the perspective of a friend rather than an authority figure. Examples include *Brio* (for girls ages twelve and up) and *Breakaway* (for boys ages twelve and up), both of which are available through Focus on the Family.

Q209 If you were a parent and knew that your son or daughter was thinking about engaging in sexual intercourse, wouldn't you talk to them about condom usage? If our kids are going to have sex anyway, shouldn't we make sure they are properly protected?

I would not, because that approach has an unintended

consequence. By recommending condom usage to teenagers, we inevitably convey five dangerous ideas: (1) that "safe sex" is achievable; (2) that everybody is doing it; (3) that responsible adults *expect* them to do it; (4) that it's a good thing; and (5) that their peers *know* they *know* these things, breeding promiscuity. Those are very destructive messages to give our kids.

Furthermore, Planned Parenthood's own data shows that the number-one reason teenagers engage in intercourse is peer pressure![62] Therefore, anything we do to imply that "everybody is doing it" results in more—not fewer—teens who give the game a try. What I'm saying is that our condom-distribution programs do not reduce the number of kids exposed to the disease—they radically increase it!

Since the Planned Parenthood–type programs began in 1970, unwed pregnancies have increased 87 percent among fifteen- to nineteen-year-olds.[63] Likewise, abortions among teens rose 67 percent;[64] unwed births went up 83.8 percent.[65] And venereal disease has infected a generation of young people. The statistics speak for themselves.

And consider this: Research indicates that where disease prevention is concerned, the failure rate of condoms is incredibly high, perhaps 50 percent or greater.[66] Condoms also fail to protect against some STDs that are transmitted from areas not covered (the base of the male genitalia, for example). After twenty-five years of teaching safe-sex ideology, and more than 2 billion federal dollars invested in selling this notion, we have a medical disaster on our hands. More than 500,000 cases of herpes occur annually,[67] and the number of reported cases of chlamydia has risen 281 percent since 1987. Forty-six percent of chlamydia cases occur in teenage girls ages fifteen to nineteen.[68] In addition, there are now over 24 million cases of HPV (human papilloma virus) in the United States, with a higher prevalence among teens.[69]

Having acknowledged these problems, why in the world would I recommend this so-called solution to my son or daughter? Look at it this way. Suppose my kids were sky divers whose parachutes had been demonstrated to fail 50 percent of the time. Would I suggest that they simply buckle the chutes tighter? Certainly not. I would say, "Please don't jump. Your life is at stake!" How could I, as a loving father, do less?

I should add that, despite the popular myth to the contrary, teens can understand, accept, and implement the abstinence message. It's not true that young people are sexual robots, hopelessly incapable of controlling their own behavior. As a matter of fact, almost 50 percent of all high school students are virgins today,[70] even though hardly anybody has told them it is a good thing. These kids desperately need to be affirmed in their decision and held up as positive examples for others. None of this will be accomplished by pushing condoms.

But there is another reason for talking to teens about abstinence rather than "safe sex." It is even more important than the life-and-death issue cited above. I'm referring, of course, to the Creator's design, God's expressed will for human sexuality. "Protected promiscuity" has no part in that plan. Sex within the context for which it was intended—lifelong, monogamous marriage—is always safe. This is the message our kids need to hear from the earliest days of childhood! Anything less is worse than third-rate!

Q210 Given the problems with condom usage and the epidemic of STDs that infect the human family, why is there so much resistance to teaching abstinence-based educational programs in our schools?

What do we have to lose by telling kids what's at stake for them?

If you ask the sex-education gurus that question, most will tell you that teenagers are going to be sexually active no matter what we do. Therefore, they say, we should teach them to do it in a safer way. I don't believe that answer is entirely honest, however. It won't explain the blatant and aggressive promotion of promiscuity among the young, or why they would recommend reliance on fragile rubber sheaths to protect against potentially deadly diseases. There is something else behind their motivation. These people become incensed when the word *abstinence* is even mentioned.

I began to understand their passion during the Reagan era when I was appointed by the Health and Human Services secretary, Otis Bowen, to a panel on the prevention of teen pregnancy. I accepted that responsibility because I thought our purpose was to prevent teen pregnancies. But during our first meeting in Washington, D.C., I learned that fifteen of the eighteen panel members had another agenda. They wanted to spend additional millions of federal dollars to put condoms in every pocket and purse of the nation's teenagers. I can't describe how emotional they were about this objective. It didn't take long to figure out their underlying point of view.

Millions of jobs and entire industries are supported by teen sexual irresponsibility. The abortion business alone generates up to one billion dollars annually. Why would physicians and nurses working in abortion clinics, and medical suppliers, and school-based sex-education counselors prefer that adolescents abstain until marriage? And what about the organizations that owe their existence to teen sexual irresponsibility, such as Planned Parenthood and

SIECUS? They receive upwards of $600 million per year, domestically and internationally, from the U.S. federal government.[71] Added to that incentive are uncounted millions in corporate grants and individual contributions that flow to the problem. Imagine how many jobs would be lost if kids quit playing musical beds with one another! This is, I'm convinced, why so many professionals who advise young people about sex become angry when abstinence rears its ugly head. If that idea ever caught on, who would need the services of Planned Parenthood and their ilk?

Q211 Someone told me the other day that there are more than twenty sexually transmitted diseases at an epidemic level, and many of them are incurable. I've been through five years of sex-education classes, and no one has ever told me this. I think that is scandalous!

It *is* scandalous that these facts are withheld from today's young people. That's what motivated our organization, Focus on the Family, to create a full-page advertisement that attempted to get the word out. It presented the dangers of viral and bacterial infections and was documented throughout with respected medical references. That ad, entitled "In Defense of a Little Virginity," has now run in 1,300 newspapers, including *USA Today*. We've received thousands of letters of appreciation from students and from parents thanking us for sharing the truth with them for the first time.

Meanwhile, 56 million Americans—one out of every five—are suffering from incurable viruses.[72] Even more have bacterial and fungal infections that cause infertility and other physical problems. And of course, 1.5 million babies are aborted each year.[73] Clearly, it's time we told young people the truth.

That need for information is especially evident to those of us at Focus on the Family. We receive heartbreaking mail from very young people who have been lured into destructive behavior. Some of them are still children, like the girl who sent us this letter. She wrote:

> This has been on my mind for a long time. I've heard that if you have sex during your period you won't get pregnet [sic]. If not, I have a problem. I'm only 11.
>
>   [signed] Really Worried

What a disgrace that we have permitted innocent kids like this one to be dragged into destructive behavior before they've even gotten started in life. We have to begin giving them the whole truth about premarital sex and the difficulties it can cause.

Q212 When I've tried to argue the "abstinence" position with the advocates of safe sex, they have said, "You just don't live in the real world. Kids are going to do what comes naturally. It is ridiculous to ask them to abstain, so we might as well show them how to do it right." Is it really a waste of time to try to teach principles of morality to this generation?

I've heard the same rationale from the advocates of safe sex. They don't want kids to abstain, so they tell us it is foolish to promote that behavior. Nothing could be further from the truth.

I remember a reporter from the *New York Times* coming to Focus on the Family several years ago to get a quote from us. She was writing a story about today's sexually active kids, making the point that morality is dead and gone. We disagreed and invited her to come to Lexington, Kentucky, to attend a youth rally we were cosponsoring with local ministries. It offered teenagers straight talk about sex, drugs, their choice of friends, and other concerns.

The reporter accepted our invitation and was blown away by what she saw. The stadium was designed to hold eighteen thousand people, but twenty-six thousand kids showed up for the rally. Several thousand who couldn't get inside stood listening to a speaker system outside the arena as they were urged to live a responsible life and stay out of bed until they were married.

The reporter went back to New York and—you guessed it—wrote that morality is dead among the young. It isn't true. But it will be soon if we continue to promote immoral principles to young people.

Q213 The spread of sexually transmitted diseases is very unsettling to me. I have three teenage daughters and am afraid they don't understand how easily these organisms are spread and what they can do to the body. This is a very scary subject.

Like you, I wonder what it will take to awaken our young people. I interviewed Dr. C. Everett Koop in the mid-eighties while he was surgeon general of the United States. He said, "The AIDS epidemic will soon change the behavior of everyone. When infected young people begin dying around us, others will be afraid to even kiss anyone."[74]

The epidemic has spread since those days, just as Dr. Koop predicted. But he was wrong about the fear of sex. People continue jumping in and out of bed with each other as though they were immune to all the viruses and bacteria that stalk the human family.

Q214 Why are young people so oblivious to the danger? Why do they put themselves at such risk?

For one thing, their idols in movies, television, and rock music tell them absolutely everyone is having sex. Unfortunately, these voices from the culture never reveal what it's like to have herpes or HPV or the other incurable viruses that are at epidemic proportions today. Also the safe-sex gurus have convinced kids that these terrible diseases can be prevented with the simple use of condoms. So why not?

Thank goodness for a few physicians who are sounding the alarm and trying to get the uncensored facts to our kids. They don't get much press, but someday they will be vindicated. One of the most vocal of these concerned doctors is my good friend Dr. Joe McIlhaney, an obstetrician-gynecologist who heads an organization called Medical Institute for Sexual Health (MISH). A frequent *Focus on the Family* broadcast guest, he talked about the fallacy of "safe sex" on a recent program:

> What you hear mostly from the press is what science is going to do for people who have a sexually transmitted disease (STD), how science is going to come up with a vaccine or treatment for AIDS, how antibiotics will kill gonorrhea and chlamydia. What is not discussed is how these STDs leave women's pelvic structures scarred for life, and they end up infertile or having to do expensive procedures to get pregnant later on.
>
> I could name patient after patient in the twenty-two years I've been in practice where I've had to perform a hysterectomy before a woman had the children she wanted because of

pelvic inflammatory disease, which is caused by chlamydia and gonorrhea. The public announcements about "safe sex" infuriate me, because what they're saying is that you can safely have sex outside of marriage if you use condoms, and you don't have to worry about getting an STD. The message is a lie. The failure rate of condoms is extremely high, and that's why married people don't use them.

He went on to say, "I see the examples of these failures in my office every day. These include victims of chlamydia, probably the most prevalent STD, and of human papilloma virus (HPV), which can cause a lasting irritation of the female organs, as well as cancer of the vulva, vagina, and cervix. It is one of the most difficult diseases to treat and kills more than 4,800 women a year. I also see victims of herpes, which some studies indicate is present in up to 30–40 percent of single, sexually active people, as well as victims of syphilis, which is at a forty-year high."[75]

Rather than expecting science to solve our problems, Dr. McIlhaney said a better solution involves a return to spiritual and moral guidelines that have been with us for thousands of years. Dr. McIlhaney concluded, "The people who made my automobile know how it works best and what I need to do to avoid car problems. They tell me that in my Ford manual. Likewise, God knows how we work best and gave us an 'owner's manual' for the human race: the Bible. In it, He tells us not to have sex until we are married; not to have sex with anybody other than the one man/one woman to whom we are married; and to stay married the rest of our lives. That's the one and only prescription for safe sex."[76]

Note: The Medical Institute for Sexual Health has a
variety of materials for physicians and others who
have opportunities to teach students and testify before legislators and school-board members. They include photographic slides, a curricular guide, and
other helpful aids. They can be contacted at
www.medinstitute.org or at P.O. Box 162306,
Austin, TX 78716-2306 or by calling 1-800-892-
9484.

Q215 We've all become aware of the AIDS epidemic, but I recently heard that a college
friend of mine who used to sleep around has been diagnosed with something called HPV. I'm not exactly sure
what it is, but it sounded serious. Are you familiar with
this disease?

Yes, I am—and I'm afraid it's very serious. You've
heard that HIV is deadly because it leads to AIDS, but
the human papillomavirus (HPV) causes far more
deaths among women in the U.S. each year.[77] Thousands of American women die from it every year. It
causes genital warts and in some patients leads to
cancer of the cervix. In fact, it is estimated that 90
percent of cervical-cancer cases are caused by HPV,
and the virus itself cannot be eradicated once it is in
the system.[78]

A medical investigation of this virus was conducted at the University of California at Berkeley
in 1992. Averaging twenty-one years of age, all the
young women coming to the campus health center
for routine gynecological examinations for one year
were tested for HPV. Would you believe that 47
percent of these female students were found to carry
this virus?[79] Some will die of cervical and uterine
cancer.

The most disturbing news is that HPV can be

transmitted while the male is wearing a condom. The virus lurks around the portion of the genitalia that is not covered by the condom. This is one of the reasons some of us object strenuously to the campaign to get young people to have "protected sex." It gives them a false sense of security. There is no such thing as safe sex when it occurs promiscuously and outside the marital relationship. Abstinence before marriage is the only safe way to go.

Q216 This information about HPV is alarming. If there are really thousands of women dying every year from cancer of the cervix caused by this virus, it seems unconscionable that it isn't being talked about in schools and on today's TV talk shows.

I heartily agree, and I can assure you that the victims of HPV feel the same. Let me share a letter that I received from a woman who has this virus but doesn't yet have cervical cancer. She makes the case very dramatically and asked me to share her story with as many people as possible.

Dear Dr. Dobson,

In one of your radio broadcasts you covered the fact that it [HPV] can cause cervical dysplasia leading to cancer of the cervix. Certainly, that's tragic. But it has many other effects that I have not read anything about.

Let me tell you about this disease and what it's done to my life. I'm a twenty-five-year-old college graduate. I've remained single and childless. That singleness is imposed on me by my physical condition. The last four years of my life have been lived with chronic pain, two outpatient surgeries, multiple office biopsies, thousands of dollars in prescriptions, and no hope. The effect of this problem is one of severe relentless infection. This condition can be so severe that the pain is almost unbearable. A sexual relationship, or the possibility of marriage, is out of the question.

The isolation is like a knife that cuts my heart out daily. Depression, rage, and hopelessness, and a drastically affected social and religious life are the result. Physicians say they are seeing this condition more commonly. Females are being sentenced to a life of watching others live, marry, and have babies. Please take what I have written to the airwaves.

Thank you for listening, Dr. Dobson. This obstacle has been the one that I cannot gain victory over.

12

SPIRITUAL LIFE
OF THE FAMILY

Q.217 Sometimes I wish there were a place where I could go to protect my kids from all the evil in the world—a place where I could raise them like I was brought up. But there is no such place to hide, is there?

No, the negative influences on young people cross all cultural and international boundaries today. As I have traveled in other countries, I've been surprised to see how much teenagers are alike wherever they live. They write the same kind of graffiti on walls and billboards; their values, their attitudes, and even their clothing are similar. Why? Because they watch the same movies, listen to the same music, admire the same idols, play the same video and cyber games, and see the same television shows. For example, MTV is the most-watched cable network in the world. Unbelievably, some little Masai tribal children in Kenya sit in their grass huts and watch the wretched Beavis and Butthead stammer through obscenities and utter foolishness.[80]

Today's youth culture is on display in all the major cities of the world, including London, where my family visited a few years ago. That wonderful and historic city serves as a living museum where more than a thousand years of cultural evolution are on display. But it is also the home of some of the most pitiful young people I've ever seen. Rockers and punkers and druggies are on the streets in search of something. Who knows what? Girls with green-and-orange hair walk by with strange-looking boy-friends. (At least I think they are boys.) They wear blue Mohawk haircuts that stick four inches in the air. While gazing at that sight, a *clang! clang! clang!* sound is heard from the rear. The Hare Krishnas are coming. They dance by with their shaved heads and monklike robes. Gays parade arm in arm, and prosti-tutes advertise their services. On a recent visit, I stood there in downtown London thinking, *What in heaven's name have we allowed to happen to the next gen-eration?*

The same phenomenon is occurring in the United States, Canada, and other parts of the world, of course. It is shocking to see what has happened to a value system that served us so well. When my daugh-ter was eighteen, I attended a program put on by the music department at her high school. Sitting in front of me was one of Danae's girlfriends. At intermission we chatted about her plans, and she told me she would soon enroll at one of the state universities in California. She had just returned from a visit to the school and mentioned that something had bothered her about the dormitory in which she would reside. She had learned that the men and women lived side by side and that they also shared the same bathrooms. What concerned this pretty young lady was that there was no curtain on the shower stall!

This is the world in which our children are grow-ing up. Obviously, conservative communities still exist, where traditional values are honored. Millions of kids want to do what is right. But dangerous en-ticements are there, too, and parents know it. So we live with the apprehension that the counterculture will consume our sons and daughters before they have even gotten started in life. That anxiety can take the pleasure out of raising children.

Q218 I have heard you say that the most important responsibility for Christian parents is to teach their children about Jesus Christ. We are new Christians and new parents. How do we go about introducing our little girl to what we believe?

The best approach is found in the instruction given to the children of Israel by Moses more than four thousand years ago. He wrote, "Impress them on your children. Talk about them when you sit at home and when you walk along the road, when you lie down and when you get up. Tie them as symbols on your hands and bind them on your foreheads. Write them on the doorframes of your houses and on your gates" (Deuteronomy 6:7-9).

This commandment provides the key to effective spiritual training at home. It isn't enough to pray with your children each night, although family devotions are important. We must live the principles of faith throughout the day. References to the Lord and our beliefs should permeate our conversation and our interactions with our kids. Our love for Jesus should be understood to be the first priority in our lives. We must miss no opportunities to teach the components of our theology and the passion that is behind it. As you've said, I believe this teaching task is the most important assignment God has given to us as parents.

The reason this is such a critical responsibility is that the world will be giving your children very different messages in the days ahead. It will take them to hell if not counterbalanced by a firm spiritual foundation at home. This is one task about which we can't afford to be lackadaisical.

Q219 It is difficult for us to have meaningful devotions as a family because our young children seem so bored and uninvolved. They yawn and squirm and giggle while we are reading from the Bible. On the other hand, we feel it is important to teach them to pray and study God's Word. Can you help us deal with this dilemma?

Brevity is the watchword. Children can't be expected to comprehend and appreciate lengthy adult spiritual activities. Four or five minutes devoted to one or two Bible verses, followed by a short prayer, usually represent the limits of attention during the preschool years. To force young children to comprehend eternal truths in an eternal devotional can be eternally dangerous.

Q220 The concept of who God is has always been difficult for me to comprehend. I'm still not sure I understand Him as I should. How can my children possibly grasp who He really is?

Remember that Jesus said, "Anyone who has seen me has seen the Father" (John 14:9). The best way to introduce our children to the character of God, therefore, is by introducing them to the person of Jesus. Even preschool kids can understand the imagery of Him given in the Gospels. Not only are children capable of comprehending things of the spirit, but Jesus said, "Anyone who will not receive the kingdom of God *like a little child* will never enter it" (Luke 18:17, italics added). They are inherently better at understanding it than are their elders.

The second way children learn about God is from what they see in Mom and Dad. It is a well-known fact that kids identify their parents—and especially their fathers—with God. That makes us grown-ups uncomfortable, of course, because we are aware of our imperfections and shortcomings. Nevertheless, we have been given the awesome responsibility of representing God to our vulnerable little children. The mistakes we make are often translated into spiritual problems for the next generation. For example, it is tough for the sons and daughters of oppressive or abusive parents to perceive God as being loving and compassionate. Likewise, permissive parents make it hard for children to understand the justice of God.

One of our most difficult tasks as mothers and fathers is to represent these two aspects of God's nature, His love and His justice, to our kids. To show our little ones love without authority is as serious a distortion of God's nature as to reveal an ironfisted authority without love.

If you put your mind and heart to it, I believe you can give your children the understanding they need. You might even get a better grasp of God's nature in the process of conveying it to your kids.

Q221 How can a parent ever live up to the perception by a young child that we are Godlike? None of us can match that expectation!

I know. It's scary, isn't it? I remember being shocked when I realized that my two-year-old son, Ryan, identified me with God. He had watched his mother and me pray before we ate each meal, but he had never been asked to say grace. One day when I was out of town on a business trip, Shirley spontaneously turned to our toddler and asked if he would like to pray before he and his sister ate. The invitation startled him, but he folded his little hands, bowed his head, and said reverently, "I love you, Daddy. Amen."

When I returned home and Shirley told me what had happened, the story unsettled me. I hadn't realized the degree to which Ryan linked me with his "heavenly Father." I wasn't even sure I wanted to stand in those shoes. The job was too big, and I didn't want the responsibility. But I had no choice, nor do you. God has given us the assignment of representing Him during the formative years of parenting. That's why it is so critically important for us to acquaint our kids with God's two predominant natures . . . His unfathomable love and His justice. If we love our children but permit them to treat us disrespectfully and with disdain, we have distorted their understanding of the Father. On the other hand, if we are rigid disciplinarians who show no love, we have tipped the scales in the other direction. What we teach our children about the Lord is a function, to a significant degree, of how we model love and discipline in our relationship with them.

Q222 What is the most important period in the spiritual training of young children?

Each is important, but I believe the fifth year is often the most critical. Up to that time, a child believes in God because his or her parents say it is the right thing to do. She accepts the reality of Christ like she would a story about Santa Claus or the Easter Bunny—uncritically and innocently. At about five or six years of age, however, she begins to think more about what she is told. Some kids come to a fork in the road about that time. Either they begin to internalize what they've been taught and make it their own or else the Bible stories become like the fables that don't exist in the real world. It is a time for careful instruction at home and in church.

I certainly don't mean to imply that parents

should wait until the child is five or six to begin spiritual training. Nor are subsequent years insignificant. But I am convinced that our most diligent efforts within the family and our best teachers in Sunday school ought to be assigned to the child of five or six years. There will be crucial crossroads after that, but this one is vital.

Q223 As a child, Christmas was always my favorite time of the year. I really enjoyed hearing stories about the birth of the Savior. I also have special family memories associated with the anticipation of Santa's arrival on Christmas Eve. I would very much like to offer these same happy experiences to my young children, but it seems many of my Christian friends think it's wrong or harmful to include any mythical characters as part of the Christmas celebration. How do you feel about this?

My sentiments mirror yours exactly. Christmas memories are among the most cherished of all my childhood reminiscences. The fantasy of Santa Claus coming on Christmas Eve was an important part of the fun. I'm reluctant to deprive today's kids of an experience that was so exciting for me.

On the other hand, I understand the concerns expressed by many Christian parents about the pagan celebration of Christmas. They don't want to link Santa Claus, a mythical figure, with the reality of the baby Jesus who was born in Bethlehem of Judea. They have good reason to fear that they might weaken the validity of the Christmas story by mixing it with fantasy.

So this is the dilemma—Santa is fun, but Santa could be confusing. What are Christian parents to do? This is a judgment call to be made by a given family. Shirley and I chose to play the "Santa game" with our kids, and we had no difficulties teaching them who Jesus was and is. Other families regret mixing the two images.

What is best? I don't know. But if I had to do it over, I would still let my children thrill to the excitement of Santa's arrival down the chimney on Christmas Eve.

Q224 What about Halloween?

Halloween is a rather different story. Whereas it can be argued that Christmas is a Christian holiday with Christian origins that has suffered the effects of growing secularism, Halloween can be traced to distinctly pagan sources. It is reasonable, then, that many believers would find some aspects of its celebration disturbing. I agree with them in that regard. The traditional emphasis upon the occult, witches, devils, death, and evil sends messages to our kids that godly parents can only regard with alarm. There is clearly no place in the Christian community for this "darker side" of Halloween.

Even here, however, there is a place for some harmless fun. Kids love to dress up and pretend. If the Halloween experience is focused on fantasy rather than the occult, I see no harm in it. Make costumes for your children that represent fun characters, such as Mickey Mouse or an elderly grandmother, and then let them go door-to-door asking for treats. This side of Halloween can be thoroughly enjoyable for the little ones.

Let me add, again, that I've given you my personal opinion. I realize that the topic is controversial among committed Christians, and I'm sensitive to the reasons for their misgivings. My final word to parents on the subject would be "Stay true to your own convictions."

Q.225 Should a child be allowed to "decide for himself" on matters related to his concept of God? Aren't we forcing our religion down his throat when we tell him what he must believe?

Let me answer the question with an illustration from nature. A little gosling (baby goose) has a peculiar characteristic that is relevant at this point. Shortly after he hatches from his shell he will become attached, or "imprinted," to the first thing that he sees moving near him. From that time forward, the gosling follows that particular object when it moves in his vicinity. Ordinarily, it becomes imprinted to the mother goose who was on hand to hatch the new generation.

If she is removed, however, the gosling will settle for any mobile substitute, whether alive or not. In fact, a gosling will become most easily attached to a blue football bladder dragged by on a string. A week later, it'll fall in line behind the bladder as it scoots by.

Time is the critical factor in this process. The gosling is vulnerable to imprinting for only a few seconds after it hatches from the shell; if that opportunity is lost, it cannot be regained later. In other words, there is a brief "critical period" in the life of a gosling when this instinctual learning is possible.

Coming back to your question now, there is also a critical period when certain kinds of instruction are easier in the life of children. Although humans have no instincts (only drives, reflexes, urges, etc.), there is a brief period during childhood when youngsters are vulnerable to religious training. Their concepts of right and wrong are formulated during this time, and their view of God begins to solidify. As in the case of the gosling, the opportunity of that period must be seized when it is available. Leaders of the Catholic church have been widely quoted as saying,

"Give us a child until he is seven years old, and we'll have him for life"; they are usually correct, because permanent attitudes can be instilled during these seven vulnerable years.

Unfortunately, however, the opposite is also true. The absence or misapplication of instruction through the prime-time period may place a severe limitation on the depth of a child's later devotion to God. When parents withhold indoctrination from their small children, allowing them to "decide for themselves," the adults are almost guaranteeing that their youngsters will "decide" in the negative. If parents want their children to have a meaningful faith, they must give up any misguided attempts at objectivity. Children listen closely to discover just how much their parents believe what they preach. Any indecision or ethical confusion from the parent is likely to be magnified in the child.

After the middle-adolescent age (ending at about fifteen years), children sometimes resent heavy-handedness about anything—including what to believe. But if the early exposure has been properly conducted, they should have an anchor to steady them. Their early indoctrination, then, is the key to the spiritual attitudes they carry into adulthood.

Q226 You have said that the children of godly parents sometimes go into severe rebellion and never return to the faith they were taught. I have seen that happen to some wonderful families that loved the Lord and were committed to the church. Still, it appears contradictory to Scripture. How do you interpret Proverbs 22:6 (KJV), which says, "Train up a child in the way he should go: and when he is old, he will not depart from it"? Doesn't that verse mean, as it implies, that the children of wise and dedicated Christian parents will never be lost?

Doesn't it promise that all wayward offspring will return, sooner or later, to the fold?

I wish Solomon's message to us could be interpreted that definitively. I know that the common understanding of the passage is to accept it as a divine guarantee, but it was not expressed in that context. Psychiatrist John White, writing in his excellent book *Parents in Pain,* makes the case that the proverbs were never intended to be absolute promises from God. Instead, they are *probabilities* of things that are likely to occur.[81] Solomon, who wrote Proverbs, was the wisest man on the earth at that time. His purpose was to convey his divinely inspired observations on the way human nature and God's universe work. A given set of circumstances can be expected to produce a set of specific consequences. Unfortunately, several of these observations, including Proverbs 22:6, have been lifted out of that context and made to stand alone as promises from God. If we insist on that interpretation, then we must explain why so many other proverbs do not inevitably prove accurate. For example:

"Lazy hands make a man poor, but diligent hands bring wealth" (10:4). (Have you ever met a diligent—but poor—Christian? I have.)

"The blessing of the Lord brings wealth, and he adds no trouble to it" (10:22).

"The fear of the Lord adds length to life, but the years of the wicked are cut short" (10:27). (I have watched some beautiful children die with a Christian testimony on their lips.)

"No harm befalls the righteous, but the wicked have their fill of trouble" (12:21).

"Plans fail for lack of counsel, but with many advisers they succeed" (15:22).

"Gray hair is a crown of splendor; it is attained by a righteous life" (16:31).

"The lot is cast into the lap, but its every decision is from the Lord" (16:33).

"A tyrannical ruler lacks judgment, but he who hates ill-gotten gain will enjoy a long life" (28:16).

We can all think of exceptions to the statements above. To repeat, the proverbs appear to represent likelihoods rather than absolutes with God's personal guarantee attached. This interpretation of the Scripture is somewhat controversial among laymen, but less so among biblical scholars. For example, *Bible Knowledge Commentary: Old Testament,* prepared by the faculty of the Dallas Theological Seminary, accepts the understanding I have suggested. This commentary is recognized for its intense commitment to the literal interpretation of God's Word, yet this is what the theologians wrote:

> Some parents, however, have sought to follow this directive but without this result. Their children have strayed from the godly training the parents gave them. This illustrates the nature of a "proverb." A proverb is a literary device whereby a general truth is brought to bear on a specific situation. Many of the proverbs are not absolute guarantees for they express truths that are necessarily conditioned by prevailing circumstances. For example, verses 3, 4, 9, 11, 16, 29 of Proverbs 22 do not express promises that are always binding. Though the proverbs are generally and usually true, occasional exceptions may be noted. This may be because of the self-will or deliberate disobedience of an individual who chooses to go his own way the way of folly instead of the way of wisdom. For that he is held responsible. It is generally true, however, that most children

who are brought up in Christian homes, under the influence of godly parents who teach and live God's standards, follow that training.[82]

Those who believe that Proverbs 22:6 offers a guarantee of salvation for the next generation have assumed, in essence, that a child can be programmed so thoroughly as to determine his course inevitably. If they bring him up "in the way he should go," the outcome is guaranteed. But think about that for a moment. Didn't the Creator handle Adam and Eve with infinite wisdom and love? He made no mistakes in "fathering" them. They were also harbored in a perfect environment with none of the pressures we face. They had no in-law problems, no monetary needs, no frustrating employers, no television, no pornography, no alcohol or drugs, no peer pressure, and no sorrow. They had no excuses! Nevertheless, they ignored the explicit warning from God and stumbled into sin. If it were ever possible to avoid the ensnarement of evil, it would have occurred in that sinless world. But it didn't. God in His love gave Adam and Eve a choice between good and evil, and they abused it. Will He now withhold that same freedom from your children? No. Ultimately, they will make their own choices. That time of decision is a breathtaking moment for parents, when everything they have taught appears to be on the line. But it must come for us all.

Q227 You obviously feel very strongly about this misinterpretation of Scripture. What are its implications?

I am most concerned for dedicated and sincere Christian parents whose grown sons and daughters have rebelled against God and their own families.

Many of these mothers and fathers did the best they could to raise their children properly, but they lost them anyway. That situation produces enormous guilt in itself, quite apart from scriptural understandings. They are led to believe that God has promised—absolutely guaranteed—the spiritual welfare of children whose parents do their jobs properly. What are they to conclude, then, in light of continued rebellion and sin in the next generation? The message is inescapable! It must be their fault. They have damned their own kids by failing to keep their half of the bargain. They have sent their beloved children to hell by their parenting failures. This thought is so terrible for a sensitive believer that it could actually undermine his or her sanity.

I simply do not believe God intended for the total responsibility for sin in the next generation to fall on the backs of vulnerable parents. When we look at the entire Bible, we find no support for that extreme position. Cain's murder of Abel was not blamed on his parents. Joseph was a godly man and his brothers were rascals, yet their father and mothers (Jacob, Leah, and Rachel) were not held accountable for the differences between them. The saintly Samuel raised rebellious children, yet he was not charged with their sin. And in the New Testament, the father of the Prodigal Son was never accused of raising his adventuresome son improperly. The boy was apparently old enough to make his own headstrong decision, and his father did not stand in his way. This good man never repented of any wrongdoing—nor did he need to.

It is not my intention to let parents off the hook when they have been slovenly or uncommitted during their child-rearing years. There is at least one biblical example of God's wrath falling on a father who failed to discipline and train his sons. That incident is described in 1 Samuel 2:22-36, where Eli, the priest, permitted his two sons to desecrate the temple. All three were sentenced to death by the Lord. Obviously, He takes our parenting tasks seriously and expects us to do likewise. But He does not intend for us to grovel in guilt for circumstances beyond our control!

Q228 Our three children were prayed for before they were conceived, and we have held their names before the Lord almost every day of their lives. Yet our middle daughter has chosen to reject our faith and do things she knows are wrong. She's living with a twice-divorced man and apparently has no intention of marrying him. She has had at least two abortions that we know about, and her language is disgraceful. My wife and I have prayed until we're exhausted, and yet she has shown no interest in returning to the church. At times, I become very angry at God for allowing this terrible thing to happen. I have wept until there are just no more tears. Tell me what intercessory prayer accomplishes, if anything. Is there a realm into which the Father will not intrude?

I can certainly understand your pain. Perhaps more people have become disillusioned with God over the waywardness of a son or daughter than any other issue. There is nothing more important to most Christian parents than the salvation of their children. Every other goal and achievement in life is anemic and insignificant compared to this transmission of faith to their offspring. That is the only way the two generations can be together throughout eternity, and those parents, like you, have been praying day and night for spiritual awakening. Unfortunately, if God does not answer those prayers quickly, there is a tendency to blame Him and to struggle with intense feelings of bitterness. The "betrayal barrier" claims another victim!

Often, this anger at the Lord results from a misunderstanding of what He will and won't do in the lives of those for whom we intercede. The key question is this: Will God require our offspring to serve Him if they choose a path of rebellion? It is a critically important question.

Let me explain again that God will not force Himself on anyone. If that was His inclination, no person would ever be lost. Second Peter 3:9 says, "He is patient with you, not wanting anyone to perish, but everyone to come to repentance." Nevertheless, to claim this great salvation, there is a condition. An individual must reach out and take it. He or she must repent of sins and believe on the name of the Lord Jesus Christ. Without that step of faith, the gift of forgiveness and eternal life is impossible.

Now let me deal with your question about what intercessory prayer accomplishes. Referring again to Dr. White's insightful book *Parents in Pain,* he wrote:

> Here lies a key to understanding how we may pray for our own children or for anyone else. We may ask with every confidence that God will open the eyes of the morally and spiritually blind. We may ask that the self-deceptions which sinners hide behind may be burned away in the fierce light of truth, that dark caverns may be rent asunder to let the sunlight pour in, that self-disguises may be stripped from a man or woman to reveal the horror of their nakedness in the holy light of God. We may ask above all that the glory of the face of Christ will shine through the spiritual blindness caused by the god of this world (2 Corinthians 4:4). All of this we can ask with every assurance that God will not only hear but will delight to answer.

But we may not ask him to force a man, woman, or child to love and trust him. To deliver them from overwhelming temptation: yes. To give them every opportunity: yes. To reveal his beauty, his tenderness, his forgiveness: yes. But to force a man against his will to bow the knee: not in this life. And to force a man to trust him: never.[83]

Said another way, the Lord will not save a person against his will, but He has a thousand ways of making him more willing. Our prayers unleash the power of God in the life of another individual. We have been granted the privilege of entering into intercessory prayer for our loved ones and of holding their names and faces before the Father. In return, He makes the all-important choices crystal clear to that individual and brings positive influences into his or her life to maximize the probability of doing what is right. Beyond that, He will not go.

Q229 That is deep theological water, isn't it? Who knows exactly how God responds to intercessory prayer and how He deals with a wayward heart?

You are certainly right about that, and I don't claim to have answered all of my own questions. How can I explain the prayers of my great-grandfather (on my mother's side), who died the year before I was born? This wonderful man of God, G. W. McCluskey, took it upon himself to spend the hour between 11:00 A.M. and 12:00 noon every day in prayer specifically for the spiritual welfare of his family. He was talking to the Lord not only about those loved ones who were then alive—McCluskey was also praying for generations not yet born. This good man was talking to the Lord about me, even before I was conceived.

Toward the end of his life, my great-grandfather made a startling announcement. He said God had promised him that every member of four generations—both those living and those not yet born—would be believers. Well, I represent the fourth generation down from his own, and it has worked out more interestingly than even he might have assumed.

The McCluskeys had two girls, one of whom was my grandmother and the other, my great-aunt. Both grew up and married ministers in the denomination of their father and mother. Between these women, five girls and one boy were born. One of them was my mother. All five of the girls married ministers in the denomination of their grandfather, and the boy became one. That brought it down to my generation. My cousin H. B. London and I were the first to go through college, and we were roommates. In the beginning of our sophomore year, he announced that God was calling him to preach. And I can assure you, I began to get very nervous about the family tradition!

I never felt God was asking me to be a minister, so I went to graduate school and became a psychologist. And yet, I have spent my professional life speaking, teaching, and writing about the importance of my faith in Jesus Christ. At times as I sit on a platform waiting to address a church filled with Christians, I wonder if my great-grandfather isn't smiling at me from somewhere. His prayers have reached across four generations of time to influence what I am doing with my life day by day.

What does that say about free moral agency and the right to choose? I don't have a clue. I only know that God honors the prayers of His righteous followers, and we should stay on our faces before Him until each child has been granted every opportunity to repent. We must remember, however, that God will not ride roughshod over the will of any individual. He deals respectfully with each person and seeks to attract him or her to Himself. It is wrong, therefore, to blame God if that process takes years to accomplish—or even if it never comes to pass. That is the price of freedom.

Q230 Your answer implies that we should continue to pray for our daughter year after year until she comes back to her faith. Does that mean that God will not be offended by our asking Him repeatedly for the same request? Is that what He wants of us on her behalf?

Yes. If what you are requesting is undeniably in the will of God, such as praying for the salvation of your daughter, I think you should keep the matter before Him until you receive the answer. There is a continuing spiritual battle under way for her soul, and your prayers are vital in winning that struggle. Paul admonished us to "pray without ceasing" (1 Thessalonians 5:17, NKJV). Isn't that what Jesus was teaching in the parable of the unjust judge? Let's read it in the book of Luke:

> Then Jesus told his disciples a parable to show them that they should always pray and not give up. He said: "In a certain town there was a judge who neither feared God nor cared about men. And there was a widow in that town who kept coming to him with the plea, 'Grant me justice against my adversary.'
>
> "For some time he refused. But finally he said to himself, 'Even though I don't fear God or care about men, yet because this widow keeps bothering me, I will see that she gets justice, so that she won't eventually wear me out with her coming!' "

And the Lord said, "Listen to what the unjust judge says. And will not God bring about
justice for his chosen ones, who cry out to him
day and night? Will he keep putting them off? I
tell you, he will see that they get justice, and
quickly. However, when the Son of Man
comes, will he find faith on the earth?" (Luke
18:1-8)

I love that Scripture because it tells us that God is
not irritated by our persistence in prayer. He urges
us not to give up but to bombard heaven with the desires of our hearts. That is encouragement enough to
keep me praying for a lifetime.

Winston Churchill said during World War II,
"Never give up. Never, never, never give up!"[84] That
advice applies not only to nations under siege but
also to believers seeking a touch from the Almighty.
I'll say it again: Moms and dads, your highest priority
is to lead your children into the fold. Don't stop
praying until that objective is fulfilled.

Q231 My wife and I have been praying for the salvation of our children for more than twenty-five years, and there is no sign that God has even heard those prayers. I know He loves our family, but I'm quite discouraged. Can you tell us anything that will jump-start our faith again?

I *do* have an encouraging word for you and others
who have asked the Lord for a miracle that hasn't yet
come. It is found in one of my favorite Scriptures located in the book of Genesis. You'll remember that
when Abraham was seventy-five years of age he began receiving promises from God that he would become the father of a great nation and that in him, all
the nations of the world would be blessed. That was

great news to an aging man and his barren wife, Sarah, who longed to be a mother.

Yet these exciting promises were followed by Sarah's continued infertility and many years of silence from God. What she and Abraham faced at this point was a classic case of "God contradicting God." The Lord hadn't honored His word or explained His delay. The facts didn't add up. The pieces didn't fit. Sarah had gone through menopause, effectively ending her hope of motherhood. By then, she and her husband were old, and we can assume that their sexual passion had diminished. There was no realistic probability that they were to be given an heir.

Abraham's response at that discouraging moment was described nearly two thousand years later in the writings of the apostle Paul. These are the inspirational words that he wrote:

> Without weakening in his faith, [Abraham] faced the fact that his body was as good as dead—since he was about a hundred years old—and that Sarah's womb was also dead. Yet he did not waver through unbelief regarding the promise of God, but was strengthened in his faith and gave glory to God, being fully persuaded that God had power to do what he had promised. This is why "it was credited to him as righteousness." (Romans 4:19-22)

In other words, Abraham believed God even when He made no sense. The facts clearly said, "It is impossible for this thing to happen." The Lord had made "empty promises" for nearly twenty-five years, and still there was no sign of their fulfillment. Unanswered questions and troubling contradictions swirled through the air. Nevertheless, Abraham "did not waver through unbelief." Why? Because he was convinced that God could transcend reason and factual evidence. And this is why he is called the "father of our faith."

Isn't that a wonderful example of faith under fire? It should give us courage to retain our spiritual confidence even when the pieces don't fit. Remember that with God, even when nothing is happening, something is happening. And if we don't waver, someday we'll understand, and "it will be credited to [us] as righteousness" for our faithfulness.

Stay on your knees. And hang on to your faith like a life preserver! The Lord is at work in the lives of your children, even though you see no evidence of it at the moment.

Q.232 My wife and I are new Christians, and we now realize that we raised our kids by the wrong principles. They're grown now, but we continue to worry about the past, and we feel great regret for our failures as parents. Is there anything we can do at this late date?

Let me deal first with the awful guilt you are obviously carrying. There's hardly a parent alive who does not have some regrets and painful memories of their failures as a mother or a father. Children are infinitely complex, and we can no more be perfect parents than we can be perfect human beings. The pressures of living are often enormous. We get tired and irritated; we are influenced by our physical bodies and our emotions, which sometimes prevent us from saying the right things and being the models we should be. We don't always handle our children as unemotionally as we wish we had, and it's very common to look back a year or two later and see how wrong we were in the way we approached a problem.

All of us experience these failures! No one does the job perfectly! That's why each of us should get alone with God and say:

> Lord, You know my inadequacies. You know my weaknesses, not only in parenting, but in every area of my life. I did the best I could, but it wasn't good enough. As You broke the fishes and the loaves to feed the five thousand, now take my meager effort and use it to bless my family. Make up for the things I did wrong. Satisfy the needs that I have not satisfied. Wrap Your great arms around my children, and draw them close to You. And be there when they stand at the great crossroads between right and wrong. All I can give is my best, and I've done that. Therefore, I submit to You my children and myself and the job I did as a parent. The outcome now belongs to You.

I know the Father will honor that prayer, even for parents whose job is finished. The Lord does not want you to suffer from guilt over events you can no longer influence. The past is the past. Let it die, never to be resurrected. Give the situation to God, and let Him have it. I think you'll be surprised to learn that you're no longer alone!

> Forgetting what is behind and straining toward what is ahead, I press on toward the goal to win the prize for which God has called me heavenward in Christ Jesus. (Philippians 3:13-14)

Q233 I am a grandmother who is blessed to have fourteen grandchildren. I often take care of them and love just having them over. However, I would

like to do more for them than just baby-sit. What can I do to really make an impact on their lives?

Above all else, I would hope you would help lead your grandchildren to Jesus Christ. You are in a wonderful position to do that. My grandmother had a profound impact on my spiritual development— even greater in my early years than my father, who was a minister. She talked about the Lord every day and made Him seem like a very dear friend who lived in our house. I will never forget the conversations we had about heaven and how wonderful it would be to live there throughout eternity. That little lady is on the other side today, waiting for the rest of her family to join her in that beautiful city.

You can have that kind of impact on your family too. Grandparents have been given powerful influence on their grandchildren if they will take the time to invest in their lives. There is so much to be accomplished while they are young. Another of the great contributions you can make is to preserve the heritage of your family by describing its history to children and acquainting them with their ancestors.

The lyrics of an African folk song say that when an old person dies, it's as if a library has burned down. It is true. There's a richness of history in your memory of earlier days that will be lost if it isn't passed on to the next generation.

To preserve this heritage, you should tell them true stories of days gone by. Share about your faith, about your early family experiences, about the obstacles you overcame or the failures you suffered. Those recollections bring a family together and give it a sense of identity.

I spoke earlier about my grandmother. There was another wonderful lady in our family, my great-grandmother (Nanny), who helped raise me from babyhood. She was already old when I was born and lived to be nearly one hundred years of age. I loved for her to tell me tales about her early life on the frontier. A favorite story involved mountain lions that would prowl around her log cabin at night and attack the livestock. She could hear them growling and moving past her window as she lay in bed. Nanny's father would try to shoot the cats or chase them away before they killed a pig or a goat. I sat fascinated as this sweet lady described a world that had long vanished by the time I came onto the scene. Her accounts of plains life helped open me to a love of history, a subject that fascinates me to this day.

The stories of your past, of your childhood, of your courtship with their grandfather, etc., can be treasures to your grandchildren. Unless you share those experiences with them, that part of their history will be gone forever. Take the time to make yesterday come alive for the kids in your family, and by all means, pass your faith along to the next generation.

13

SIBLING RIVALRY

Q234 Why do my kids have to fight all the time? I have three of them, and they drive me crazy. Why can't they be nice to each other?

Good question! All I can tell you is that sibling rivalry has been going on for a long time. It was responsible for the first murder on record (when Cain killed Abel) and has been represented in virtually every two-child family from that time to this. The underlying source of this conflict is old-fashioned jealousy and competition between children. Marguerite and Willard Beecher, writing in their book *Parents on the Run,* expressed the inevitability of this struggle as follows:

> It was once believed that if parents would explain to a child that he was having a little brother or sister, he would not resent it. He was told that his parents had enjoyed him so much that they wanted to increase their happiness. This was supposed to avoid jealous competition and rivalry. It did not work. Why should it? Needless to say, if a man tells his wife he has loved her so much that he now plans to bring another wife into the home to "increase his happiness," she would not be immune to

jealousy. On the contrary, the fight would just begin—in exactly the same fashion as it does with children.[85]

Q235 If jealousy between kids is so common, then how can parents minimize the natural antagonism children feel for their siblings?

It's helpful to avoid circumstances that compare them unfavorably with each other. They are extremely sensitive to the competitive edge of their relationship. The question is not "How am I doing?" it is "How am I doing compared with John or Steven or Marion?" The issue is not how fast I can run, but who crosses the finish line first. A boy does not care how tall he is; he is vitally interested in who is tallest. Each child systematically measures himself against his peers and is tremendously sensitive to failure within his own family. Accordingly, parents should guard against comparative statements that routinely favor one child over another.

Perhaps an illustration will help make the case. When I was about ten years old, I loved to play with a couple of dogs that belonged to two families in the neighborhood. One was a black Scottie who liked to chase and retrieve tennis balls. The other was a pug bulldog who had a notoriously bad attitude. One day as I was tossing the ball for the Scottie, it occurred to me that it might be interesting to throw it in the direction of the ol' grouch. It was not a smart move. The ball rolled under the bulldog, who grabbed the Scottie by the throat when he tried to retrieve it. It was an awful scene. Neighbors came running as the Scottie screamed in pain. It took ten minutes and a garden hose to pry the bulldog's grip loose, and by then the Scottie was almost dead. He spent two weeks in the hospital, and I spent two weeks in "the doghouse." I regret throwing that ball to this day.

I have thought about that experience many times and have begun to recognize its application to human relationships. Indeed, it is a very simple thing to precipitate a fight between people. All that is necessary is to toss a ball, symbolically, under the more aggressive of the two and prepare for the battle that ensues. This is done by repeating negative comments one has made or by baiting one in the presence of the other. It can be accomplished in business by assigning overlapping territory to two managers. They will tear each other to pieces in the inevitable rivalry. Alas, it happens every day.

This principle is also applicable to siblings. It is remarkably easy to make them mortal enemies. All a parent must do is toss a ball in the wrong direction. Their natural antagonism will do the rest.

Q236 What are the areas of potential conflict that should be handled with care? How can we keep the bulldog and the Scottie apart?

There are three areas that are most delicate. First, children are extremely sensitive about the matter of physical attractiveness and body characteristics. It is highly inflammatory to commend one child at the expense of the other. Suppose, for example, that Sharon is permitted to hear the casual remark about her sister, "Betty is sure going to be a gorgeous girl." The very fact that Sharon was not mentioned will probably establish the two girls as rivals. If there is a significant difference in beauty between the two, you can be assured that Sharon has already concluded, "Yeah, I'm the ugly one." When her fears are then confirmed by her parents, resentment and jealousy are generated.

Beauty is the most significant factor in the self-esteem of Western children. Anything that a parent utters on this subject within the hearing of children should be screened carefully. It has the power to make brothers and sisters hate one another.

Second, the matter of intelligence is another sensitive nerve to be handled with care. It is not uncommon to hear parents say in front of their children, "I think the younger boy is actually brighter than his brother." Adults find it difficult to comprehend how powerful that kind of assessment can be in a child's mind. Even when the comments are unplanned and are spoken routinely, they convey how a child is seen within his family. We are all vulnerable to that bit of evidence.

Third, children (and especially boys) are extremely competitive with regard to athletic abilities. Those who are slower, weaker, and less coordinated than their brothers are rarely able to accept "second best" with grace and dignity. Consider, for example, the following note given to me by the mother of two boys. It was written by her nine-year-old son to his eight-year-old brother the evening after the younger child had beaten him in a race.

Dear Jim:

I am the greatest and your the badest. And I can beat everybody in a race and you can't beat anybody in a race. I'm the smartest and your the dumbest. I'm the best sport player and your the badest sport player. And your also a hog. I can beat anybody up. And that's the truth. And that's the end of this story.

Yours truly,
Richard

This note is humorous to me because Richard's motive was so poorly disguised. He had been badly stung by his humiliation on the field of honor, so he came home and raised the battle flags. He will probably spend the next eight weeks looking for opportunities to fire torpedoes into Jim's soft underbelly. Such is the nature of humankind.

Q.237 My older child is a great student and earns straight A's year after year. Her younger sister, now in the sixth grade, is completely bored in school and won't even try. The frustrating thing is that the younger girl is probably brighter than her older sister. Why would she refuse to apply her ability like this?

There could be many reasons for her academic disinterest, but let me suggest the most probable explanation. Children will often refuse to compete when they think they are likely to place second instead of first. Therefore, a younger child may avoid challenging an older sibling in his area of greatest strength. If Son Number One is a great athlete, then Son Number Two may be more interested in collecting butterflies. If Daughter Number One is an accomplished pianist, then Daughter Number Two may be a boy-crazy goof-off.

This rule does not always hold true, of course, depending on the child's fear of failure and the way he estimates his chances of successful competition. If his confidence is high, he may blatantly wade into the territory owned by big brother, determined to do even better. However, the more typical response is to seek new areas of compensation that are not yet dominated by a family superstar.

If this explanation fits the behavior of your younger daughter, then it would be wise to accept something less than perfection from her school performance. Ev-

ery child need not fit the same mold—nor can we
force them to do so.

Q238 Sometimes I feel as though my children fight and argue as a method of attracting my attention. If this is the case, how should I respond?

You are probably correct in making that assumption.
Sibling rivalry often represents a form of manipulation of parents. Quarreling and fighting provide an
opportunity for both children to "capture" adult attention. It has been written, "Some children had
rather be wanted for murder than not wanted at all."
Toward this end, a pair of obnoxious kids can tacitly
agree to bug their parents until they get a response—
even if it is an angry reaction.

One father told me that his son and his nephew
began to argue and then beat each other with their
fists. Both fathers were nearby and decided to let the
fight run its natural course. During the first lull in the
action, one of the boys glanced sideways toward the
passive men and said, "Isn't anybody going to stop us
before we get hurt?!" The fight, you see, was something neither boy wanted. Their violent combat was
directly related to the presence of the two adults and
would have taken a different form if the boys had
been alone. Children will "hook" their parents' attention and intervention in this way.

Believe it or not, this form of sibling rivalry is easiest to control. The parent must simply render the
behavior unprofitable to each participant. I would
recommend that you review the problem (for example, a morning full of bickering) with the children
and then say, "Now listen carefully. If the two of you
want to pick on each other and make yourselves miserable, then be my guests [assuming there is a fairly
equal balance of power between them]. Go outside

and fight until you're exhausted. But it's not going to occur under my feet anymore. It's over! And you know that I mean business when I make that kind of statement. Do we understand each other?"

Having made the boundaries clear, I would act decisively the instant either boy returned to his bickering. If they had separate bedrooms, I would confine one child to each room for at least thirty minutes of complete boredom without radio, computer, or television. Or I would assign one to clean the garage and the other to mow the lawn. Or I would make them take a nap. My purpose would be to make them believe me the next time I asked for peace and tranquillity.

It is simply not necessary to permit children to destroy the joy of living. And what is most surprising, children are the happiest when their parents enforce reasonable limits with love and dignity.

Q239 I've been very careful to be fair with my children and give them no reason to resent one another. Nevertheless, they continue to fight. What can I do?

The problem may rest in your lack of disciplinary control at home. Sibling rivalry is at its worst when there is an inadequate system of justice among children—where the "lawbreakers" do not get caught or if apprehended, are set free without standing trial. It is important to understand that laws in a society are established and enforced for the purpose of protecting people from each other. Likewise, a family is a minisociety with the same requirement for protection of human rights.

For purposes of illustration, suppose that I live in a frontier community where there is no established law. Policemen do not exist, and there are no courts to whom disagreements can be appealed. Under those circumstances, my neighbor and I can abuse each other with impunity. He can steal my horses and throw rocks through my windows, while I raid the apples from his favorite tree and take his plow late at night. This kind of mutual antagonism has a way of escalating day by day, becoming ever more violent with the passage of time. When permitted to run its natural course, as in early American history, the end result can be feudal hatred and murder.

As indicated, individual families are similar to societies in their need for law and order. In the absence of justice, "neighboring" siblings begin to assault one another. The older child is bigger and tougher, which allows him to oppress his younger brothers and sisters. But the junior member of the family is not without weapons of his own. He strikes back by breaking the toys and prized possessions of the older sibling and interfering when friends are visiting. Mutual hatred then erupts like an angry volcano, spewing its destructive contents on everyone in its path.

In many homes, the parents do not have sufficient disciplinary control to enforce their judgments. In others, they are so exasperated with constant bickering among siblings that they refuse to get involved. In still others, parents require an older child to live with an admitted injustice "because your brother is smaller than you." Thus, they tie his hands and render him utterly defenseless against the mischief of his bratty little brother or sister. Even more commonly today, mothers and fathers are both working while their children are home busily disassembling each other.

I will say it again to parents: One of your most important responsibilities is to establish an equitable system of justice and a balance of power at home.

There should be reasonable "laws" that are enforced fairly for each member of the family. For purposes of illustration, let me list the boundaries and rules that evolved through the years in my own home.

1. Neither child was ever allowed to make fun of the other in a destructive way. Period! This was an inflexible rule with no exceptions.
2. Each child's room was his or her private territory. There were locks on both doors, and permission to enter was a revocable privilege. (Families with more than one child in each bedroom can allocate available living space for each youngster.)
3. The older child was not permitted to tease the younger child.
4. The younger child was forbidden to harass the older child.
5. The children were not required to play with each other when they preferred to be alone or with other friends.
6. We mediated any genuine conflict as quickly as possible, being careful to show impartiality and extreme fairness.

As with any plan of justice, this plan requires (1) children's respect for leadership of the parent, (2) willingness by the parent to mediate, (3) occasional enforcement of punishment. When this approach is accomplished with love, the emotional tone of the home can be changed from one of hatred to (at least) tolerance.

14

HELP FOR SINGLE PARENTS AND STEPPARENTS

Q240 What encouragement can you offer to those of us who are single parents? Each day seems more difficult than the one before it. Can you help plead our case to those who don't understand what we're facing?

In my view, single parents have the toughest job in the universe! Hercules himself would tremble at the range of responsibilities people like you must handle every day. It's difficult enough for two parents with a solid marriage and stable finances to satisfy the demands of parenting. For a single mother or father to do that task excellently over a period of years is evidence of heroism.

The greatest problem faced by single parents, especially a young mother like yourself, is the overwhelming amount of work to be done. Earning a living, fixing meals, caring for kids, helping with homework, cleaning house, paying bills, repairing the car (if she has one), handling insurance, and doing the banking, the income tax, marketing, etc., can require twelve hours a day or more. She must continue that schedule seven days per week all year long. Some have no support from family or anyone else. It's enough to exhaust the strongest and healthiest woman. Then where does she find time and energy to meet her social and emotional needs—and how does she develop the friendships on which that part of her life depends? This job is no easier for most fathers, who may find themselves trying to comb their daughter's hair and explain menstruation to their preteen girls.

There is only one answer to the pressures single parents face. It is for the rest of us to give them a helping hand. They need highly practical assistance, including the friendship of two-parent families who will take their children on occasion to free up some time. Single moms need the help of young men who will play catch with their fatherless boys and take them to the school soccer game. They need men who will fix the brakes on the Chevy and patch the leaky roof. They need prayer partners who will hold them accountable in their walk with the Lord and bear their burdens with them. They need an extended family of believers to care for them, lift them up, and remind them of their priorities. Perhaps most important, single parents need to know that the Lord is mindful of their circumstances.

Clearly, I believe it is the responsibility of those of us in the church to assist you with your parenting responsibilities. This requirement is implicit in Jesus' commandment that we love and support the needy in all walks of life. He said, "Inasmuch as ye have done it unto one of the least of these my brethren, ye have done it unto me" (Matthew 25:40, KJV). That puts it in perspective. Our effort on behalf of a fatherless or motherless child is seen by Jesus Christ as a direct service to Himself!

The biblical assignment is even more explicitly stated in James 1:27: "Religion that God our Father accepts as pure and faultless is this: to look after orphans and widows in their distress and to keep oneself from being polluted by the world."

Thankfully, churches today are becoming more sensitive to the needs of single parents. More congregations are offering programs and ministries geared to the unique concerns of those with special needs. I'd advise every single parent to find such a church or fellowship group and make himself or herself at home there. Christian fellowship and support can be the key to survival.

Those among my readers who want to help mothers or fathers raising kids alone might start by giving them a subscription to the Single-Parent Family edition of *Focus on the Family* magazine. Write us in Colorado Springs for information.

Q241 My husband died three years ago, leaving me to raise my ten-year-old son and nine-year-old daughter alone. For the past year I have been dating a very gentle, godly man who has three kids of his own. We have recently begun to talk about marriage, which really excites me. I have a major concern, however, that my children are not in favor of the relationship, even though Bill has been very good to them and quick to include them in many of our activities. I know Chuck and Laura miss their father and don't want to give up his memory, but I need companionship, and this is definitely a good thing. How should I handle this situation?

If you love Bill and he loves you, I think you should press forward with your marriage plans—especially if you have made it a matter of prayer. I do need to tell you unequivocally that the blending of your two families will not be easy. I have seen fewer than five "reconstituted families" in my professional career that didn't experience major adjustments and struggles. The myth of *The Brady Bunch*—the old television sitcom based on the harmonious blending of six children—just doesn't happen. There are highly predictable points of conflict that must be anticipated and dealt with early in the relationship. One of them is the situation you've described, where the children of one parent refuse to accept the new stepparent. These problems can be sorted out, but you must set your mind to doing it.

Q.242 Where should we start to build this new family? And could you identify the issues that are likely to be most difficult for us?

I would strongly suggest that you get some outside help as you bring your two families together. It is extremely difficult to do that on your own, and for some people, it is impossible. If you can afford professional counseling from a marriage, family, and child counselor who has dealt with blended families, it would be wise to get that assistance. A pastor also might be able to guide you, although there are some tough relationship issues to be handled by a professional who has "been there" before.

You're already experiencing the thorny issue of conflict between Bill and your children, which is common. One of the kids is likely to see him as a usurper. When a mother or father dies or when a divorce occurs, one child often moves into the power vacuum left by the departing parent. That youngster becomes the surrogate spouse. I'm not referring to sexual matters. Rather, that boy or girl becomes more mature than his or her years and relates to the remaining parent more as a peer. The status that comes with that supportive role is very seductive, and he or she is usually unwilling to give it up. The stepfather becomes a threat to that child. Much work must be done to bring them together.

The kids' loyalty to the memory of their dad is another issue that requires sensitive handling. In their eyes, to welcome the newcomer with open arms would be an act of betrayal. That's certainly understandable and something that must be worked through with your children. It will require time, patience, understanding, and prayer.

I would say the greatest problem you will face, however, is the way you and Bill will feel about your kids. Each of you is irrationally committed to your own, and you're merely acquainted with the others. When fights and insults occur between the two sets of children, you will be tempted to be partial to those you brought into the world, and Bill will probably favor his own flesh and blood. The natural tendency is to let the blended family dissolve into armed camps—us against them. If the kids sense any tension between you and Bill over their clashes, they will exploit and exaggerate it to gain power over the other children, etc. Unless there are some ways to ventilate these issues and work through them, battles will occur that will be remembered for a lifetime.

I have painted a worst-case scenario in order to prepare you for what could occur. Now let me encourage you. Many of these problems can be anticipated and lessened. Others can be avoided altogether. It is possible to blend families successfully, and millions have done it. But the task is difficult, and you will need some help in pulling it off.

Q243 I'd like to leave my children with friends or relatives for a few days and get some time for myself, but I'm worried about how this might affect them. Will they feel deserted again?

Not only is a brief time away from your children not likely to be hurtful—it will probably be healthy for them. One of the special risks faced by single parents is the possibility of a dependency relationship developing that will trap their children at an immature stage. This danger is increased when wounded people cling to each other exclusively for support in stressful times. Spending a reasonable amount of time apart can teach independence and give everyone a little relief from the routine. Therefore, if you have a clean, safe place to leave your children for a week or two, by all means, do it. You'll be more refreshed and better able to handle your usual "homework" when you return.

Q244 My former wife and I were married for thirteen years before we divorced two years ago. She has since remarried and has custody of our twelve-year-old daughter. Recently, I've learned that my ex-wife is saying things to our daughter that I feel are damaging to her spirit. She frequently blames her weight problem, smoking addiction, and financial woes on our daughter ("I wouldn't be in this mess if it weren't for you"). She also has no respect for our daughter's boundaries and routinely confiscates cash gifts that are received for birthday or Christmas presents. Since I am no longer recognized as the primary care provider, I am somewhat hesitant to raise objections. Still, she is my daughter, and it pains me to see her subjected to this kind of abuse. Should I step in and make things right?

I'm sure what you are witnessing is extremely distressing, and I wish there were legal remedies to help you protect your daughter. Within certain limits, however, your ex-wife is permitted by the court to be a bad mother and even do things that are harmful to the child. If you attack her or try to place her on the defensive, you could even make things tougher for your daughter. Apart from what you can accomplish with your wife through negotiation and personal influence, then, your hands are tied.

There is, however, so much that you can do directly with your daughter—even though you don't have custody over her. Work hard on that relationship. Be there for her when she needs you. Give her the best of your love and attention when she visits. At twelve years of age, she is at the most vulnerable time of her life, and she needs a father who thinks she is very special. You can have a profound influence on her if you demonstrate your love and concern consistently during this difficult period of her life. Remember, too, that the present situation may be temporary. Teenagers are given greater latitude in deciding which parent they want to live with. By your daughter's choice, you might have custody of her in a year or two. Until then, all you can do is the best you can do. I pray that it will be enough.

Q245 I am a single mother with a five-year-old son. How can I raise him to be a healthy man who has a good masculine image?

As I think you recognize from your question, your son has needs that you're not properly equipped to meet. Your best option, then, is to recruit a man who can act as a mentor to him—one who can serve as a masculine role model.

In her book *Mothers and Sons,* the late Jean Lush talked about the challenges single mothers face in raising sons. She says the ages four to six are especially important and difficult.[86] I agree. A boy at that age still loves his mother, but he feels the need to separate from her and gravitate toward a masculine model. If he has a father in the home, he'll usually want to spend more time with his dad apart from his mother and sisters. If his dad is not accessible to him, a substitute must be found.

Admittedly, good mentors can be difficult to recruit. Consider your friends, relatives, or neighbors who can offer as little as an hour or two a month. In a pinch, a mature high schooler who likes kids could even be "rented" to play ball or go fishing with a boy in need.

If you belong to a church, you should be able to find support for your son among the male members of the Christian community. Scripture commands people of faith to care for children without fathers. Isaiah 1:17 states, "Defend the cause of the fatherless, plead the case of the widow." Jesus Himself took boys and girls on His lap and said, "And whoever welcomes a little child like this in my name welcomes me" (Matthew 18:5). I believe it is our responsibility as Christian men to help single mothers with their difficult parenting tasks.

Certainly single mothers have many demands on their time and energy, but the effort to find a mentor for their sons might be the most worthwhile contribution they can make.

Q246 I am a single mom who is struggling to survive. Of all the things that frustrate me, I am bothered most by having to send my kids to visit their dad for three weeks in the summer. That will happen next month, and I'm already uptight about putting them on the plane. Can you help me accept what I'm about to go through?

Maybe it will help to know that many other single parents have similar feelings. One of these mothers expressed her frustration this way:

I stand in the terminal, and I watch the kids' airplane disappear into the clouds. I feel an incredible sense of loss. The loneliness immediately starts to set in. I worry constantly about their safety, but I resist the urge to call every hour to see how they're doing. And when they do call me to tell me how much fun they're having, I grieve over the fact that they're living a life completely separate from my own. My only consolation is knowing that they're returning soon. But I'm haunted by the fear that they won't want to come home with me.

If the anxieties of that mother represent your own feelings, let me offer some suggestions for how you might make the most of your days alone. Instead of seeing the next three weeks as a period of isolation, view them as an opportunity to recharge your batteries and reinvigorate the spirit. Single parenting is an exhausting responsibility that can cause burnout if it knows no relief. Take this time to enjoy some relaxed evenings with your friends. Read an inspirational book, or return to a hobby that you've set aside. Fill your day with things that are impossible amidst the pressures of child care, recognizing that your children will benefit from your rehabilitation. They'll return to a reenergized parent, instead of one coming off three weeks of depression.

Q247 There are several single parents in my church who seem to be so needy. I would like to help them, but, honestly, I am barely able to do everything necessary to care for my own family. What responsibility do you think I have as a Christian woman to help these other families?

Everyone is busy today. I don't know any families that aren't experiencing fatigue and time pressure. None of us need new things to do, certainly, but I do believe it is our duty to reach out to those who are going through hard times. This is especially true of single parents because their vulnerable children are the ones who suffer. I'm sure Jesus would have us care for these little families, financially and with our love and concern.

Many years ago, my wife, Shirley, was working around the house one morning, when a knock came at the front door. When she opened it, there stood a young woman in her late teens, who called herself Sally.

"I'm selling brushes," she said, "and I wonder if you'd like to buy any."

Well, my wife told her she wasn't interested in buying anything that day, and Sally said, "I know. No one else is, either." And with that, she began to cry.

Shirley invited Sally to come in for a cup of coffee, and she asked her to share her story. She turned out to be an unmarried mother who was just struggling mightily to support her two-year-old son. That night, we went to her shabby little apartment above a garage to see how we could help this mother and her toddler. When we opened the cupboards, there was nothing there for them to eat, and I mean nothing. That night, they both had dined on a can of SpaghettiOs. We took her to the market, and we did what we could to help get her on her feet.

Sally is obviously not the only single mother out there who is desperately trying to survive in a very hostile world. All of these mothers could use a little kindness—from baby-sitting to providing a meal to repairing the washing machine or even to just showing a little thoughtfulness.

Raising kids alone is like climbing a mountain a mile high. Can you find it in your heart to baby-sit for that single mother one afternoon a week? Or maybe you can fix extra food when you cook and take it over some evening. Imagine what that kindness will convey to a mom or dad who comes home exhausted and discovers that someone cares about his or her little family. Not only will it bring encouragement to the parent, but one or more children will bless you as well.

15

LIVING WITH
A TEENAGER

Q248 Why do you think kids are more sexually active today than when I was young? Lust is certainly not new. What is causing this generation to be so promiscuous?

There are many factors that have brought on the epidemic we're seeing, not the least of which is the trash that is beamed to teenagers on television, in movies, and from the rock-music industry. Young people today are bombarded by immoral entertainment that models promiscuous behavior and teaches them that "everyone is doing it." The diminishing influence of traditional Christian teaching is also responsible for the changing mores of our kids.

There is another extremely important consideration that has been identified recently by behavioral research. A team of researchers from the Oregon Social Learning Center has found that parental divorce plays a direct role in fostering sexual experimentation among adolescents.

The investigators tracked the behavior of 201 junior high and high school boys who lived in "higher-crime areas." They found that the boys who had sexual intercourse at an early age tended to be those who had experienced two or more "parental transitions" (divorce, remarriage, or repartnering). Only 18 percent of these promiscuous boys came from intact families. By contrast, 57 percent of the virgins came from homes where divorce had not occurred. On average, these abstinent boys had experienced fewer than one parental transition.[87]

A similar study was conducted on young women by sociologist Lawrence L. Wu of the University of Wisconsin—Madison. He studied 2,441 white women and 1,275 black women, and found that there was a strong correlation between those who bore babies out of wedlock and those who had been through a "change in family structure" when growing up. Wu concluded that the stresses of divorce and/or remarriage on children are directly implicated in out-of-wedlock childbearing.[88]

In study after study now, we are seeing that divorce, single parenting, and family disruption are unhealthy for children. This is not to criticize those who find themselves in those circumstances, but neither can we continue to deny that intact, two-parent families are the most healthy and contribute directly to a stable society. If that is true (and the evidence for it is overwhelming), then our public policies and governmental agencies should favor and encourage traditional families. Anything that undermines or weakens them, such as confiscatory taxes or governmental intrusion, should be viewed with suspicion. The future of the nation depends, quite literally, on millions of strong, committed, and loving families.

To those who remember the vice president's controversial speech on family values during the election of 1992, we can now say unequivocally, "Dan Quayle was dead right!"

Q.249 Children seem to be growing up at a younger age today than in the past. Is this true, and if so, what accounts for their faster development?

Yes, it is true. Statistical records indicate that our children are growing taller today than in the past, probably resulting from better nutrition, medicine, exercise, rest, and recreation. And this more ideal physical environment has apparently caused sexual maturity to occur at younger and younger ages. It is thought that puberty in a particular child is triggered when he or she reaches a certain level of growth; therefore, when environmental and general health factors propel a youngster upward at a faster rate, sexual maturation occurs earlier.

For example, in 1850 the average age of menarche (first menstruation) in Norwegian girls was 17.0 years of age; in 1950, it was 13.0. The average age of puberty in females had dropped four years in one century. In the United States the average age of menarche dropped from 16.5 in 1840 to 12.9 in 1950.[89] More recent figures indicate that it now occurs on average at 12.8 years of age![90] Thus, the trend toward younger dating and sexual awareness is a result, at least in part, of this "fast-track" mechanism.

Q.250 Are there limits to this trend toward younger and younger sexual development? If not, the kids of the future may enter puberty in the middle of childhood. That could create enormous problems when sexual awareness precedes emotional maturity by a decade or more.

It could happen, but that isn't likely. Actually, studies now indicate that a leveling off and perhaps a reversal of the trend is occurring. As of 1988, the average age of menarche reached a low point of 12.5.[91] By 1993, however, researchers Dann and Roberts found that the curve had begun to swing back in the other direction. Puberty appears to be arriving slightly later again. Why? Well, just as better nutrition and health care caused the average age to drop in the recent past, the present emphasis on ultrathin bodies and intense exercise is apparently delaying development somewhat.[92] Many physicians are concerned about today's obsession with what used to be called "skinniness." Extremes, they say, are rarely beneficial to human beings—whether they be manifested in grossly overweight bodies or those that are bone thin.

A famous biochemist at the University of Southern California, Dr. Sam Bessman, once told me, "Remember that the body never stops eating. If you don't feed it properly, it will begin to consume itself." That is precisely what happens in the girl who consumes too few calories; she may have no periods for years at a time.

Q251 What is the most difficult period of adolescence, and what is behind the distress?

The eighteenth year is the time of greatest conflict between parent and child, typically. But the thirteenth and fourteenth years commonly are the most difficult twenty-four months in life for the youngster. It is during this time that self-doubt and feelings of inferiority reach an all-time high, amidst the greatest social pressures yet experienced. An adolescent's sense of worth as a human being hangs precariously on peer-group acceptance, which can be tough to garner. Thus, relatively minor evidences of rejection or ridicule are of major significance to those who already see themselves as fools and failures. It is difficult to overestimate the impact of having no one to sit with on the school-sponsored bus trip or of not being invited to an important event or of being laughed at by the "in" group or of waking up in the morning to find seven shiny new pimples on your forehead or of being slapped by the girl you thought had liked you as much as you liked her. Some boys and girls consistently face this kind of social catastrophe throughout their teen years.

Dr. Urie Bronfenbrenner, eminent authority on child development at Cornell University, told a Senate committee that the junior high years are probably the most critical to the development of a child's mental health. It is during this time of self-doubt that the personality is often assaulted and damaged beyond repair. Consequently, said Bronfenbrenner, it is not unusual for healthy, happy children to enter junior high school but then emerge two years later as broken, discouraged teenagers.[93]

Q252 Talk about the social pressures that beset many early adolescents. Why do they seem to overreact to almost everything at that time?

It is common knowledge that a twelve- or thirteen-year-old child suddenly awakens to a brand-new world around him, as though his eyes were opening for the first time. That world is populated by age-mates who scare him out of his wits. His greatest anxiety, far exceeding the fear of death, is the possibility of rejection or humiliation in the eyes of his peers. This ultimate danger will lurk in the background for years, motivating him to do things that make absolutely no sense to the adults who watch. It is impossible to comprehend the adolescent mind without understanding this terror of the peer group.

I'll never forget a vulnerable girl named Lisa who was a student when I was in high school. She attended modern-dance classes and was asked to perform during an all-school assembly program. Lisa was in the ninth grade and had not begun to develop sexually. As she spun around the stage that day, the unthinkable happened! The top of her strapless blouse suddenly let go (it had nothing to grip) and dropped to her waist. The student body gasped and then roared with laughter. It was terrible! Lisa stood clutching frantically at her bare body for a moment and then fled from the stage in tears. Years later she hadn't recovered from the tragedy. And you can bet that her "friends" made sure she remembered it for the rest of her life.

Such a situation would also humiliate an adult, of course, but it was worse for a teenager like Lisa. An embarrassment of that magnitude could even take away the desire to live, and indeed, thousands of adolescents are killing themselves every year. That is how forceful the need to be respected and accepted during the teen years is. Those who are mocked and rejected by the peer group are often devastated well into the adult years.

Q253 You obviously have a great empathy for kids who are in the junior high years—especially those who are rejected and ridiculed by their peers. Have you always felt that way about that age-group, which many adults don't like to be around?

My concern for early adolescents dates back to the years I spent teaching in junior high school. I was only twenty-five years old at the time, and I fell in love with 250 science and math students. The day I left to accept other responsibilities I fought back the tears. Some of the kids were hurting badly, and I developed a keen sensitivity to their plight. Let me illustrate how I saw them.

Years later, I was sitting in my car at a fast-food

restaurant, eating a hamburger and French fries. I happened to look in the rearview mirror. There I saw the most pitiful, scrawny, dirty little kitten on a ledge behind my car. I was so touched by how hungry she looked that I got out, tore off a piece of my hamburger, and tossed it to her. But before this kitten could reach it, a huge gray tomcat sprang out of the bushes, grabbed the morsel, and gobbled it down. I felt sorry for the kitten, who turned and ran back into the shadows, still hungry and frightened.

I was immediately reminded of those kids I used to teach. They were just as needy, just as deprived, just as lost as that little kitten. It wasn't food that they required; it was love and attention and respect that they needed, and they were desperate for it. And just when they opened up and revealed the pain inside, one of the more popular kids would abuse and ridicule them, sending them scurrying back into the shadows, frightened and alone.

We, as adults, must never forget the pain of trying to grow up and of the competitive world in which many adolescents live today. Taking a moment to listen, to care, and to direct such a youngster may be the best investment of a lifetime.

Q254 Why are kids so vulnerable? How do you explain this paralyzing social fear at an age when they are notoriously gutsy? There is very little else that scares them. Teenagers drive their cars like maniacs, and the boys make great combat soldiers. Why is it that an eighteen-year-old can be trained to attack an enemy gun emplacement or run through a minefield, and yet he panics in the noisy company of his peers? Why are they so frightened of each other?

I believe the answer is related to the nature of power and how it influences human behavior. Adolescent

society is based on the exercise of raw force. That is
the heart and soul of its value system. It comes in various forms. For girls, there is no greater social dominance than physical beauty. A truly gorgeous young
woman is so powerful that even the boys are often
terrified of her. She rules in a high school like a queen
on her throne, and in fact, she is usually given some
honor with references to royalty in its name (Homecoming Queen, Homecoming Princess, All-School
Queen, Sweetheart's Queen, Football Queen, etc.).
The way she uses this status to intimidate her subjects
is in itself a fascinating study in adolescent behavior.

Boys derive power from physical attractiveness
too, but also from athletic accomplishment in certain
prescribed sports. Those that carry the greatest status are usually skilled in sports that exhibit sheer
physical strength (football) or size (basketball).

Do you remember what the world of adolescence
was like for you? Do you recall the power games that
were played—the highly competitive and hostile environment into which you walked every day? Can
you still feel the apprehension you experienced
when a popular (powerful) student called you a
creep or a jerk, or he put his big hand in your face and
pushed you out of the way? He wore a football jersey
that reminded you that the entire team would eat
you alive if you should be so foolish as to fight back.
Does the memory of the junior-senior prom still
come to mind occasionally, when you were either
turned down by the girl you loved or were not asked
by the boy of your dreams? Have you ever had the
campus heroes make fun of the one flaw you most
wanted to hide, and then threaten to mangle you on
the way home from school?

Perhaps you never went through these stressful
encounters. Maybe you were one of the powerful

elite who oppressed the rest of us. But your son or daughter could be on the receiving end of the flak. A few years ago I talked to a mother whose seventh-grade daughter was getting butchered at school each day. She said the girl awakened an hour before she had to get up each morning and lay there thinking about how she could get through her day without being humiliated.

Typically, power games are more physical for adolescent males than females. The bullies literally force their will on those who are weaker. That is what I remember most clearly from my own high school years. I had a number of fights during that era just to preserve my turf. The name of the game was power! And not much has changed for today's teenagers.

Q255 Explain in greater detail the role of power in the life of a teenager.

Let's begin with a definition. *Power* is the ability to control others, to control our circumstances, and especially, to control ourselves. The lust for it lies deep within the human spirit. We all want to be the boss, and that impulse begins very early in life. Studies show that one-day-old infants actually reach for control of the adults around them. Even at that tender age, they behave in ways designed to get their guardians to meet their needs.

The desire for power is evident when a toddler runs from his mother in a supermarket or when a ten-year-old refuses to do his or her homework or when a husband and wife fight over money. We see it when an elderly woman refuses to move to a nursing home. The common thread between these and a thousand other examples is the passion to run our own lives—and everything else, if given the chance.

People vary in the intensity of this urge, but it seems to motivate all of us to one degree or another.

Now, what about your sons and daughters? Have you wondered why they come home from school in such a terrible mood? Have you asked them why they are so jumpy and irritable through the evening? Perhaps they are unable to describe their feelings to you, but they may have engaged in a form of combat all day. Even if they haven't had to fight with their fists, it is likely that they are embroiled in a highly competitive, openly hostile environment where emotional danger lurks on every side. Am I overstating the case? Yes, for the kid who is coping well. But for the powerless young man and woman, I haven't begun to tell their stories.

That's why they are nervous wrecks on the first day of school or before the team plays its initial game or any other time when their power base is on the line. The raw nerve, you see, is not really dominance but self-worth. One's sense of value is dependent on peer acceptance at that age, and that is why the group holds such enormous influence over the individual. If he or she is mocked, disrespected, ridiculed, and excluded—in other words, if that individual is stripped of power—he or she feels it deeply.

Q.256 If power is so important to teenagers, then it must play a key role in family dynamics. How does it work itself out at home?

You've asked a very perceptive question. It is a wise parent who knows intuitively how to transfer power, or independence, to the next generation. That task requires a balancing act between two equally dangerous extremes. They dare not set their teenagers free before they are mature enough to handle the autonomy—even though they are screaming for it. Adolescents still need parental leadership, and parents are obligated to provide it—that's the law of the land. One of the characteristics of those who acquire power too early is a prevailing attitude of disrespect for authority. It extends to teachers, ministers, policemen, judges, and even to God Himself. Such an individual has never yielded to parental leadership at home. Why should he or she submit himself or herself to anyone else? For a rebellious teenager, it is only a short step from there to drug abuse, sexual experimentation, running away, and so on. The early acquisition of power has claimed countless young victims by this very process.

On the other hand, there is an equally dangerous mistake to be avoided at the latter end of adolescence. We must not wait too long to set our young adults free. Self-determination is a basic human right to which every adult is entitled. To withhold that liberty too long is to incite wars of revolution.

My good friend Jay Kesler observed that Mother England made that specific mistake with her children in the American colonies. They grew to become rebellious "teenagers" who demanded their freedom. Still she refused to release them, and unnecessary bloodshed ensued. Fortunately, England learned a valuable lesson from that painful experience. Some 171 years later, she granted a peaceful and orderly transfer of power to another tempestuous offspring named India. Revolution was averted.[94]

At the risk of being redundant, let me summarize our goal as parents: First, we must not transfer power too early, even if our children take us daily to the battlefield. Mothers who make that mistake are some of the most frustrated people on the face of the earth. On the other hand, we must not retain parental power too long. Control will be torn from our grasp if we refuse to surrender it voluntarily. The granting of self-determination should be matched stride for stride with the arrival of maturity, culminating with complete release during early adulthood.

Sounds easy, doesn't it? We all know better. I consider this orderly transfer of power to be one of the most delicate and difficult responsibilities in the entire realm of parenthood.

Q.257 What guidelines can you offer to help us transfer power at the right time—neither early nor late?

There are some approaches that have been successful in lessening this conflict. The Amish people have developed a unique tradition that has succeeded for them. Their children are kept under very tight control when they are young. Strict discipline and harsh standards of behavior are imposed from infancy. When children turn sixteen years of age, however, they enter a period called "Rumspringa." Suddenly, all restrictions are lifted. They are free to drink, smoke, date, marry, or behave in ways that horrify their parents. Some do just that. But most don't. They are even granted the right to leave the Amish community if they choose. But if they stay, it must be in accordance with the social order. The majority accept the heritage of their families, not because they must, but because they choose to.

Although I admire the Amish and many of their approaches to child rearing, I believe the Rumspringa concept is implemented too quickly for children raised in a more open society. To take a teenager overnight from rigid control to complete emancipation is an invitation to anarchy. It works in the controlled environment of Amish country, but it would be disastrous for most of the rest of us. I've seen families grant "instant adulthood" to their adolescents, to their regret. The result has been similar to what occurred in African colonies when European leadership was suddenly withdrawn. Bloody revolutions were often fought in the power vacuum that was created.

If it doesn't work to transfer power suddenly to young people, how can they be established as full-fledged adults without creating a civil war in the process? I have recommended that parents begin granting tiny elements of independence literally in toddlerhood. When a child can tie his shoes, he should be permitted—yes, required—to do it. When she can choose her clothes, she should make her own selections, within reason. When he can walk safely to school, he should be allowed to do so. Each year, more responsibility and freedom (they are companions) must be given to the child so that the final release in early adulthood is merely a small, final release of authority. This is the theory, at least. Pulling it off is sometimes quite another matter.

In the final analysis, your own son or daughter will let you know when the time is right for independence. You must judge his or her maturity, wisdom, and emotional readiness for full-fledged adulthood. Then you grant it—and pray diligently for the next thirty years.

Q.258 My thirteen-year-old daughter has become increasingly lazy in the past couple of years. She lies around the house and will sleep half a day on Saturday. She complains about being tired a lot. Is this typical of early adolescence? How should I deal with it?

It is not uncommon for boys and girls to experience fatigue during the years of puberty. Their physical

resources are being invested in a rapid growth process during that time, leaving less energy for other
activities. This period doesn't last very long and is
usually followed by the most energetic time of life.

I would suggest, first, that you schedule your
daughter for a routine physical examination to rule out
the possibility of a more serious explanation for her fatigue. If it does turn out to be a phenomenon of puberty, as I suspect, you should "go with the flow." See
that she gets plenty of rest and sleep. This need is often
not met because teenagers feel that they shouldn't
have to go to bed as early as they did when they were
children. Therefore, they stay up too late and then
drag through the next day in a state of exhaustion. Surprisingly, a thirteen- or fourteen-year-old actually
needs more rest than when he or she was nine or ten,
simply because of the acceleration in growth.

In summary, your daughter is turning overnight
from a girl into a woman. Some of the physical characteristics you are observing are part of the transformation. Do everything you can to facilitate it.

Q.259 We have a very athletic junior high school
boy who loves every kind of physical
activity. He gets most of his exercise in a P.E. class every
morning, but I happen to know that he doesn't shower
afterward. The school no longer makes him or the other
kids do it. When I was a student we were required to
clean up after sweating in the gym. How come this is no
longer considered necessary?

Like you, I was required to shower after every gym
class. The coach would look us over to make sure we
were clean before sending us on our way. Students
who didn't shower didn't pass. But those days are
just about over. The reason is that because junior
highers are so sensitive about their bodies today, it is

very painful for them to have to strip in front of one another. They vary so much in development at that age that some are grown-up adults and others are still little prepubescent kids. It is nightmarish for the immature youngster to have to put his or her body on display in front of the wolf pack. They would tear him to pieces. Others feel fat or skinny or hairy or (fill in the blank). Increasingly, they resist having to take it all off in the locker room.

When I was a school psychologist, I met with a high school sophomore who absolutely refused to shower. His recalcitrance violated district policy, and I was asked to identify his problem. After talking to this boy and seeing how vulnerable he was to the ridicule of his peers, I agreed that he should not be required to humiliate himself five days a week. Twenty years ago, this lad was an exception. Now, given the body consciousness of our culture, his attitude is common.

Another factor is that coaches and teachers have become very leery of false charges of sexual abuse. Even if untrue, a person's entire career could go down the drain just by the suggestion that he or she was enjoying looking at the kids. This is another reason mandatory showers in schools are being phased out.

The result? Teachers have to work in a classroom full of sweaty adolescents who smell like a gymnasium—or worse.

Q.260 I hear so much about communicating with our children and making sure we stay on the same wavelength. How can I do that during the teen years?

You can expect communication to be very difficult for several years. I said adolescence was sometimes like a tornado. Let me give you a better analogy. This time of life reminds me in some ways of the very early space probes that blasted off from Cape Canaveral in Florida. I remember my excitement when Colonel John Glenn and the other astronauts embarked on their perilous journeys into space. It was a thrilling time to be an American.

People who lived through those years will recall that a period of maximum danger occurred as each spacecraft was reentering the earth's atmosphere. The fliers inside were entirely dependent on the heat shield on the bottom of the capsule to protect them from temperatures in excess of one thousand degrees Fahrenheit. If the craft descended at the wrong angle, the astronauts would be burned to cinders. At that precise moment of anxiety, negative ions would accumulate around the capsule and prevent all communication with the earth for approximately seven minutes. The world waited breathlessly for news of the astronauts' safety. Presently, the reassuring voice of a man named Chris Craft broke in to say, "This is Mission Control. We have made contact with Friendship Seven. Everything is A-OK. Splashdown is imminent." Cheers and prayers went up in restaurants, banks, airports, and millions of homes across the country. Even CBS news anchor Walter Cronkite seemed relieved.

The application to the teen years should be apparent. After the training and preparation of childhood are over, a pubescent youngster marches out to the launching pad. His parents watch apprehensively as he climbs aboard a capsule called adolescence and waits for his rockets to fire. His father and mother wish they could go with him, but there is room for just one person in the spacecraft. Besides, nobody invited them. Without warning, the mighty rocket engines begin to roar and the "umbilical cord" falls away. "Liftoff! We have liftoff!" screams the boy's father.

Junior, who was a baby only yesterday, is on his way to the edge of the universe. A few weeks later, his parents go through the scariest experience of their lives: They suddenly lose all contact with the capsule. "Negative ions" have interfered with communication at a time when they most want to be assured of their son's safety. Why won't he talk to them?

This period of silence lasts much longer than a few minutes, as it did with Colonel Glenn and friends. It may continue for years. The same kid who used to talk a mile a minute and ask a million questions has now reduced his vocabulary to nine monosyllabic phrases. They are, "I dunno," "Maybe," "I forget," "Huh?" "No!" "Nope," "Yeah," "Who—me?" and "He did it." Otherwise, only static comes through the receivers—groans, grunts, growls, and gripes. What an apprehensive time it is for those who wait on the ground!

Years later, when Mission Control fears the spacecraft has been lost, a few scratchy signals are picked up unexpectedly from a distant transmitter. The parents are jubilant as they hover near their radio. Was that really his voice? It is deeper and more mature than they remembered. There it is again. This time the intent is unmistakable. Their spacey son has made a deliberate effort to correspond with them! He was fourteen years old when he blasted into space and now he is nearly twenty. Could it be that the negative environment has been swept away and communication is again possible?

Yes. For most families, that is precisely what happens. After years of quiet anxiety, parents learn to their great relief that everything is A-OK on board the spacecraft. The "splashdown" occurring during the early twenties can then be a wonderful time of life for both generations.

Q261 Isn't there some way to avoid this blackout period and the other stresses associated with the adolescent voyage?

Not with some teenagers; perhaps not with the majority. Tension occurs in the most loving and intelligent of families. Why? Because it is driven by powerful hormonal forces that overtake and possess boys and girls in the early pubescent years. I believe parents and even some behavioral scientists have underestimated the impact of the biochemical changes occurring in puberty. We can see the effect of these hormones on the physical body, but something equally dynamic is occurring in the brain. How else can we explain why a happy, contented, cooperative twelve-year-old suddenly becomes a sullen, angry, depressed thirteen-year-old? Some authorities would contend that social pressure alone accounts for this transformation. I simply don't believe that.

The emotional characteristics of a suddenly rebellious teenager are rather like the symptoms of premenstrual syndrome or severe menopause in women or perhaps a tumultuous midlife crisis in men. Obviously, dramatic changes are going on inside! Furthermore, if the upheaval were caused entirely by environmental factors, its onset would not be so predictable in puberty. The emotional changes I have described arrive right on schedule, timed to coincide precisely with the arrival of sexual maturation. Both characteristics, I contend, are driven by a common hormonal assault. Human chemistry apparently goes haywire for a few years, in some more than others, affecting mind as much as body.

Q262 If that explanation is accurate, then what implications does it have for parents of early adolescents?

First, understanding this glandular upheaval makes it easier to tolerate and cope with the emotional reverberations that are occurring. For several years, some kids are not entirely rational! Just as a severely menopausal woman may accuse her innocent and bewildered husband of infidelity, a hormonally depressed teenager may not interpret his world accurately either. His social judgment is impaired. Therefore, parents shouldn't despair when it looks like everything they have tried to teach their kid seems to have been forgotten. He is going through a metamorphosis that has turned everything upside down. But stick around. He'll get his legs under him again!

I strongly recommend that parents of strong-willed and rebellious females, especially, quietly keep track of the particulars of their daughters' menstrual cycles. Not only should you record when their periods begin and end each month, but also make a comment or two each day about moods. I think you will see that the emotional blowups that tear the family apart are cyclical in nature. Premenstrual tension at that age can produce a flurry of skirmishes every twenty-eight days. If you know they are coming, you can retreat to the storm cellar when the wind begins to blow. You can also use this record to teach your girls about premenstrual syndrome and how to cope with it. Unfortunately, many parents never seem to notice the regularity and predictability of severe conflict with their daughters. Again, I recommend that you watch the calendar. It will tell you so much about your girls.

Q263 How about adolescent boys? Do they have a hormonal cycle too?

Their emotions and behavior are certainly driven by hormones. Everything from sexual passion to aggressiveness is motivated by the new chemicals that surge through their veins. There is, however, no cyclical fluctuation that parallels a menstrual calendar in girls. As a result, they can be more volatile and less predictable throughout the month than their female counterparts.

Q264 My fourteen-year-old boy is flighty, mischievous, irresponsible, and lazy. If I don't watch him very carefully, he'll find ways to get into trouble—not really bad stuff, just stupid kid behavior. But I'm afraid I could lose him right at this time. What can I do to keep him on track?

It is most important to keep your rambunctious youngster moving. If you let him get bored, he'll find destructive ways to use unstructured and unsupervised time. My advice is to get him involved in the very best church youth program you can find. If your local congregation only has four bored kids in its junior high department and seven sleepy high schoolers, I would consider changing churches. I know doing that could be disruptive to the rest of your family, but it might help save your volatile kid. This can be done not only through church activities but also by involvement with athletics, music, horses or other animals, and part-time jobs. The hope is that one of those options will grab his fancy at some point, and his boundless energy will be channeled into something constructive. Until then, you must keep that energetic kid's scrawny legs churning!

Q.265 It is commonly understood that peer pressure causes teenagers to begin smoking or using drugs. Is that what really motivates them to pick up dangerous habits?

That precise question was the subject of a recent survey. The researchers studied more than sixteen thousand schoolchildren in Orange County, California. They found that it was family members, not classmates or teachers, who had the biggest influence on whether children used drugs, alcohol, or tobacco. If teenagers felt that their parents or siblings approved of smoking, they were likely to follow suit. And if there was one person who could convince them not to participate, it was usually a member of their own family. Many parents feel that this is an area that can be left to the schools, and they neglect to talk about it at home. But this study and others have shown that family pressure, not peer pressure, has the greatest effect on children.[95]

Another finding to come out of the investigation is that children are still dangerously unaware of the hazards of smoking. Obviously, the antismoking advertising campaign has not reached their tender ears.

Like other messages we want our children to hear, the responsibility to communicate them lies with parents. Talk to your sons and daughters when they are young about the dangers of cigarette smoking. Tell them that you don't approve of the habit. Discuss the health hazards, including the risk of cancer and lung disease. And offer them professional help in quitting if they've already started. Warn them repeatedly about drug abuse and what it can do to the body. Parents can make a difference in avoiding addictive behavior in their children if they take the time to teach them. Most of them can even counterbalance the peer group.

Q266 My thirteen-year-old son is in the full bloom of adolescence. I'm suspicious that he may be masturbating when he's alone, but I don't quite know how to approach him about it. Should I be concerned, and if so, what should I say to him?

I don't think you should invade that private world at all unless there are unique circumstances that lead you to do so. I offer that advice while acknowledging that masturbation is a highly controversial subject and Christian leaders differ widely in their perspectives on it. I will answer your question but hope you understand that some Bible scholars will disagree emphatically with what I will say.

First, let's consider masturbation from a medical perspective. We can say without fear of contradiction that there is no scientific evidence to indicate that this act is harmful to the body. Despite terrifying warnings given to young people historically, it does not cause blindness, weakness, mental retardation, or any other physical problem. If it did, the entire male population and about half of females would be blind, weak, simpleminded, and sick. Between 95 and 98 percent of all boys engage in this practice—and the rest have been known to lie. It is as close to being a universal behavior as is likely to occur. A lesser but still significant percentage of girls also engage in what was once called "self-gratification."

As for the emotional consequences of masturbation, only four circumstances should give us cause for concern. The first is when it is associated with oppressive guilt from which the individual can't escape. That guilt has the potential to do considerable psychological and spiritual damage. Boys and girls who labor under divine condemnation can gradually become convinced that even God couldn't love them. They promise a thousand times with great sincerity never again to commit this despicable act. Then a week or two passes, or perhaps several months. Eventually, the hormonal pressure accumulates until nearly every waking moment reverberates with sexual desire. Finally, in a moment (and I do mean a moment) of weakness, it happens again. What then, dear friend? Tell me what a young person says to God after he or she has just broken the one thousand first solemn promise to Him? I am convinced that some teenagers have thrown over their faith because of their inability to please God at this point of masturbation.

The second circumstance in which masturbation might have harmful implications is when it becomes extremely obsessive. That is more likely to occur when it has been understood by the individual to be "forbidden fruit." I believe the best way to prevent that kind of obsessive response is for adults not to emphasize or condemn it. Regardless of what you do, you will not stop the practice of masturbation in your teenagers. That is a certainty. You'll just drive it underground—or under covers. Nothing works as a "cure." Cold showers, lots of exercise, many activities, and awesome threats are ineffective. Attempting to suppress this act is one campaign that is destined to fail—so why wage it?

The third situation around which we should be concerned is when the young person becomes addicted to pornographic material. The kind of obscenity available to teenagers today has the capacity to grab and hold a boy for the rest of his life. Parents will want to intervene if there is evidence that their son or daughter is heading down that well-worn path.

The fourth concern about masturbation refers not to adolescents but to us as adults. This habit has the

capacity to follow us into marriage and become a
substitution for healthy sexual relations between a
husband and wife. This, I believe, is what the apostle
Paul meant when he instructed us not to "deprive"
one another as marital partners: "Do not deprive
each other except by mutual consent and for a time,
so that you may devote yourselves to prayer. Then
come together again so that Satan will not tempt you
because of your lack of self-control" (1 Corinthians
7:5).

As for the spiritual implications of masturbation, I
will have to defer to the theologians for a more definitive response. It is interesting to me, however, that
Scripture does not address this subject except for a
single reference in the Old Testament to a man
named Onan. He interrupted sexual intercourse
with his sister-in-law and allowed his semen to fall
on the ground to keep from producing offspring for
his brother, which was his "duty" (Genesis 38:8).
Though that verse is often cited as evidence of God's
disapproval of masturbation, the context doesn't
seem to fit.

So, what should parents say to their kids about this
subject? My advice is to say nothing after puberty has
occurred. You will only cause embarrassment and
discomfort. For those who are younger, it would be
wise to include the subject of masturbation in the
"Preparing for Adolescence" conversation I have recommended on other occasions. I would suggest that
parents talk to their twelve- or thirteen-year-old
boys, especially, in the same general way my mother
and father discussed this subject with me. We were
riding in the car, and my dad said, "Jim, when I was a
boy, I worried so much about masturbation. It really
became a scary thing for me because I thought God
was condemning me for what I couldn't help. So I'm

telling you now that I hope you don't feel the need to engage in this act when you reach the teen years, but if you do, you shouldn't be too concerned about it. I don't believe it has much to do with your relationship with God."

What a kind thing my father did for me that night in the car. He was a very conservative minister who never compromised his standards of morality to the day of his death. He stood like a rock for biblical principles and commandments. Yet he cared enough about me to lift from my shoulders the burden of guilt that nearly destroyed some of my friends in the church. This kind of "reasonable" faith taught to me by my parents is one of the primary reasons I never felt it necessary to rebel against parental authority or defy God.

Well, those are my views, for what they are worth. I know my recommendations will be inflammatory to some people. If you are one of them, please forgive me. I can only offer the best advice of which I'm capable. I pray that in this instance, I am right.

Q267 My oldest son is approaching the age when we had previously agreed to allow him to date. The more I think about it, though, the more the whole idea concerns me. It seems that even in the best of dating situations, the negatives exceed the positives. I can't help but feel that I'm setting my son up for failure. Several of my church friends have adopted the concept of "courtship" rather than dating. Could you please explain this idea to me and suggest which of the two arrangements you favor?

Simply put, the "courtship" concept is a reaction to the dating model that is thought by many to be unhealthy. Dating couples go through a series of short-term and often unsatisfying relationships over a period of five or ten years or longer. They are being taught to flit from one relationship to another like a honeybee buzzing from flower to flower. Why would they not be inclined later to bail out on a marriage partner when bored or frustrated? Dating also encourages sexual familiarity and experimentation. It isn't difficult to understand why an increasing number of parents feel this traditional model undermines commitment, exclusivity, and permanence in marriage.

The courtship model, by contrast, seeks to postpone emotional and physical entanglements until they occur with the probable husband or wife. The family is very supportive in helping to choose that special individual for a serious courtship when the time is right. Until then, relationships between the sexes are limited to group situations in carefully controlled settings. Physical intimacy for the sake of titillation and experimentation is considered to be most inappropriate. It is the ultimate in "saving oneself" for the man or woman with whom a lifetime will be spent.

Many parents, and undoubtedly the majority of teenagers, would consider the courtship model to be extreme and terribly restrictive. Not every teenager would tolerate it. I believe it is a good idea in those settings where both generations are committed to it and are willing to work together to make it successful. Courtship is not recommended in cases of adolescent rebellion or where there is great resistance to the idea. Whether or not to take this approach, therefore, is a matter for individual families to determine.

Q.268 How do you feel about the changes in the way boys and girls relate to each other? When I was a kid, guys always did the telephoning. My

mother would never have allowed me to call a boy when I was fourteen. Now, girls ask boys for dates and are sometimes very pushy in getting what they want. Does it matter? What should I teach my daughter?

You are right. Relationships between the sexes at all ages have changed radically. Historically, young girls were taught to be reserved—to keep a tight rein on their impulses—especially when it came to matters of the heart. Boys have traditionally been the initiators, and girls were quite content to be the responders. But what we're seeing now is a new sexual aggressiveness among females that has many parents worried. I am one of them.

Some hard-charging girls are so bold that they intimidate the boys they pursue. The male ego is constructed in such a way as to be uncomfortable if in retreat. Even in this day, when the old restrictions and taboos for women have fallen away, I believe it's still appropriate for parents to teach their girls a certain reserve, a certain self-respect, when it comes to romantic relationships. This is especially true during the awkward experiences of early adolescence.

It may be difficult for a girl to cool down a bit, but she'll be more successful and less vulnerable by attracting the object of her affection, rather than trying to run him down. If that is an old-fashioned notion, I still believe in it.

Q269 Do you believe in what is known as "the double standard"? In other words, is it okay for guys to do things that girls can't do?

I emphatically do *not* believe in the double standard. The Scripture makes no distinction between the sexes when it prohibits immoral behavior. It is just as wrong for a boy to engage in premarital sex as it is for a girl to do it. Still, there is a reason why girls have been given a different code of behavior than boys in the past.

The double standard came into being, I would think, because parents understood that girls are more likely to get hurt from premarital sexual encounters. Only females get pregnant, of course, and their complex reproductive system is more vulnerable to venereal diseases and infections. Girls and women also have more to lose emotionally. They often feel wounded and used after casual sex, whereas guys may think of the experience as another trophy to brag about. That is why parents and teachers used to worry more about girls and took steps to guard their virginity. Many still do.

Given these differences between the sexes, the sexual revolution was the biggest joke men ever played on women. By convincing them that the old rules didn't apply, men enticed women to do what men have always wanted women to do. But what a price was paid for the new "freedom." And predictably, women were the ones who got stuck with most of the bill.

Again, the moral significance of sexual promiscuity is the same for both sexes, and sin is devastating to whoever engages in it. Nevertheless, the physical and emotional consequences of immorality are disproportionate. Women are usually the bigger losers.

Q270 I was watching an old black-and-white movie on television the other night that was made in the late 1930s. What jumped out at me was the respectful way the teenagers related to their parents. These kids, who appeared to be seventeen or eighteen years old, were downright deferential and looked to their father to make final decisions regarding their own

behavior. I know this was just fiction, but I got the impression that that's the way families functioned back then. Today, even "good kids" from strong families are often more independent and disrespectful to their parents. If I'm right about this change, why has it occurred and how do you see it?

The movie you saw is characteristic of others made during that era, because children in most nations of the world responded that way to their parents. There were exceptions, of course. Rebellion has occurred throughout history—even in biblical times. Remember that King David's son Amnon raped his half sister Tamar and Absalom tried to overthrow the reign of his father. While some of yesterday's families had to deal with upheavals of this nature, they have typically been the exception rather than the rule. But today, as you indicated, children and young people are taught to be disrespectful and rebellious by the culture. One of the most effective teachers is the rock-music industry and the excesses it embraces.

It is difficult to overestimate the negative impact contemporary music is having. Rock stars are the heroes, the idols, that young people want to emulate. And when they are depicted in violent and sexual roles, many teenagers and preadolescents are pulled along in their wake.

What could possibly be wholesome about showing explicit sex scenes—especially those involving perversion—to twelve- and thirteen-year-old kids? Yet videos come into the home via MTV and other channels that feature men and women in blatantly sexual situations, or even in depictions of sadism.

One study showed that more than half of all MTV videos featured violence or implied violence, and 35 percent revealed violence against women.[96] A steady diet of this garbage will pollute the minds of even the healthiest of teenagers.

I believe that this perpetual and pernicious exposure to rock music is responsible, at least in part, for many of the social problems now occurring among the young, including the high suicide rate, the reported willingness of young men to rape women if given an opportunity, and the moral undermining of the next generation.

Q271 I don't believe kids are as easily influenced as you say. What they see does not necessarily determine how they behave.

Well, look at it this way. Back in the early eighties, the most popular movie was a science-fiction film entitled *E.T. The Extra-Terrestrial*. It included a brief scene where the little creature from outer space was given a few pieces of the candy Reese's Pieces. The brand was not named, but children recognized it during its few seconds on the screen. In the months that followed, the sale of Reese's Pieces went through the ceiling. Isn't that a clear example of a movie's influence on children's thinking?

Why do advertisers spend billions of dollars to put their products before the people if what we see and hear does not influence our behavior? Why do schools and colleges purchase textbooks for children and young adults if what they read does not translate into influence of one form or another? Of course children are vulnerable to what they witness! We all are. How much greater impact is made by dramatic, sexually oriented, no-holds-barred musical and theatrical presentations that are aimed at the hearts and souls of our kids? Whom are we kidding when we say they are not harmed by the worst of it?

Q.272 I remember adults complaining about the music of my day. Doesn't every generation of parents think their kids have gone too far?

Yes, but we're dealing with something especially vile today. As a case in point, you may remember the flap that occurred over the rap group 2 Live Crew and their album *As Nasty As They Wanna Be*. A Florida judge reviewed the filthy lyrics of this album, and, for the first time ever, a piece of "music" was declared to be obscene and illegal.[97]

Predictably, Phil Donahue (shortly before his first show was canceled) and his cronies in the press threw their usual temper tantrums when the news broke. "Censorship!" they cried from the rooftops. Hundreds of newspaper editors and television commentators carried editorials and feature stories about the audacity of the judge who imposed his standard of morality on the rest of us.

Dan Rather, on his show *48 Hours,* made outlandish statements about our loss of freedoms in this era of oppression. And Geraldo Rivera risked getting his nose broken again by bringing 2 Live Crew and their critics face-to-face on his television show.

What the media did not tell the American people, however, was the content of 2 Live Crew's album. They censored that information from the public, choosing instead to talk abstractly about "First-Amendment rights" and "right-wing fundamentalists."

Isn't it interesting that those who were accusing concerned citizens of censorship were themselves editing the truth? Millions of words were spoken about the obscene lyrics to a single album, yet no one would quote them directly. Why not? Because adults would be shocked and outraged by their filth and debauchery. Thus, language that was unfit to print or utter on television was considered perfectly acceptable for the consumption of young minds. That is the logic of Phil, Dan, and Geraldo.

At the risk of upsetting our readers, let me list for you—as discreetly as possible—the words that appeared in the album *As Nasty As They Wanna Be*. They included

- 226 uses of the *f*-word
- 117 explicit terms for male or female genitalia
- 87 descriptions of oral sex
- 163 uses of the word for female dog
- 15 uses of *ho* (slang for *whore*) when referring to women
- 81 uses of the vulgarity *s—t*
- 42 uses of the word *ass*
- 9 descriptions of male ejaculation
- 6 references to erections
- 4 descriptions of group sex
- 3 mentions of rimming (oral-anal sex)
- 2 inclusions of urination or feces
- 1 reference to incest
- over 12 illustrations of violent sex

Please understand that these words did not appear singularly in the album. They were used to describe specific acts and attitudes. Remember, too, that youngsters—some only eight to ten years of age—buying this "music" typically listened to it dozens, or perhaps hundreds, of times.

Descriptions of oral sex and extreme violence against women were thereby memorized and burned into the conscious experience of kids barely out of elementary school. More than two million albums were sold, and with the exception of Florida and a few other locations where it was banned, no restrictions were placed on the album's distribution. A child of any age could purchase it.

This is merely one salvo in an industry that has helped to destroy the moral code of Western civilization. It has been accomplished methodically and deliberately during the past thirty years, in cooperation with television and movie producers. The damage has been incalculable!

I feel like the patriarch Lot, who the Bible says was "vexed with the filthy conversation of the wicked" (2 Peter 2:7, KJV), in Sodom and Gomorrah more than four thousand years ago.

Oh, by the way. The conviction of 2 Live Crew on obscenity charges was overturned by an appeals court.[98] It turns out that the offensive language used in their album is protected by the U.S. Constitution. Imagine what the framers of that document would have thought about that.

Q273 My sister's daughter went off to college at eighteen and immediately went a little crazy. She had always been a good kid, but when she was on her own, she drank like a lush, was sexually promiscuous, and flunked three of her classes. My daughter is only twelve, but I don't want her to make the same mistakes when she is beyond our grasp. How can I get her ready to handle freedom and independence?

Well, you may already be twelve years late in beginning to prepare your daughter for that moment of release. The key is to transfer freedom and responsibility to her little by little from early childhood so she won't need your supervision when she is beyond it. To move suddenly from tight control to utter liberty is an invitation to disaster.

I learned this principle from my own mother, who made a calculated effort to teach me independence and responsibility. After laying a foundation during the younger years, she gave me a "final examination" when I was seventeen years old. Mom and Dad went on a two-week trip and left me at home with the family car and permission to have my buddies stay at the house. Wow! Fourteen slumber parties in a row! I couldn't believe it. We could have torn the place apart—but we didn't. We behaved rather responsibly.

I always wondered why my mother took such a risk, and after I was grown, I asked her about it. She just smiled and said, "I knew in one year you would be leaving for college, where you would have complete freedom with no one watching over you. I wanted to expose you to that independence while you were still under my influence."

I suggest that you let your daughter test the waters of freedom occasionally as she's growing up, rather than tossing her into the big wide ocean all at once. It takes wisdom and tact to pull that off, but it can be done. If you do the job properly, the time of release in six or seven years will be a gentle transition rather than a cataclysmic event.

Q274 My sixteen-year-old daughter is driving me crazy. She is sassy, noisy, and selfish. Her room looks like a pigpen, and she won't work any harder in school than absolutely necessary to get by. Everything I taught her, from manners to faith, seems to have sailed through her ears. What in the world do my husband and I do now?

I'm going to offer you some patented advice that may not make sense or seem responsive to the problem you've described. But stay with me. The most important thing you can do for your daughter is to "just get her through it." The concept is a bit obscure, so let me make an effort to explain it.

Imagine your daughter riding in a small canoe called *Puberty* on the Adolescent River. She soon comes to a turbulent stretch of white water that rocks her little boat violently. There is a very real danger that she will capsize and drown. Even if she survives today's rapids, she will certainly be caught in swirling currents downstream and plunge over the falls. That is the apprehension harbored by millions of parents with kids bouncing along on the wild river. It's the falls that worry them most.

Actually, the typical journey down the river is much safer than believed. Instead of the water becoming more violent downstream, it eventually transitions from frightening rapids to tranquillity once more. What I'm saying is that I believe your daughter is going to be okay even though she is now splashing and thrashing and gasping for air. Her little boat is more buoyant than you might think. Yes, a few individuals do go over the falls, usually because of drug abuse or other addictive behavior. But even some of them climb back in the canoe and paddle on down the river. Most will regain their equilibrium in a few years. In fact, the greatest danger of sinking a boat could come from . . . parents!

Q275 Why do you focus your comments on parents? It's the kids who do crazy things.

I'm particularly concerned about idealistic and perfectionistic moms and dads who are determined to make their adolescent perform and achieve and measure up to the highest standard. In so doing, they rock a boat that is already threatened by the rapids. Perhaps another child could handle the additional turbulence, but the unsteady kid—the one who lacks common sense for a while and may even lean toward irrational behavior—could capsize if you're not careful. Don't unsettle his boat any more than you must!

I'm reminded of a waitress who recognized me when I came into the restaurant where she worked. She was not busy that day and wanted to talk about her twelve-year-old daughter. As a single mother, she had gone through severe struggles with the girl, whom she identified as being very strong willed.

"We have fought tooth and nail for this entire year," she said. "It has been awful! We argue nearly every night, and most of our fights are over the same issue."

I asked her what had caused the conflict, and she replied, "My daughter is still a little girl, but she wants to shave her legs. I feel she's too young to be doing that, and she becomes so angry that she won't even talk to me. This has been the worst year of our lives together."

I looked at the waitress and said, "Lady, buy your daughter a razor!"

That twelve-year-old girl was paddling into a time of life that would rock her canoe good and hard. As a single parent, Mom would soon be trying to keep this rebellious kid from getting into drugs, alcohol, sex and pregnancy, early marriage, school failure, and the possibility of running away. Truly, there would be many ravenous alligators in her river within a year or two. In that setting, it seemed unwise to make a big deal over what was essentially a nonissue. While I agreed with the mother that adolescence should not be ushered in prematurely, there were higher goals than maintaining a proper developmental timetable.

I have seen other parents fight similar battles over nonessentials such as the purchase of a first bra for a flat-chested preadolescent girl. For goodness' sake! If she wants it that badly, she probably needs it for social reasons. Run, don't walk, to the nearest department store, and buy her a bra. The objective, as Charles and Andy Stanley wrote, is to keep your kids on your team.[99] Don't throw away your friendship over behavior that has no great moral significance. There will be plenty of real issues that require you to stand like a rock. Save your big guns for those crucial confrontations.

Let me make it very clear, again, that this advice is not relevant to every teenager. The compliant kid who is doing wonderfully in school, has great friends, is disciplined in his conduct, and loves his parents is not nearly so delicate. Perhaps his parents can urge him to reach even higher standards in his achievements and lifestyle. My concern, however, is for that youngster who could go over the falls. He is intensely angry at home and is being influenced by a carload of crummy friends. Be very careful with him. Pick and choose what is worth fighting for, and settle for something less than perfection on issues that don't really matter. Just get him through it!

Q276 What does this mean in practical terms? Give me some examples of demands that would rock my daughter's boat unnecessarily.

Well, you will have to decide what the nonnegotiables are to you and your husband. Defend those demands, but lighten up on lesser matters. That may indicate a willingness to let her room look like a junkyard for a while. Close the door and pretend not to notice. Does that surprise you? I don't like lazy, sloppy, undisciplined kids any more than you do, but given the possibilities for chaos that this girl might precipitate, spit-shined rooms may not be all that important.

You have to ask yourself this question: "Is the behavior to which I object bad enough to risk turning the canoe upside down?" If the issue is that important, then brace yourself and make your stand. But think through those intractable matters in advance, and plan your defense of them thoroughly.

Someday, when the river has smoothed out again, you may look back with satisfaction that you didn't add to the turbulence when your daughter was bobbing like a cork on a stormy sea.

Q277 I think I understand what you're recommending. You're not suggesting that my husband and I let this kid run wild. Instead, we should choose our battles very carefully and not push her into further rebellion by trying to make her something she can't be right now.

That's it. The philosophy we applied with our teenagers (and you might try with yours) can be called "loosen and tighten." By this I mean we tried to loosen our grip on everything that had no lasting significance and tighten down on everything that did. We said yes whenever we possibly could, to give support to the occasional no. And most important, we tried never to get too far away from our kids emotionally.

It is simply not prudent to write off a son or daughter, no matter how foolish, irritating, selfish, or insane a child may seem to be. You need to be there, not only while their canoe is bouncing precariously, but after the river runs smooth again. You have the remainder of your life to reconstruct the relationship that is now in jeopardy. Don't let anger fester for too long. Make the first move toward reconciliation. And try hard not to hassle your kids. They hate to be nagged. If you follow them around with one complaint after another, they are almost forced to protect themselves by appearing deaf. And finally, continue to treat them with respect, even when punishment or restrictions are necessary.

Then wait for the placid water in the early twenties.

Q.278 Give me your shortest answer to the question: How can I best survive the tumultuous years of my three teenagers?

This is my best shot:

1. Keep the family schedule simple.
2. Get plenty of rest.
3. Eat nutritious meals.
4. Keep your teenager involved in nonstop, wholesome activities.
5. Stay on your knees.

When fatigue and ill health lead adults to act like hot-tempered teenagers, anything can happen at home.

Q.279 Would you speak about the impact of what has been called "the absentee father"—especially during the tougher years of adolescence?

It is stating the obvious, I suppose, to say that fathers are desperately needed at home during the teen years. In their absence, mothers are left to handle disciplinary problems alone. This is occurring in millions of families headed by single mothers today, and heaven only knows how difficult their task has become. Not only are they doing a job that should have been shouldered by two, they must also deal with

behavioral problems that fathers are more ideally
suited to handle. It is generally understood that a
man's larger size, deeper voice, and masculine demeanor make it easier for him to deal with defiance
in the younger generation. Many mothers raise their
teenagers alone and do the job with excellence, but it
is a challenging assignment.

Q280 As a father, what should I be trying to accomplish with my son in these teen years?

Someone has said, "Link a boy to the right man and
he seldom goes wrong." I believe that is true. If a dad
and his son can develop hobbies together or other
common interests, the rebellious years can pass in
relative tranquillity. What they experience may be
remembered for a lifetime.

I recall a song, written by Dan Fogelberg, that
told about a man who shared his love of music with
his elderly father. It is called "Leader of the Band,"
and its message touches something deep within me.
The son talks of a father who "earned his love
through discipline, a thundering, velvet hand." The
father's "song is in my soul." The son himself has become a "living legacy to the leader of the band."[100]

Can't you see this man going to visit his aged father today, with a lifetime of love passing between
them? That must have been what God had in mind
when he gave dads to boys.

Let me address your question directly: What
common ground are you cultivating with your impressionable son? Some fathers build or repair cars
with them; some construct small models or make
things in a woodshop. My dad and I hunted and
fished together. There is no way to describe what
those days meant to me as we entered the woods in

the early hours of the morning. How could I get angry at this man who took time to be with me? We had wonderful talks while coming home from a day of laughter and fun in the country. I tried to maintain that kind of contact with my son.

Opportunities to communicate openly and build the father-son relationship have to be created. It's a goal that's worth whatever it takes to achieve.

Q281 My wife works hard to teach my sons to respect me as their father, and that makes my job with them easier. Even when she is upset with me, she never lets the kids know about it. Don't you think that is generous of her?

She's not only generous—she's a wise woman, too. Mothers can help bond the generations together, or they can drive a wedge between them. This concept was expressed beautifully in a book entitled *Fathers and Sons* by Lewis Yablonsky. The author observed that mothers are the primary interpreters of fathers' personality, character, and integrity to their sons. In other words, the way boys see their fathers is largely a product of the things their mothers have said and the way they feel about their husbands. In Yablonsky's case, his mother destroyed the respect he might have had for his father. This is what he wrote:

> I vividly recall sitting at the dinner table with my two brothers and father and mother and cringing at my mother's attacks on my father. "Look at him," she would say in Yiddish, "his head and shoulders are bent down. He's a failure. He doesn't have the courage to get a better job or make more money. He's a beaten man." He would keep his eyes pointed toward his plate and never answer her. She never extolled

his virtues or persistence or the fact that he worked so hard; instead she constantly focused on the negative and created an image to his three sons of a man without fight, crushed by a world over which he had no control.

His not fighting back against her constant criticism had the effect of confirming its validity to her sons. I have to add that my mother's treatment and depiction of my father did not convey to me that marriage was a happy state of being, or that women were very supportive people. I was not especially motivated to assume the role of husband and father myself from my observations of my whipped father.

My overall research clearly supports the fact that the mother is a basic filter and has enormous significance in the father-son relationship.[101]

Though Yablonsky did not say so, it is also true that a father can do great damage to his wife's relationship with their children. Very early on I found that when I was irritated with Shirley for some reason, my attitude was instantly picked up by our son and daughter. They seemed to feel, *If Dad can argue with Mom, then we can, too.* It became clear to me just how important it was for me to express my love and admiration for Shirley. However, I could never do that job of building respect for my wife as well as she did for me! She made me a king in my own home. If our son and daughter had believed half of what she told them about me, I would have been a fortunate man. The close relationship I enjoy with Danae and Ryan today is largely a product of Shirley's great love for me and the way she "interpreted" me to our kids. I will always be grateful to her for doing that!

Q282 How about a little equal time? Talk about a father's impact on his daughter and what he should hope to accomplish through that relationship.

Fathers have an incalculable impact on their daughters. Most psychologists believe, and I am one of them, that all future romantic relationships are influenced positively or negatively by the way a girl interacts with her dad in the childhood years.

If that is true, then fathers should give careful thought to this responsibility and seek to be what their daughters need of them. There are, I believe, at least seven components to that assignment.

First, a dad's leadership at home should be a model of strength and authority, but always tempered by love and compassion. Harsh discipline tends to close down a sensitive feminine spirit, but permissiveness and capriciousness can create lifelong disdain for men.

Second, a dad must remember that he is being watched closely by that little girl around his knees. The way he treats her mother will teach her volumes about how men and women should relate to one another. Blatant disrespect toward his wife will not be missed by the child.

Third, I think it is good to begin "dating" a daughter when she is six years of age, or even earlier. Dad should let the child help plan their evenings and then see that they occur when and where promised. These times together are not intended simply for fun, although that is important. The father can also use them to show his daughter how a man treats a woman he respects. He can open doors for her, help her with her chair, and listen attentively when she speaks. Later, when she is a teenager, she will know what to expect—or insist on—from the boys she dates.

Fourth, a dad should always look for ways to build

the self-confidence of his little girl. If she believes he thinks she is pretty and "special," she will be inclined to see herself that way. He holds the key to her self-acceptance.

Fifth, a father should keep the lines of communication open throughout childhood so that he is seen as someone to whom his daughter can turn when she needs advice. She will need that counsel before she is grown.

Sixth, God designed men to be the "providers and protectors" of their families. Their daughters should perceive them that way. Dad is often his little girl's "hero," and it is wonderful when that kind of relationship develops.

Seventh, a father must be the spiritual leader of his family, making clear his devotion to Jesus Christ and to the principles in Scripture. He should give the highest priority to bringing up his daughters, and his sons, in the nurture and admonition of the Lord.

It's not an easy responsibility raising girls, is it? But those who do the job properly can rest in the knowledge that they have given their daughters the best chance for a successful marriage, if they choose to wed.

Q283 My teen daughter, Cynthia, and I have incredible fights sometimes. No one has ever gotten to me in quite the way she can. We actually yell at each other when these battles are going on. How unusual is that kind of conflict between mothers and daughters? And is there hope for us?

Unfortunately, it is very common. Many psychologists have described a "thing" that occurs between some mothers and teenage daughters. Even though they love each other, the friction between them can generate a lot of heat. It probably results from a phenomenon that has been called "two women in the kitchen"—a kind of natural competitiveness that occurs between females in the family. It can also be caused by a mother's inability to cope with an extremely difficult and antagonistic kid. Whatever the source, it can make life unpleasant for several years. I know women who would give their lives for their daughters, yet they say, with fire in their eyes, "I don't even *like* her very much right now." That appears to be what you and your teenager are experiencing at this time.

Is there hope for a better relationship in years to come? Yes, I believe you will overcome it. Getting Cynthia through adolescence and into adulthood will change everything. I wouldn't be surprised if she became one of your best friends down the road. So take heart. A better day is coming.

Q.284 What can we do in the meantime? How can I deal with this wildcat who lives under my roof?

Before I answer, tell me what your husband's relationship with Cynthia is.

Q.285 It's very good. She doesn't pull the same stuff on him that she does with me. What are you getting at?

He may hold the key to the tension in your home. Fathers can play a valuable role as peacemakers and mediators at a time like this. They can help you ventilate anger and find acceptable compromises where they are appropriate. Cynthia may listen to her dad. When teenagers are greatly irritated with one parent, they will sometimes seek to draw closer to the other. It's like a nation at war that seeks supportive allies. If fathers are favored in that way, they can calm the troubled waters and keep two women from killing each other. Without this masculine influence, routine skirmishes can turn into World War III.

Q.286 You have recommended that parents be willing to apologize to their kids when they are wrong and to "stay on your child's team" even when it's a losing team. This is difficult for me because my son is in full-blown rebellion at this time. He's using drugs, flunking his classes, and giving us fits at home. Is there a time to forget the nicey-nice stuff and get tough with a teenager?

No doubt about it. There are moments when it is appropriate to apologize, to accommodate, to compromise, and to negotiate. But there comes a time to draw a line in the dirt and say, "Enough is enough!" For youngsters who have tyrannized their families, their parents' willingness to "forgive and forget" repeatedly is interpreted as weakness. Appeasement, as we know, is never successful in pacifying a bully. It only makes him or her more angry and disrespectful.

Behavioral research has now validated that statement. Dr. Henry Harbin and Dr. Denis Madden, working at the University of Maryland's medical school, studied the circumstances that surround violent attacks on parents by teenagers.[102] They found that "parent battering" usually occurs when "one or both parents have abdicated the executive position" and left no one in charge. No one, that is, except the violent child. Rebellious, mean-spirited teenagers respect strength and disdain weakness—especially that borne of love.

Harbin and Madden also observed that "an almost universal element" in the parent-battering cases was the parents' unwillingness to admit the seriousness of the situation. They did not call the police, even when their lives were in danger; they lied to protect the children, and they continued to give in to their demands. Parental authority had collapsed.

One father was almost killed when his angry son pushed him down a flight of stairs. He insisted that the boy did not have a bad temper. Another woman was stabbed by her son, missing her heart by an inch. Nevertheless, she continued letting him live at home.

Drs. Harbin and Madden concluded that appeasement and permissiveness are related to youthful violence and that both parents should lead with firmness. "Someone needs to be in charge," they said.[103]

I agree wholeheartedly with these psychiatrists. Having been appointed by President Ronald Reagan to serve on the National Advisory Commission to the Office of Juvenile Justice and Delinquency Prevention, I am very familiar with the pattern of youthful violence. I've seen cold-blooded killers who were no more than thirteen years of age. Many of them came from homes where authority was weak or nonexistent. It is a formula for cranking out very tough criminals at an early age.

When you are faced with a potentially violent situation at home, you must weigh your options and take decisive action. The organization Tough Love, founded by Phyllis and David York, has been helpful to parents whose backs are to the wall. Tough Love is dedicated to helping out-of-control parents regain the upper hand in their own homes. Their basic philosophy is one of confrontation that is designed to bring a belligerent teenager to his or her senses. You might give them a call. To do nothing is to risk the unthinkable.

Q.287 I read in the paper the other day that a fourteen-year-old boy shot a woman in the face for no reason at all. Things like that are happening all

around us. When I was a kid I wouldn't even have sassed a teacher, much less assaulted one. Today the level of violence among the young is like nothing I've ever seen! What is going on?

You are right; an epidemic of violence is occurring among the young that is expected to actually worsen in the next few years. During a recent meeting of Prison Fellowship workers in our city, a group of hardened former criminals said the kids growing up today scare them because they have no consciences. They can kill without a hint of remorse. It is true.

In Seattle a few years ago, two boys, twelve and thirteen, beat to death a person coming out of a convenience store. There was no motive except a desire to brutalize someone—anyone—with a baseball bat.[104]

In Virginia, a fourteen-year-old shot the driver of a nearby car six times in the face. Why? "Because he looked at me," the boy said.[105]

In 1995 a family made a wrong turn down a street in Los Angeles and was subjected to a hail of gunfire that killed their little girl. Gang members poured bullets into the car for the sheer fun of it.[106]

And finally, who can forget the five-year-old Chicago boy who was pushed from an upper-story window and fell to his death? His killers were ten and eleven years old.[107]

This kind of random violence is more common among children and adolescents today than ever before in our history.

Q288 But why? What has caused many members of the younger generation to be so violent?

Hundreds of millions of dollars have been invested in research to answer that question. The findings are startling. In addition to the violence children have

seen on television and in the movies, and apart from
the drug wars they have witnessed, the tendency toward violence is a function of the neglect and abuse so
many have experienced. That is especially true of
those raised in the inner city. What has been learned is
that millions of children, many of them born to drug-
and alcohol-dependent parents, have been subjected
to unimaginable deprivation. They were left in cribs
for days with dirty diapers burning their buttocks and
legs. Some were hit repeatedly, or they were scalded
or starved. Others simply had no one to love and hold
them when they were frightened. Many were sexually
exploited from their earliest days—some even in infancy. If they survived, they grew up on the streets
with no adult guidance and care. At night, they slept
in bathtubs to avoid bullets sprayed by drive-by shootings.[108] If this description sounds exaggerated, talk to
social workers or police officers who work every day
in the slums of large cities.

What does it do to a child to experience intense
pain, fear, and deprivation at a very early age? The
answers are beginning to come in. What has been
learned is that kids who go through these traumas in
the first year or two of life produce high levels of
stress hormones—notably cortisol and adrenaline.
Those substances put the body in an "alarm reaction
state" in order to cope with the crisis at hand. But in
a small child, the brain is a vacuum cleaner for
stress-related hormones. The human neurological
apparatus is bombarded with chemicals that
shouldn't be there in a child that age. The result is
impairment of the boy or girl's thinking apparatus
and emotional development. Specifically, the "fir-
ing mechanism" of certain portions of the brain is
rendered inoperable.

What I'm saying is that many of today's abused

kids can kill and destroy without pangs of conscience because they are literally brain damaged. They don't feel what you and I feel. They can't empathize with helpless victims the way they should, because the emotion of compassion flows from cognitive functions that no longer operate. Some of them are, at that point, potential killers waiting for the time and place to shoot or stab or bludgeon.

I am not excusing their violent behavior, of course, and society can't afford to tolerate it. But this explains some of the mayhem occurring day after day in inner cities.

The bottom line is this: We are paying a terrible price for the disintegration of the family and for the victimization of children. Any society that doesn't protect the most vulnerable in their midst can expect to suffer at the hands of those abused individuals when they get old enough to strike back.

So lock your doors and avoid eye contact when you drive through certain sections of your city. There are kids there who would just as soon kill you as look at you.

Q289 You stated earlier that you do not favor spanking a teenager. What would you do to encourage the cooperation of my thirteen-year-old, who deliberately makes a nuisance of himself? He throws his clothes around, refuses to help out with any routine tasks in the house, and pesters his little brother incessantly. If I can't spank him, how can I get his attention?

If any approach will succeed in charging his sluggish batteries or motivating him to live within the rules, it will probably involve an incentive-and-disincentive program of some variety. The following three steps might be helpful in initiating such a system:

1. Decide what is important to the youngster for use as a motivator. Two hours with the family car on date night is worth the world to a sixteen-year-old who has just gotten his or her license. (This could be the most expensive incentive in history if the young driver is a bit shaky behind the wheel.) An allowance is another easily available source of inspiration. Teenagers have a great need for cold cash today. A routine date with Helen Highschool might cost twenty dollars or more—in some cases far more. Yet another incentive may involve a fashionable article of clothing that would not ordinarily be within your teen's budget. Offering him or her a means of obtaining such luxuries is a happy alternative to the whining, crying, begging, complaining, and pestering that might occur otherwise. Mom says, "Sure you can have the ski sweater, but you'll have to earn it." Once an acceptable motivator is agreed upon, the second step can be implemented.

2. Formalize the agreement. A contract is an excellent means of settling on a common goal. Once an agreement has been written, it is signed by the parent and teen. The contract may include a point system that enables your teenager to meet the goal in a reasonable time period. If you can't agree on the point values, you could allow for binding arbitration from an outside party. Let's examine a sample agreement in which Marshall wants a compact-disc player, but his birthday is ten months away, and he's flat broke. The cost of the player is approximately $150. His father agrees to buy the device if Marshall earns ten thousand points over the next six to ten weeks doing various tasks. Many of these opportunities are outlined in advance, but the list can be lengthened as other possibilities become apparent:

a) For making bed and straightening
room each morning . . . . 50 points
b) For each hour of studying . . . . . 150 points
c) For each hour of housecleaning
or yard work done . . . . 300 points
d) For being on time to breakfast
and dinner . . . . 40 points
e) For baby-sitting siblings (without
conflict) per hour . . . . 150 points
f) For washing the car each week . . 250 points
g) For arising by 8 A.M. Saturday . . . 100 points

While the principles are almost universally effective, the method of application must be varied. With a little imagination, you can create a list of chores and point values that work in your family. It's important to note that points can be gained for cooperation and lost for resistance. Disagreeable and unreasonable behavior can be penalized fifty points or more. (However, penalties must be imposed fairly and rarely or the entire system will crumble.) Also, bonus points can be awarded for behavior that is particularly commendable.

3. Finally, establish a method to provide immediate rewards. Remember that prompt reinforcement achieves the best results. This is necessary to sustain teens' interest as they move toward the ultimate goal. A thermometer-type chart can be constructed, with the point scale listed down the side. At the top is the ten-thousand-points mark, beside a picture of a compact-disc player or other prize. Each evening, the daily points are totaled and the red portion of the thermometer is extended upward. Steady, short-term progress might earn Marshall a bonus of some sort—perhaps a CD of his favorite musician or a special

privilege. If he changes his mind about what he wishes to buy, the points can be diverted to another purchase. For example, five thousand points is 50 percent of ten thousand and would be worth $75 toward another purchase. However, do not give your child the reward if he does not earn it. That would eliminate future uses of reinforcement. Likewise, do not deny or postpone the goal once it is earned.

This system described above is not set in concrete. It should be adapted to the age and maturity of the adolescent. One youngster would be insulted by an approach that would thrill another. Use your imagination and work out the details with your youngster. This suggestion won't work with every teenager, but some will find it exciting. Lots of luck to you.

Q290 Generally speaking, what kind of discipline do you use with a teenager who is habitually miserable to live with?

The general rule is to use action—not anger—to reach an understanding. Anytime you can get teenagers to do what is necessary without becoming furious at them, you are ahead of the game. Let me provide a few examples of how this might be accomplished.

1. In Russia, I'm told that teenagers who are convicted of using drugs are denied driver's licenses for years. It is a very effective approach.
2. When my daughter was a teenager, she used to slip into my bathroom and steal my razor, my shaving cream, my toothpaste, or my comb. Of course, she never brought them back. Then after she had gone to school, I would discover the uten-

sils missing. There I was with wet hair or "fuzzy" teeth, trying to locate the confiscated items in her bathroom. It was no big deal, but it was irritating at the time. Can you identify?

I asked Danae a dozen times not to do this but to no avail. Thus, the phantom struck without warning one cold morning. I hid everything she needed to "put on her face" and then left for the office. My wife told me she had never heard such wails and moans as were uttered that day. Our daughter plunged desperately through bathroom drawers looking for her toothbrush, comb, and hair dryer. The problem never resurfaced.

3. A family living in a house with a small hot-water tank was continually frustrated by their teenager's endless showers. Screaming at him did no good. Once he was locked behind the bathroom door, he stayed in the steamy stall until the last drop of warm water had been drained. Solution? In midstream, Dad stopped the flow of hot water by turning a valve at the tank. Cold water suddenly poured from the nozzle. Junior popped out of the shower in seconds. Henceforth, he tried to finish bathing before the faucet turned frigid.

4. A single mother couldn't get her daughter out of bed in the morning until she announced a new policy: The hot water would be shut off promptly at 6:30 A.M. The girl could either get up on time or bathe in ice water. Another mother had trouble getting her eight-year-old out of bed each morning. She then began pouring bowls of frozen marbles under the covers with him each morning. They gravitated to wherever his body lay. The boy arose quite quickly.

5. Instead of standing in the parking lot and screaming at students who drive too fast, school officials

now put huge bumps in the road that jar the teeth of those who ignore them. It does the job quite nicely.

6. You as the parent have the car that a teenager needs, the money that he covets, and the authority to grant or withhold privileges. If push comes to shove, these chips can be exchanged for commitments to live responsibly, share the workload at home, and stay off little brother's back. This bargaining process works for younger kids, too. I like the one-to-one trade-off for television-viewing time. It permits a child to watch one minute of television for every minute spent reading.

The possibilities are endless, and they depend not at all on anger, threats, and unpleasantries.

Q.291 Our fourteen-year-old recently came to my husband and me to say, "I'm pregnant." Nothing has ever upset us more than hearing those words. What should our attitude toward her be now?

Responding to a teenage pregnancy is one of the most difficult trials parents are ever asked to face. When the news breaks, it's reasonable to feel anger at the girl who has brought this humiliation and pain into her life. How dare this kid do something so stupid and hurtful to herself and the entire family!

Once you have caught your breath, however, a more rational and loving response is appropriate. This is no time for recrimination. Your daughter needs your understanding and wisdom now more than ever. She'll face many important decisions in the next few months, and you can't afford to alienate yourselves from her. She will also need your spiritual guidance as you point her to the Lord for forgiveness and direction.

If you can summon a measure of strength and love at this stressful time, you should be able to create the bond that often develops between those who have survived a crisis together.

Q292 I am suspicious that my sixteen-year-old son may be using some kind of illegal drugs. He's just not himself lately, and his friends are some of the weirdest guys you ever saw. Can you summarize the most common symptoms of drug abuse for me? What should I look for?

A complete answer to that question would fill a book, because there are so many illegal substances on the market today and each has its own characteristic "fingerprint." But there are eight common physical and emotional symptoms you might look for in your son:

1. Inflammation of the eyelids and nose is common. The pupils of the eyes are either very wide or very small, depending on the kind of drugs internalized.
2. Extremes of energy may be evident. Either the individual is sluggish, gloomy, and withdrawn or he may be loud, hysterical, and jumpy.
3. The appetite is extreme—either very great or very poor. Weight loss may occur.
4. The personality suddenly changes; the individual may become irritable, inattentive, and confused, or aggressive, suspicious, and explosive.
5. Body and breath odor is often bad. Cleanliness is generally ignored.
6. The digestive system may be upset—diarrhea, nausea, and vomiting may occur. Headaches and double vision are also common. Other signs of physical deterioration may include change in skin tone and body stance.

7. Needle marks on the body, usually appearing on the arms, are an important symptom. These punctures sometimes get infected and appear as sores and boils.
8. Moral values often crumble and are replaced by new, avant-garde ideas and values.

Let me caution you that some kids are able to hide their drug use better than others. You might stop by to see the officer in charge of narcotics enforcement for your local police department. He or she may be able to give you more specific information applicable to your son.

Q293 What about snooping through my son's room to see what he might be doing? Do you think parents should do that?

There are definitely times when mothers and fathers need to conduct their own quiet investigation, even though it might invade the privacy of the teenager. This issue was discussed widely in the media some years ago when comedienne Carol Burnett discovered that her teenage daughter was a drug user. When the problem finally came to light, Carol was regretful that she hadn't taken steps to inform herself of what was going on. She appeared on many talk shows to say, in effect, that kids desperately need their parents to "catch them" in a moment like that. Don't let your respect for their privacy cause you to stick your head in the sand and fail to notice what is going on right in front of you.[109] I strongly agree.

Of course, parents have to know their children, too. There are some who would never do anything illegal or harmful. It's just not in them. In those cases, I would not recommend snooping through their room and private stuff. But in situations where a secretive

boy or girl is doing suspicious things, running with
the wrong crowd, and then demanding utter privacy
at home, I would gather whatever information I
needed in order to know how to respond.

Q.294 I heard you say that we have shamefully mismanaged the present generation of children. Explain what you meant by that.

I was referring to the many harmful influences that
previous generations didn't have to confront—at
least not to the degree that we see today. That in-
cludes safe-sex ideology and violence and sexual imagery in movies, rock music, and television; it refers
to gang activity and drug abuse, and many other dangerous aspects of the culture. I was speaking also
about the extreme emphasis on physical attractiveness and body consciousness in Western nations that
is having a terrible impact on children. It can even be
life-threatening to them.

A study done at the University of California
showed that 80 percent of girls in the fourth grade
have attempted to diet because they see themselves
as fat. One elementary school girl justified her dieting by saying she just wanted to be skinny so that no
one would tease her.[110] How sad it is that children in
this culture have been taught to hate their bodies—
to measure their worth by comparison to a standard
that they can never achieve. At a time when they
should be busy being kids, they're worried about
how much they weigh, how they look, and how
they're seen by others.

For young girls this insistence on being thin is
magnified by the cruelties of childhood. Dozens of
studies now show that overweight children are held
in low regard by their peers, even at an early age. According to one investigation, silhouettes of obese

children were described by six-year-olds as "lazy," "stupid," and "ugly."[111]

This overemphasis on beauty does not occur in a vacuum, of course. Our children have caught our prejudices and our system of values. We, too, measure human worth largely on a scale of physical attractiveness. It's bad enough when adults evaluate each other that way. It's tragic when millions of children have already concluded that they're hopelessly flawed, even before life has gotten started.

We must take the blame for the many pressures on today's kids. Fifty years ago, parents and other adults acted in concert to protect kids—from pornography, from sexual abuse, from harmful ideas, and from dangerous substances. Millions of husbands and wives stayed together "for the benefit of the children." It was understood that tender minds and bodies needed to be shielded from that which could hurt them. But now, child abuse, date rape, and sexually transmitted disease are rampant. As the family unravels and as adults become more self-centered and preoccupied, children are often left to fend for themselves in a very dangerous world. It may be our greatest failing as a people.

Q295 I'm convinced that mothers of preschoolers should stay home with them if finances and temperaments permit. But what about after they are off to school? Do you feel it is still important to have Mom at home, we'll say, in the teen years?

Many will not agree with my opinion on that subject, but it is borne of experience with thousands of families. All things being equal, I believe Mom is still needed at home as the kids grow. Why? Because the heavy demands of child rearing do not slacken with the passage of time. In reality, the teen years generate as much pressure on the parents as any other era. An adolescent turns a house upside down—literally and figuratively. Not only is the typical rebellion of those years a stressful experience, but the chauffeuring, supervising, cooking, and cleaning required to support a teenager can be exhausting. Someone within the family must reserve the time and energy to cope with those new challenges. Mom is the candidate of choice. Remember, too, that menopause and a man's midlife crisis are scheduled to coincide with adolescence, which can make a wicked soup! It is a wise mother who doesn't exhaust herself at a time when so much is going on at home.

Let me illustrate why moms are needed at home during the teen years. A good military general will never commit all his troops to combat at the same time. He maintains a reserve army that can relieve the exhausted soldiers when they falter on the front lines. I wish parents of adolescents would implement the same strategy. Instead, they commit every moment of their time to the business of living, holding nothing back for the challenge of the century. It is a classic mistake that can be even more difficult for parents of strong-willed adolescents.

This is my point: A woman in this situation has thrown all her troops into frontline combat. There is no reserve on which to call. In that fatigued condition, the routine stresses of raising an adolescent can be overwhelming. Let me say it again. Raising boisterous teenagers is an exciting and rewarding experience but also a frustrating one at times. Their radical highs and lows affect our moods. The noise, the messes, the complaints, the arguments, the sibling rivalry, the missed curfews, the paced floors, the wrecked car, the failed test, the jilted lover, the wrong friends, the busy telephone, the pizza on the carpet, the ripped new blouse, the rebellion, the slammed doors, the mean words, the tears—it enough to drive a rested mother crazy. But what about our career woman who already "gave at the office," then came home to this chaos? Any unexpected crisis or even a minor irritant can set off a torrent of emotion. There is no reserve on which to draw. In short, the parents of adolescents should save some energy with which to cope with aggravation!

Whether or not you agree with my advice at this point is your business. It is my responsibility simply to offer it. Generally speaking, the working mother has a challenging task before her. Admittedly, many women are able to maintain a busy career and keep the home fires burning, some with the assistance of involved husbands or domestic help. Other low-energy mothers with unhelpful husbands don't cope so well. Each family must decide for itself how best to deal with life's pressure points and opportunities.

16

BUILDING SELF-CONFIDENCE
IN CHILDREN AND TEENS

Q.296 You have said that children and young people are experiencing an epidemic of self-doubt and feelings of low self-esteem. Why do you think this is true?

It has resulted, in part, from an unjust system of evaluating human worth now prevalent in our society. Not everyone is seen as worthy; not everyone is accepted. Instead, we reserve our praise and admiration for those who have been blessed from birth with the characteristics we value most highly. It is a vicious system, and we, as parents, must counterbalance its impact.

At the top of the list of the most highly respected and valued attributes in our culture is physical attractiveness. Those who happen to have it are often honored and even feared; those who do not may be disrespected and rejected through no fault of their own. This measure of human worth is evident from the earliest moments of life, when an attractive infant is considered more valuable than a homely one. For this reason, it is not uncommon for a mother to be depressed shortly after the birth of her first baby. She had hoped to give birth to a beautiful six-week-old Gerber baby, having four front teeth and rosy, pink cheeks. Instead, they hand her a red, toothless, bald, prune-faced, screaming little individual who isn't exactly what Mom expected.

As the child grows, his or her value as a person will be assessed not only by parents but also by those outside the home. Beauty contests offering scholarships and prizes for gorgeous babies are now common, as if the attractive child didn't already have enough advantages in life. What a distorted system for evaluating human worth. As author George Orwell has written, "All [people] are equal, but some [people] are more equal than others."[112] The real tragedy today is how often this statement is proven true in the lives of our children.

Q297 What are the prospects for the very pretty or handsome child? Does he or she usually have smooth sailing all the way?

Well, that child has some remarkable advantages, as I have described. She is much more likely to accept herself and enjoy the benefits of self-confidence. However, she also faces some unique problems that the homely child never experiences. Beauty in our society is power, and power can be dangerous in immature hands. A fourteen-year-old young woman, for example, who is prematurely curved and rounded in all the right places may be pursued vigorously by males who would exploit her beauty. As she becomes more conscious of her flirtatious power, she is sometimes urged toward promiscuity. Furthermore, women who have been coveted physically since early childhood often become bitter and disillusioned as they age. I'm thinking particularly of Hollywood's most glamorous sex queens, such as Marilyn Monroe and Brigitte Bardot, who had difficulty dealing with the depersonalization of body worship as the years passed.

Research also indicates some interesting consequences in regard to marital stability for the "beautiful people." In one important study, the more attractive college girls were found to be less happily married twenty-five years later.[113] It is apparently difficult to reserve the "power" of sex for one mate, ignoring the ego gratification that awaits outside the marriage bonds. And finally, the more attractive a person is in his or her youth, the more painful is the aging process.

My point is this: The measurement of worth on a scale of beauty is wrong, often damaging to the haves and have-nots.

Q.298 If beauty is the most important attribute in determining personal worth in this culture, what is in second place?

It is intelligence as expressed in scholastic aptitude. When the birth of a firstborn child is imminent, his parents pray that he will be normal . . . that is, "average." But from that moment on, average will not be good enough. Their child must excel. He must succeed. He must triumph. He must be the first of his age to walk or talk or ride a tricycle. He must earn a stunning report card and amaze his teachers with his wit and wisdom. He must do well in Little League, and later he must be a track star or first-chair trombone player or the valedictorian. His sister must be a cheerleader or the senior-class president or the soloist or the best pupil in her advanced-placement class.

Throughout the formative years of childhood, parents give their kids the same message day after day: "We're counting on you to do something fantastic. Now don't disappoint us!" The hopes, dreams, and ambitions of an entire family sometimes rest on the shoulders of an immature child. And in this atmosphere of fierce competition, the parent who produces an intellectually gifted child is clearly holding the winning sweepstakes ticket.

Unfortunately, exceptional children are just that—exceptions. Seldom does a five-year-old memorize the King James Version of the Bible or play chess blindfolded or compose symphonies in the Mozart manner. To the contrary, the vast majority of our children are not dazzlingly brilliant, extremely witty, highly coordinated, tremendously talented, or universally popular! They are just plain kids with oversized needs to be loved and accepted as they are. Thus, the stage is set for unrealistic pressure on the younger generation and considerable disappointment for their parents.

Q299 I made a little offhanded comment the other day about my daughter's hair, and she cried for an hour. I didn't mean to hurt her. I guess she's just more sensitive than I thought. Do I have to walk on eggshells around her?

You should always be mindful that your daughter is listening to what you say about her and that she's "reading" the subtle attitudes that you might like to conceal. Kids are extremely sensitive to their parents' love and respect. That's why adults must learn to guard what they say in their presence. Many times I have been consulted by a mother regarding a particular problem her child is having. As Mom describes the details of the boy or girl's problems, I notice that the subject of all this conversation is standing about a yard behind her. His ears are ten feet tall as he listens to a candid description of all his faults. The child may remember that conversation for a lifetime.

Parents often inadvertently convey disrespect to a child whom they genuinely love. For example, Mom may become tense and nervous when little Jimmy speaks to guests or outsiders. She butts in to explain what he is trying to say or laughs nervously when his remarks sound foolish. When someone asks him a direct question, she interrupts and answers for him. She reveals her frustration when she is trying to comb her daughter's hair or make her "look nice" for an important event. The daughter knows Mom thinks it is an impossible assignment. If the daughter is to spend a weekend away from the family, the mother gives her an extended lecture on how to avoid making a fool of herself. These subtle behaviors are signals to the child that the mother doesn't trust him or her with her image and that he or she must be supervised closely to avoid embarrassing the whole family. He or she reads disrespect in her manner, though it is framed in genuine love.

The first step in building a strong self-concept in your daughter is to be very careful what you say and do in her presence. Be particularly cautious about the matters of physical attractiveness and intelligence. These are two primary "soft spots" where boys and girls are most vulnerable.

Q300 How can parents prepare their younger children for the assault on self-esteem that is almost certain to come in adolescence? That was a tough time for me, and I want it to be easier for my kids.

Well, one important approach is to teach boys and girls valuable skills with which they can compensate in years to come. They can benefit from learning something that will serve as the centerpiece of their self-concept during the difficult years. This would include learning about basketball, tennis, electronics, art, music, or even raising rabbits for fun and profit. It's not so much what you teach your child.

The key is that he or she learns something with which to feel good when the whole world seems to be saying, "Who are you and what is your significance as a human being?"

The teenager who has no answer to those questions is left unprotected at a very vulnerable time of life. Developing and honing skills with which to compensate may be one of the most valuable contributions parents can make during the elementary school years. It may even be worth requiring your carefree kid to take lessons, practice, compete, and learn something he or she will not fully appreciate for a few more years.

Q301 You make a convincing case that beauty and brains are false values that demoralize kids who don't think they measure up. But what values do you suggest that I teach to my children?

I believe the most valuable contribution a parent can make to his child is to instill in him or her a genuine faith in Jesus Christ. What greater sense of self-worth could there be than knowing that the Creator of the universe is acquainted with me personally? That He values me more than the possessions of the entire world; that He understands my fears and my anxieties; that He reaches out to me in immeasurable love when no one else cares; that He actually gave His life for me; that He can turn my liabilities into assets and my emptiness into fullness; that a better life follows this one, where the present handicaps and inadequacies will all be eliminated—where earthly pain and suffering will be no more than a dim memory! What a beautiful philosophy with which to "clothe" your tender child. What a fantastic message of hope and encouragement for the broken teenager who has been crushed by life's circumstances. This is true self-worth at its richest, dependent not on the whims of birth or social judgment or the cult of the superchild but on divine decree.

Q302 My two kids are as different as night and day. You'd never even know they were born to the same parents. One of them is having trouble in school, and the other is something of a superstar. I'm very worried about the one boy. Do some kids start out doing poorly and then catch fire?

Thank goodness they often do. Let me give you an encouraging illustration. Several years ago I attended a wedding ceremony in a beautiful garden setting, and I came away with some thoughts about parents who are raising a child like yours.

After the minister had instructed the groom to kiss the bride on that day, approximately 150 colorful, helium-filled balloons were released into the blue California sky. Within a few seconds the balloons were just scattered all across the heavens, some of them rising hundreds of feet overhead and others cruising toward the horizon. A few balloons struggled to clear the upper branches of the trees while the show-offs became mere pinpoints of color on their journey to the sky.

How interesting, I thought, and how symbolic of children. Let's face it. Some boys and girls seem to be born with more helium than others. They catch all the right breezes, and they soar effortlessly to the heights, while others wobble dangerously close to the trees. Their frantic folks run along underneath, huffing and puffing to keep them airborne. It is an exhausting experience.

In short, I have a word of encouragement to you and all the parents of low-flying kids. Sometimes the child who has the greatest trouble getting off the ground eventually soars to the highest heights. That's why I urge you as parents not to look too quickly for the person your child will become.

Q303 Our fifteen-year-old daughter is getting some rough treatment at the hands of her peers these days. She wasn't invited to a party given by a girl who had been her best friend, and she cried herself to sleep that night. It's just tearing me up to see her hurt like this. Will this experience leave lifelong scars on her mind?

It's all a matter of degree. Most teenagers experience a measure of rejection like your daughter is experiencing. They typically roll with the punches and eventually get beyond the discomfort. Others, however, are wounded for life by the rejection of those adolescent experiences. I suggest you give your daughter plenty of emotional support, keep her talking, and do what you can to help her cope. I think she'll get her legs under her when the pressure of these years has passed.

Let me address the larger issue here. When we see our children struggling with the teen experience or other frustrations, it's natural to wish we could sweep aside the problems and obstacles. Sometimes we have to be reminded that the human personality grows through adversity. "No pain, no gain," as they say. Those who have conquered their problems are more secure than those who have never faced them.

I learned the value of hard times from my own experience. During my seventh and eighth grades, I lived through the most painful years of my life. I found myself in a social cross fire that gave rise to intense feelings of inferiority and doubt. And yet those two years have contributed more positive qualities to my adult personality than any other span of my life. What I learned through that experience is still useful to me today.

Though it may be hard to accept now, your child needs the minor setbacks and disappointments that come her way. How can she learn to cope with problems and frustrations if her early experiences are totally without trial? Nature tells us this is true. A tree that's planted in a rain forest is never forced to extend its roots downward in search of water. Consequently, it remains poorly anchored and can be toppled by even a moderate wind. By contrast, a mesquite tree that's planted in a dry desert is threatened by its hostile environment. It can only survive by sending its roots down thirty feet or more into the earth, seeking cool water. But through this adaptation to an arid land, the well-rooted tree becomes strong and steady against all assailants.

Our children are like the two trees in some ways. Those who have learned to conquer their problems are better anchored than those who have never faced them.

Our task as parents, then, is not to eliminate every challenge for our children but to serve as a confident ally on their behalf, encouraging them when they are distressed, intervening when the threats are overwhelming, and above all, giving them the tools they need to overcome the obstacles.

Q304 I've read that you have recommended that parents not give little girls Barbie dolls. They seem harmless to me. Why do you oppose them?

First I should tell you that my daughter played with Barbie for years, despite my views on this subject.[114] My objection was more passive and philosophical than absolute. Nevertheless, let me tell you why I wish Barbie would go away. There could be no better method for teaching the worship of beauty and materialism than is done with these dolls. If we intentionally sought to drill our little girls on the necessity of growing up rich and gorgeous, we could do no better than has already been done. Did you ever see an ugly Barbie doll? Has she ever had even the slightest imperfection? Of course not! She oozes femininity and sex appeal. Her hair is thick and gleaming—loaded with "body" (whatever in the world that is). Her long, thin legs, curvaceous bust, and delicate feet are absolutely perfect. Her airbrushed skin is without flaw or blemish (except for a little statement on her bottom that she was "Made in Hong Kong"). She never gets pimples or blackheads, and there is not an ounce of fat on her body. Such an idealized model creates an emotional time bomb set to explode the moment a real live thirteen-year-old takes her first long look in the mirror. No doubt about it—Barbie she ain't!

Yet it is not the physical perfection of these Barbie dolls (and their many competitors) that concerns me most; of much greater harm are the teenage games that they inspire. Instead of three- and four-year-old boys and girls playing with stuffed animals, balls, cars, trucks, model horses, and the traditional memorabilia of childhood, they are learning to fantasize about life as an adolescent. Ken and Barbie go on dates, learn to dance, drive sports cars, get suntans, take camping trips, exchange marriage vows, and have babies (hopefully in that order). The entire adolescent culture, with its emphasis on sexual awareness, is illustrated to tiny little girls who ought to be thinking about more childish things. This places our children on an unnatural timetable likely to reach the peak of sexual interest several years before it is due—with all the obvious implications for their social and emotional health.

Q305 Barbie isn't the only example of this adolescent influence in our culture, is it?

No, our children are saturated with commercial stuff that has the same impact. More and more, we see adolescent clothes, attitudes, and values being marketed to younger and younger children. And rock and rap music, with adolescent and adult themes, is finding eager listeners among the very young.

I believe it is desirable to postpone the adolescent experience until it is summoned by the happy hormones. Therefore, I strongly recommend that parents screen the influences to which their children are exposed, keeping activities appropriate for each age. While we can't isolate our kids from the world as it is, we don't have to turn our babies into teenyboppers.

Q306 Does the middle child really have greater adaptive problems than his or her siblings?

The middle child does sometimes find it more difficult to establish his or her identity within the family. She enjoys neither the status of the eldest nor the attention given to the baby. Furthermore, she is likely to be born at a busy period in the life of her parents, especially her mother. Then, during her preschool years, her precious territory is invaded by a cute little newborn who steals Mama from her. Is it any wonder that she often asks, "Who am I, and where is my place in life?"

Q307 What can I do to help my middle child figure out who she is?

Parents should take steps to ensure the identity of *all* their children but especially the child in the middle. That can be accomplished by relating to each boy or girl as an individual, rather than merely as a member of the group. Let me offer two suggestions that will illustrate what I mean.

1. It is meaningful for Dad to "date" each child, one at a time, every four or five weeks. The other kids should not be told where they are going until it is revealed by the boy or girl in retrospect. They can play miniature golf, go bowling, play basketball, eat tacos or pizza, or visit a skating rink. The choice should be made by the child whose turn has arrived.

2. Ask each offspring to design his or her own flag, which can be sewn in canvas or cloth. That flag is then flown in the front yard on the child's "special" days, including birthdays, after he has received an A in school, when he scores a goal in soccer or hits a home run in baseball, and so forth.

There are other ways to accomplish the same purpose. The target, again, is to plan activities that emphasize one child's individuality apart from his identity within the group.

Q308 My son is an outstanding gymnast. His high school coach says he has more natural ability than anyone he's ever seen. Yet when he is being judged in a competitive meet, he does terribly! Why does he fail during the most important moments?

If your son thinks of himself as a failure, his performance will probably match his low self-image when the chips are down. In the same way, there are many excellent golfers on the PGA tour who make a satisfactory living in tournament play, but they never win. They may even place as high as second, third, sixth, or tenth. Whenever it looks like they might come in first, however, they "choke" at the last minute, and someone else wins. It is not that they want to fail; rather, they can't conceive of themselves as winners, and their performance merely reflects this image.

I once spoke with a concert pianist with outstanding talent who has resolved never to play in public again. She knows she is blessed with remarkable talent but believes she is a loser in every other regard. Consequently, when she plays the piano on stage, her mistakes and errors creep into her performance. Each time this mortifying experience has occurred, she has become more convinced of her own unworthiness in every area. She has now withdrawn into the secluded, quiet, talentless world of have-nots.

A person's self-concept is instrumental in determining those who are "winners" and those who see themselves as "losers." Professional tennis players call this characteristic "tournament toughness," but it is really nothing more than confidence in action.

Q309 Is this true of mental ability, too? My twelve-year-old was asked to recite a poem at a school function the other day, and he went completely blank in front of the crowd. I know he knew the poem perfectly because he said it dozens of times at home. He's a bright child, but he's had this trouble before. Why does his mind "turn off" when he's under pressure?

It will be helpful to understand an important characteristic of intellectual functioning. Your son's self-confidence, or the lack of it, actually affects the way his brain operates. All of us have experienced the frustration of mental "blocking," which you described. This occurs when a name or fact or idea just won't surface to the conscious mind, even though we know it is recorded in the memory. Or suppose we are about to speak to an antagonistic group and our mind suddenly goes blank. This kind of blocking usually occurs (1) when social pressure is great, and (2) when self-confidence is low. Why? Because emotions affect the efficiency of the human brain. Unlike a computer, our mental apparatus only functions properly when a delicate biochemical balance exists between the neural cells. This substance makes it possible for a cell to "fire" its electrochemical charge across the gap (synapse) to another cell. It is now known that a sudden emotional reaction can instantly change the nature of that biochemistry, interfering with the impulse. This blockage prevents the electrical charge from being relayed, and the thought is never generated. This mechanism has profound implications for human behavior; for example, a child who feels inferior and intellectually inadequate often does not even make use of the mental power with which he has been endowed. His lack of confidence produces a disrupting mental inefficiency, and the two factors go around in an endless cycle of defeat. This is seemingly what happened to your son when he "forgot" the poem.

Q310 What can I do to help him?

Actually, it is not unusual for a twelve-year-old to "choke" in front of a crowd. I once stood before three hundred fellow teenagers with my words stuck in my throat and my mind totally out to lunch. It was a painful experience, but time gradually erased its impact. As your child matures, he will probably overcome the problem if he can experience a few successes to build his confidence. Anything that raises self-esteem will reduce the frequency of mental blocking for children and adults alike.

Q311 As an elementary school teacher, I am bothered by what I see my students doing to each other every day. They can be brutal—especially to the child who is a little different. I'm not sure what my role should be. I feel I should step in to defend the underdog, but other teachers say kids should learn to work out their own problems. What do you think?

As a former teacher, I am very familiar with the cruelty

of which you speak. Every classroom has a few boys and girls at the bottom of the social hierarchy who are subjected to frequent ridicule. Their ranks include those who are physically unattractive, intellectually challenged, uncoordinated, boys who are very small or effeminate, girls who are taller than all the boys, the foreign child, the stutterer, etc. Anyone who is different is an easy mark for the wolf pack. What is most disturbing is that adults often feel no obligation to come to the aid of these vulnerable children.

I've heard the argument that says, "Kids will be kids—adults should stay out of the conflict and let the children settle it themselves." I disagree emphatically. It is almost criminal for an adult to stand by passively while a defenseless boy or girl is shredded by peers. The damage inflicted in those moments can reverberate for a lifetime.

Some years ago a woman told me about her experience as a room mother for her daughter's fourth-grade class. She visited the classroom on Valentine's Day to assist the teacher with the traditional party on that holiday. Valentine's Day can be the most painful day of the year for an unpopular child. Every student counts the number of valentines he or she is given, which becomes a direct measure of social worth.

This mother said the teacher then announced that the class was going to play a game that required the formation of boy-girl teams. That was her first mistake, since fourth graders have not yet experienced the happy hormones that draw the sexes together. The moment the teacher instructed the students to select a partner, all the boys immediately laughed and pointed at the homeliest and least-respected girl in the room. She was overweight, had protruding teeth, and was too withdrawn even to look anyone in the eye.

"Don't put us with Nancy," they all said in mock

terror. "Anybody but Nancy! She'll give us a disease! Ugh! Spare us from Nasty Nancy." The mother waited for the teacher (a strong disciplinarian) to rush to the aid of the beleaguered little girl. But nothing was said to the insulting boys. Instead, the teacher left Nancy to cope with that painful situation in solitude.

Ridicule by one's own sex is distressing, but rejection by the opposite sex is like taking a hatchet to the self-concept. What could this devastated child say in reply? How does an overweight fourth-grade girl defend herself against nine aggressive boys? What response could she make but to blush in mortification and slide foolishly into her chair? This child, whom God loves more than the possessions of the entire world, will never forget that moment (or the teacher who abandoned her in this time of need).

I say again to teachers: Defend the most defenseless child in your classroom. We can do no less.

Q312 What would you have done if you had been the teacher on that day?

Those mocking, joking boys would have had a fight on their hands, I promise you that. Of course, it would have been better if the embarrassment could have been prevented by discussing the feelings of others from the first day of school. But if the conflict occurred as described, with Nancy's suddenly being humiliated for everyone to see, I would have thrown the full weight of my authority and respect on her side of the battle.

My spontaneous response would have carried this general theme: "Wait just a minute! By what right do any of you boys say such mean, unkind things to Nancy? I want to know which of you is so perfect that the rest of us couldn't make fun of you in some way. I know you all very well. I know about your homes and your school records and some of your personal secrets. Would you like me to share them with the class, so we can all laugh at you the way you just did at Nancy? I could do it! I could make you want to crawl into a hole and disappear. But listen to me! You need not fear. I will never embarrass you in that way. Why not? Because it hurts to be laughed at by your friends. It hurts even more than a stubbed toe or a cut finger or a bee sting.

"I want to ask those of you who were having such a good time a few minutes ago: Have you ever had a group of students make fun of you in the same way? If you haven't, then brace yourself. Someday it will happen to you, too. Eventually you will say something foolish—something that will cause everyone to point at you and laugh in your face. And when it happens, I want you to remember what happened today."

Then addressing the entire class: "Let's make sure that we learn something important from what took place here this afternoon. First, we will *not* be mean to each other in this class. We will laugh together when things are funny, but we will not do it by making one person feel bad. Second, I will never intentionally embarrass anyone in this class. You can count on that. Each of you is a child of God. You were made with His loving hands, and He has said that we all have equal worth as human beings. This means that Susie is neither better nor worse than Wade or Mary or Brent. Sometimes I think maybe you believe a few of you are more important than others. It isn't true. Every one of you is priceless to God, and each of you will live forever in eternity. That's how valuable you are. God loves every boy and girl in this room, and because of that, I love every one of you. He wants us to be kind to other people, and we're going to be practicing that kindness through the rest of this year."

When a strong, loving teacher comes to the aid of the least-respected child in the class, as I've described, something dramatic occurs in the emotional climate of the room. Every child seems to utter an audible sigh of relief. The same thought is bouncing around in many little heads: "If Nancy is safe from ridicule—even Nancy—then I must be safe too." You see, by defending the least-popular child in the room, a teacher is demonstrating (1) that she has no "pets," (2) that she respects everyone, (3) that she will fight for anyone who is being treated unjustly. Those are three virtues that children value highly and that contribute to mental health.

And may I suggest to parents: Defend the underdog in your neighborhood. Let it be known that you have the confidence to speak for the outcast. Explain this philosophy to your neighbors, and try to create an emotional harbor for the little children whose ship has been threatened by a storm of rejection. Don't be afraid to exercise leadership on behalf of a youngster who is being mauled. There is no more worthy investment of your time and energy.

Q313 Can boys and girls be taught to treat each other with respect? That seems like a tough assignment.

They certainly can! Young people are naturally more sensitive and empathetic than adults. Their viciousness is a learned response, resulting from the highly competitive and hostile world in which they live—a world we have allowed to develop. They are destructive to the weak and lowly because we adults haven't bothered to teach them to feel for one another.

One of the values children cherish most is justice. They are uneasy in a world of injustice and abuse. Therefore, when we teach children respect for others by insisting on civility in our classrooms, we're laying a foundation for human kindness in the world of adulthood to come. It is a fundamental attitude that should be taught in every classroom and every home.

Q314 Before our baby was born last month, our three-year-old daughter, April, was thrilled about having a new brother or sister. Now, however, she shows signs of jealousy, sucking her thumb sullenly when I nurse the baby and getting very loud and silly when friends drop by. Please suggest some ways I can ease her through this period of adjustment.

Your daughter is revealing a textbook reaction to the invasion that has occurred in her private kingdom. It is typical for such a preschooler to throw temper tantrums, wet the bed, suck her thumb, mess her pants, hold tightly to Mama, talk "baby talk," etc. Since the baby gets all the attention by being helpless, the older child will often try to "out-baby the baby"— behaving in immature ways from an earlier stage of development. That pattern seems to be occurring with your little girl. Here's what I would suggest:

1. Bring her feelings out in the open and help her verbalize them. When she is acting silly in front of adults, take her in your arms and say, "What's the matter, April? Do you need some attention today?" Gradually, a child can be taught to use similar words when she feels excluded or rejected. "I need some attention, Dad. Will you play with me?" By verbalizing her feelings, you also help her understand herself better.

2. Don't let infantile behavior succeed. If she cries when the baby-sitter arrives, leave her anyway. A temper tantrum can be greeted by firmness. However, reveal little anger and displeasure, re-

membering that the entire episode is motivated
by a threat to your love.

3. Meet her needs in ways that grant status to her for
being older. Take her to the park, making it clear
that the baby is too little to go; talk "up" to her
about the things she can do that the baby can't—
she can use the bathroom instead of her pants, for
example. Let her help take care of the baby so she
will feel she is part of the family process.

Beyond these corrective steps, give your daughter
some time to adjust to her new situation. Even
though it stresses her somewhat today, she should
profit from the realization that she does not sit at the
center of the universe.

Q315 My thirteen-year-old daughter is still built
like a boy, but she is insisting that I buy her a
bra. Believe me, she has no need for it, and the only reason
she wants one is because most of her friends do. Should I
give in?

Your straight-and-narrow daughter needs a bra to be
like her friends, to compete, to avoid ridicule, and to
feel like a woman. Those are excellent reasons. I
think you should buy her a bra today.

Q316 Our teenage daughter has become extremely
modest in recent months, demanding that
even her sisters leave her room when she's dressing. I
think this is silly, don't you?

No, I would suggest that you honor her requests for
privacy. Her sensitivity is probably caused by an
awareness that her body is changing, and she is embarrassed by recent developments (or the lack of
them). This is likely to be a temporary phase, and
you should not oppose her in it.

Q317 Just how much opportunity do parents have to remake the personalities of their children? Can they change characteristics that they dislike? My son is painfully shy, and I'd like him to be strong and assertive. Can we redesign him?

You can teach new attitudes and modify some behavioral patterns, but you will not be able to redesign the basic personality with which your child was born. Some characteristics are genetically programmed, and they will always be there. For example, some kids appear to be born to lead, and others seem to be made to follow. And that fact can be a cause of concern for parents at times.

One mother told me that her compliant, easygoing child was being picked on and beaten up every day in nursery school. She urged him to defend himself, but it contradicted his very nature to even think about standing up to the bullies. Finally, his frustration became so great that he decided to heed his mother's advice. As they drove to school one day he said, "Mom, if those kids pick on me again today . . . I'm . . . I'm . . . I'm going to beat them up—slightly!"

How does a kid beat up someone slightly? I don't know, but it made perfect sense to this compliant lad.

Like you, some parents worry about an easygoing, passive child—especially if he's a boy. Followers in this society are sometimes less respected than aggressive leaders and may be seen as wimpy or spineless. And yet, the beauty of the human personality is seen in its marvelous uniqueness and complexity. There is a place for the wonderful variety of temperaments that find expression in children. After all, if two people are identical in every regard, it's obvious that one of them is unnecessary.

My advice to you is to accept, appreciate, and cultivate the personality with which your little child is born. He does not need to fit a preconceived mold. That youngster is, thankfully, one of a kind.

Q318 We have always laughed a lot in our family, sometimes at each other. Is that good or bad?

It is healthy to be able to laugh together in a family. We ought to be able to tease and joke with each other without having to worry about getting an angry overreaction in response. But when the laughter is always at the expense of the most vulnerable member of the family, it can be destructive.

Even innocent humor is painful when it's the same child who is the object of ridicule. Unfortunately, that's the way it often happens. When one youngster has an embarrassing characteristic, such as bed-wetting or thumb-sucking or stuttering, the other members of the family should be encouraged to tread very softly on the exposed nerves thereabouts. And a child should never be ridiculed for his or her size, whether he's a small boy or a large girl.

This is the guiding principle: It's wise not to tease a child about the features that he or she is also defending outside the home. If that youngster is hearing about some obvious flaw all day long, he or she certainly doesn't need more flak from the family. And when that child asks for a joke to end, the request should be honored.

Being the butt of everyone's ridicule is a formula for lifelong resentment, and there's just nothing funny about that happening.

17

THE DELICATE ART
OF LETTING GO

Q319 We hear so much about mothers being depressed and unable to accept the empty nest when the kids leave home. In our family, however, it was Dad who took it hard. He went into a tailspin for more than a month. Is this unusual?

No, it happens very commonly. In a recent study, 189 parents of college freshmen were asked to report their feelings when their son or daughter left home. Surprisingly, the fathers took it harder than the mothers.[115]

That resistance to the empty nest was the theme of the movie *Father of the Bride,* which was a hilarious and touching tribute to the love of a father for his daughter. When George, the dad, sat across from his daughter at the dinner table and learned that she was engaged, he took the news hard. He couldn't believe what he was hearing. He had to clear his vision when he saw his daughter as a baby girl, and then as a ten-year-old tomboy, and finally as a beautiful young woman of eighteen. His little girl had grown up so quickly, and now she was leaving home. He would never again be the main man in the life of his precious daughter, and there was grieving to be done.

Why do men sometimes take the empty nest so

hard? One of the chief explanations is regret. They have been so busy—working so hard—that they let the years slip by almost unnoticed. Then suddenly they realize it is too late to build a relationship with the child who is leaving home forever.

For those of you who still have children or teenagers at home, take a moment regularly to enjoy your remaining time together. Those days will be gone in the blink of an eye.

Q320 Why do you think so many parents are reluctant to let their kids go after they are grown?

One reason is that parents fear their children aren't ready to stand on their own, and they worry about what will happen to them. They want to protect them as long as they can. But more important, they hate to see childhood come to an end. I'm convinced that mothers and fathers in North America are among the very best in the world. We care passionately about our kids and would do anything to meet their needs. But we are among the worst when it comes to letting go of our grown sons and daughters. In fact, those two characteristics are linked.

The same commitment that leads us to do so well when the children are small (dedication, love, concern, involvement) also causes us to hold too tightly when they are growing up. I will admit my own difficulties in this area. I understood the importance of turning loose before our kids were born. I wrote extensively on the subject when they were still young. I prepared a film series in which all the right principles were expressed. But when it came time to open my hand and let the birds fly, I struggled mightily! I had loved the experience of fatherhood, and I was not ready to give it up. Now, however, I relate to my grown children as adults and find this an exciting and rewarding era too. "There is a time for everything," Solomon wrote. There is also a time for everything to end.

Q321 I have found it very hard to turn my kids loose and face the empty nest. I know I need to release them, but it is so difficult. Can you help me?

Humorist Erma Bombeck described this difficult process in terms that were helpful to me.[116] She said that the task of raising kids is rather like trying to fly a kite on a day when the wind doesn't blow. Mom and Dad run down the road pulling the cute little device at the end of a string. It bounces along the ground and shows no inclination of getting off the ground.

Eventually, and with much effort, they manage to lift it fifteen feet in the air, but great danger suddenly looms. The kite dives toward electrical lines and twirls near trees. It is a scary moment. Will they ever get it safely on its way? Then, unexpectedly, a gust of wind catches the kite, and it sails upward. Mom and Dad feed out line as rapidly as they can.

The kite begins pulling the string, making it difficult to hold on. Inevitably, they reach the end of their line. What should they do now? The kite is demanding more freedom. It wants to go higher. Dad stands on his tiptoes and raises his hand to accommodate the tug. It is now grasped tenuously between his index finger and thumb, held upward toward the sky. Then the moment of release comes. The string slips through his fingers, and the kite soars majestically into God's beautiful sky.

Mom and Dad stand gazing at their precious "baby," who is now gleaming in the sun, a mere pinpoint of color on the horizon. They are proud of what they've done—but sad to realize that their job is finished. It was a labor of love. But where did the years go?

That is where you are today—standing on tiptoes and stretching toward the sky with the end of the string clutched between your fingers. It's time to let go. And when you do, you'll find that a new relationship will be born. Your parenting job is almost over. In its place will come a friendship that will have its own rewards.

Remember: The kite is going to break free one way or the other. It's best that you release it when the time is right!

Q.322 Our twenty-one-year-old daughter came home from college and moved back into her old bedroom. Now, three years later, she's still there. She doesn't work, she has no ambition or direction, and she seems perfectly content to freeload on her dad and me. I know she ought to get on with her life, but what can I do? I can't just force her out, can I?

Your daughter is not alone. Millions of young adults are living at home and loving it. They have no intention of growing up—and why should they? The nest is just too comfortable there. Food is prepared. Clothes are laundered, and the bills are paid. There's no incentive to face the cold world of reality, and they are determined not to budge. Some, like your daughter, even refuse to work. I know it's difficult to dislodge a homebound son or daughter. They're like furry little puppies who hang around the back door waiting for a saucer of warm milk. But to let them stay year after year, especially if they're not pursuing career goals, is to cultivate irresponsibility and dependency. That's not love, even though it may feel like it. There comes the time when you must gently but forthrightly hand the reins over to your adult daughter and force her to stand on her own. I think it's time to help her pack.

Giving a shove to a twenty-four-year-old woman

may seem cruel at the time, but I encourage you to consider emancipating her. The parental gravy train probably should go around the bend. If that never happens, lasting characteristics of dependency and immaturity may ensue.

I suggest you sit down and talk to your daughter, explaining why the time has come for her to make a life of her own. Set a deadline, perhaps two or three weeks ahead, and begin preparing for it. Then give her a big hug, a promise of prayers, and send her on her way.

Q323 Our son will be leaving for college next fall. Is there anything we can do to help ease the transition from home to dorm life?

For starters, author Joan Wester Anderson suggests that you make sure that your teen has the basic skills necessary to survive dorm life. Can he operate a washer and dryer, stick to a budget, handle a checkbook, get along with roommates, and manage his time wisely?

It's important as well to prepare your son for the negative aspects of campus life. Too often, adults present a rosy portrait of college as "the best years of life," which creates unrealistic expectations that lead to disappointment. Remind your son that homesickness is to be expected and that he can call home collect anytime, just to chat. At a dime a minute after working hours, the costs of telephone usage should be within everyone's reach financially.

During the first semester away, letters and treats from home can ease the pain of separation anxiety. And be pleasant when that young man returns for visits. If he feels like an intruder, he just might decide to visit someone else's home for future vacations. [117]

Going away to college is a milestone for those who embark on that journey. With proper planning, it can be a positive time of growth for the whole family.

ENDNOTES

1. John Locke, *An Essay Concerning Human Understanding,* 1690, and Jean-Jacques Rousseau, *Émile ou de l'Éducation,* 1762.
2. Dr. Stella Chess and Dr. Alexander Thomas, *Know Your Child: An Authoritative Guide for Today's Parents* (New York: Basic Books, 1987).
3. Blake Morrison, "From the Chill of Cold Steel to the Iron Laws of History," *The Independent* (10 February 1991): 31.
4. APA Monitor, American Psychological Association, Washington, D.C. 7:4 (1976).
5. Morton Edwards, ed., *Your Child from Two to Five* (New York: Permabooks, 1955), 95–96.
6. Ibid.
7. Willard and Marguerite Beecher, *Parents on the Run: A Commonsense Book for Today's Parents* (New York: Crown Publishers, 1955), 6–8.
8. Focus on the Family, "Helping Your Kids Say No," Josh McDowell, guest, 16 October 1987.
9. Dr. N. J. Sheers, *Infant Suffocation Project—Final Report,* U.S. Consumer Product Safety Commission, January 1995.
10. Dr. Daniel Pine, Dr. Patricia Cohen, and Dr. Judith Brook, "Emotional Problems during Youth as Predictors of Stature during Early Adulthood: Results from a Prospective Epidemiologic Study," *Pediatrics* 97, no. 6 (June 1996): 1–8.
11. Beth Ashley, "Bedwetting Often Medical, Parents Wrong to Punish," *USA Today,* 17 December 1996, 1D.
12. Ray Reed, "Abusers Often Start with Animals," *Roanoke Times and World News,* 19 January 1995, C1.
13. Harold M. Voth and Gabriel Nahas, *How to Save Your Kids from Drugs* (Middlebury, Vt.: Paul S. Ericksson, 1987).
14. Fetal Alcohol Syndrome Factsheet, Missouri Department of Mental Health, Division of Alcohol and Drug Abuse.
15. Mildred Goertzel, *Three Hundred Eminent Personalities* (San Francisco: Jossey-Bass Publishers, 1987).
16. Tim Friend, "Heart Disease Awaits Today's Soft-Living Kids," *USA Today,* 15 November 1994, 1D.
17. Childrens Hospital Los Angeles, 4650 Sunset Boulevard, Los Angeles, CA 90027.
18. Kim Painter, "Pre-Teens Want to Be Close to Their Parents," *USA Today,* 11 May 1995, 1D.

19. Dr. Edward M. Hallowell and Dr. John J. Ratey, *Driven to Distraction* (New York: Simon and Schuster, 1995), 73–76.
20. Hannah Bloch, "Life in Overdrive," *Time* (18 July 1994): 46.
21. Ibid., 48.
22. Ibid., 44.
23. Ibid., 45.
24. Grant Martin, *The Hyperactive Child* (Wheaton, Ill.: Victor Books, 1992).
25. Bloch, 48.
26. Hallowell and Ratey, 238.
27. Domeena Renshaw, *The Hyperactive Child* (Chicago: Nelson-Hall Publishers, 1974), 118–120.
28. Dr. David Larson, "Is Mild Spanking Abusive or Helpful for Young Children?" Physicians Research Forum Research Summary, 1993.
29. Edwards, 182–184.
30. Christina Hoff Sommers, professor of philosophy, Clark University, Worcester, Mass.
31. Sigmund Freud, "Three Essays on the Theory of Sexuality," 1905.
32. Focus on the Family, "The Family from Shore to Shore," 26 March 1996.
33. *TV Guide* (22–28 August 1992).
34. Ibid.
35. Mary Ellen McNeil, "The Jury Is Still Out But Video Games Are Sure to Be In for a Long Time," *Los Angeles Times,* 21 September 1989, 1E.
36. Ibid.
37. *Information Bank Abstracts,* 18 April 1976.
38. Kathleen Seligman, "More Children Than Cops Are Shot in the U.S.," *San Francisco Examiner,* 21 January 1994, A16.
39. K. Freund and R. J. Watson, "The Proportions of Heterosexual and Homosexual Pedophiles among Sex Offenders against Children: in Exploratory Study," *Journal of Sex and Marital Therapy* 18, no. 1 (Spring 1992): 34–43.
40. Ibid.
41. "Your Baby's Language," *Psychology Today* (May 1977).
42. Focus on the Family, "Rebellious Teenagers," Rev. Raul Ries, Pastor Mike MacIntosh, Rev. Franklin Graham, guests, 19–20 October 1988.
43. National Clearinghouse on Child Abuse and Neglect, Department of Health and Human Services, Washington, D.C.
44. Beecher, 6–8.
45. Ben Sherwood, "Even Spanking Is Outlawed: Once-Stern Sweden Leads Way in Children's Rights," *Los Angeles Times,* 11 August 1985, 2A.
46. Kathleen Engman, "Corporal Punishment v. Child Abuse: Society Struggles to Define 'Reasonable' Force," *The Ottawa Citizen,* 30 December 1996, C8.
47. Dr. David W. Fleming, Dr. Stephen L. Cochi, Dr. Allen W. Hightower, and Dr. Claire V. Broome, "Childhood Upper Respiratory Tract

Infections: To What Degree Is Incidence Affected by Attendance?" *Pediatrics* (January 1987): 55–60.

48. Donna Partow, *Homemade Business* (Colorado Springs, Colo.: Focus on the Family, 1991).

49. Speech given by Max Rafferty, former California state superintendent of public instruction, 1967.

50. Research performed at the University of Illinois–Urbana-Champaign, reported by J. Madeline Nash, "Fertile Minds: The First Three Years Are Critical," *Time*, 3 February 1997. (Note: While this study is over twenty years old, its findings were also reported in this article.)

51. Dr. Stanley Coopersmith, former associate professor of psychology, University of California, Berkeley.

52. Amy Kaslow, "Learning at Home," *Christian Science Monitor*, 26 February 1996, 9.

53. Focus on the Family, "Preparing Children for Learning," Cheri Fuller, guest, 29–30 August 1991.

54. David Kearns, "How to Revitalize Our Schools," *The Record*, 30 April 1991, B10.

55. Dr. Raymond Moore, *School Can Wait* (Provo, Utah: Brigham Young University Press, 1980).

56. Ibid.

57. Kaslow, 9.

58. Dr. Stan Weed and Dr. Joseph Olson, "Effects of Family Planning Programs for Teenagers on Adolescent Birth and Pregnancy Rates," *Family Research Council*, 1988.

59. Dr. Stephen A. Small, University of Wisconsin–Madison, 1992.

60. Dr. Sharon D. White and Dr. Richard R. DeBlassie, "Adolescent Sexual Behavior," *Adolescence* 27 (1992): 183–191.

61. Eleanor Rudolph, "New York City's Controversial Schools Chancellor Ousted," *Washington Post*, 11 February 1993, A3.

62. Tom Hess, "They Call This Abstinence?" Focus on the Family *Citizen* (May 1992): 1–4.

63 "Condom Roulette," Family Research Council, *In Focus* (1992): 1.

64. Gilbert L. Crouse, Office of Planning and Evaluation, U.S. Department of Health and Human Services, t.i., 12 March 1992, based on data from Planned Parenthood's Alan Guttmacher Institute.

65. *Monthly Vital Statistics Report,* National Center for Health Statistics, 41:9, supplement (25 February 1993).

66. Source: Alan Guttmacher Institute. Reported by Kim Painter in "Few Changes in Profile of Women Getting Abortions," *USA Today*, 8 August 1996, 4A.

67. U.S. Department of Health and Human Services, Public Health Service, Centers for Disease Control, *1991 Division of STD/HIV Prevention,* Annual Report, 13.

68. Centers for Disease Control, U.S. Department of Health and Human Services, reported in "Chlamydia Infections Rising," *Reuters News Service,* 10 March 1997.

69. Kay Stone, Sexually Transmitted Diseases Division, Centers for Disease Control, U.S. Department of Health and Human Services, t.i., 20 March 1992.

70. "Condom Roulette," 1.

71. Ibid.

72. Felicity Barringer, "Viral Sexual Diseases Are Found in One in Five in the U.S.," *New York Times,* 1 April 1993, A1.

73. Dr. Richard Glascow, "The Most Commonly Asked Questions about RU-486," *National Right to Life News,* 28 April 1993, 12–13.

74. Focus on the Family, "A Visit with the U.S. Surgeon General," Dr. C. Everett Koop, guest, 20 January 1984.

75. Focus on the Family, "A Doctor Speaks Out on Sexually Transmitted Diseases," Joe McIlhaney, M.D., guest, 26–27 March 1991.

76. Ibid.

77. Dr. Barbara Reed, "Factors Associated with Human Papillomarvirus Infection in Women Encountered in Community-Based Offices," *Archives of Family Medicine* 2 (December 1993): 1239.

78. Ibid.

79. Heidi M. Bauer, "Genital HPV Infection in Female University Students as Determined by a PCR-Based Method," *Journal of the American Medical Association* 265, no. 472 (1991).

80. Jill Brookes, "Its Empire Stretches Worldwide," *Los Angeles Times,* 22 April 1993, 21.

81. John White, *Parents in Pain* (Downers Grove, Ill.: InterVarsity Press, 1979), 44.

82. John Walvoord and Roy Zuck, eds., *Bible Knowledge Commentary: Old Testament* (Wheaton, Ill.: Victor Books, 1985), 953.

83. White, 47.

84. Address at Harrow School, 29 October 1941.

85. Beecher, 128.

86. Jean Lush and Pamela Vredevelt, *Mothers and Sons* (Pomona, Calif.: Focus on the Family, 1988).

87. Deborah M. Capaladi, Lynn Crosby, and Mike Stoolmiller, "Predicting the Timing of First Sexual Intercourse for At-Risk Adolescent Males," *Child Development* 67 (1996): 344–259.

88. Lawrence L. Wu, "Effects of Family Instability, Income, and Income Instability on the Risk of a Premarital Birth," *American Sociological Review* 61 (1996): 386–406.

89. Dr. Dorothy V. Whipple, *Dynamics of Development: Euthenic Pediatrics* (New York: McGraw-Hill, 1966), 98.

90. Margaret Rees, "Menarche When and Why?" *The Lancet* (journal of the British Medical Association) 342, no. 8884 (4 December 1993): 1375.

91. "Growing Needs, Diverse Needs: Discussion of Reproductive Health and Sexuality Needs of Today's Youth," The Johns Hopkins University, *Population Reports* 23, no. 3 (October 1995): 4.

92. Rees, 1375.

93. Urie Bronfenbrenner, "The Social Ecology of Human Development" in *Brain and Intelligence: The Ecology of Child Development*, ed. Fredrick Richardson (Hyattsville, Md.: National Educational Press, 1973).

94. Focus on the Family, "Too Big to Spank," Jay Kesler, guest, 5–6 December 1984.

95. Lily Eng, "Study Measures Drug Abuse by Orange County Students," *Los Angeles Times*, 16 January 1992, A1.

96. William A. Davis, "Flesh for Fantasy: Women Are Often Depicted in Music Videos as Powerless and Decorative," *Montreal Gazette*, 25 August 1991, F2.

97. Margaret Cronin Fisk, "1990 Was a Year of Uncertainty for the Profession," *National Law Journal* (31 December 1990): 53.

98. Ibid.

99. Dr. Charles Stanley, *How to Keep Your Kids on Your Team* (Nashville: Thomas Nelson, 1991).

100. Dan Fogelberg, "The Leader of the Band," copyright 1981, April Music, Inc. and Hickory Grove Music, Inc.

101. Lewis Yablonsky, *Fathers and Sons* (New York: Simon and Schuster, 1982), 134.

102. "'Giving In' Often Seen When Kids Hit Parents," *Omaha World-Herald*, 6 July 1979.

103. Ibid.

104. Focus on the Family, "The Family at the End of the 20th Century," 8–9 June 1995.

105. Ibid.

106. Sonia Nazari, "Wrong Turn Ends in Deadly Gang Ambush; Violence: Child, 3, Dies. Two Others Hurt As Youths Block Car's Escape from Dead End Street and Open Fire," *Los Angeles Times*, 18 September 1995, 1A.

107. Susan Kuczka and Flynn McRoberts, "5-Year-Old Was Killed Over Candy; Boy Refuses to Shoplift and Is Dropped 14 Floors to His Death, Police Say," *Chicago Tribune*, 15 October 1994, 1.

108. Jerry Adler, "Growing Up Scared," *Newsweek* (10 January 1994): 44.

109. Bob Thomas, "Television and Movie Viewers Are Used to a Happy, Laughing, Carol Burnett on Screen. But at Home, Things Have Been a Lot Different Since She and Her Husband Revealed Their Daughter's Addiction to Drugs," *Associated Press*, 10 December 1979.

110. Sandra Boodman, "Researchers Study Obesity in Children," *Washington Post*, 13 June 1995, Z10.

111. Patricia Long, "Kids with a Lot to Lose," *Hippocrates* (November 1988).

112. George Orwell, *Animal Farm* (London: Longman, 1945), chapter 10.

113. "Attractive Women Less Happy, Study Says," *Psychology Today* (September 1971).

114. *Barbie* is a registered trademark of Mattel.

115. Marilyn Elias, "Nest Is Emptier for Dad," *USA Today,* 23 January 1985, 1D.

116. Erma Bombeck, "Fragile Strings Join Parent, Child," *Arizona Republic,* 15 May 1977.

117. Joan Wester Anderson, "Preparing Your Child for Those College Years," *Focus on the Family* (May 1992): 8.

INDEX

Numbers indicate question numbers, not page numbers.

A

Aaron, Dr. Leonard D., 98
abortion, 5, 199, 211
  and sex education, 210
Abraham and Sarah, 231
absent fathers, 18, 279
abstinence, 204, 207, 209–210, 212, 215
abstinence-based educational programs, 210
academic disinterest, related to sibling rivalry, 237
academic marks, 186
Action for Children's Television, Peggy Charren, 98
action versus anger in discipline, 115, 290
Adam and Eve, 226
ADD, 64–74, 181, 190
  and discipline, 73
  and high-risk behavior, 69
  and prescription drugs, 72
  and self-concept, 71
  in adolescence, 69
  in adulthood, 69
  medication for, 71
  treatment of, 71
ADHD, 64, 70, 190
  and discipline, 154
adolescence, 43, 260
  and communication at home, 260
  and rebellion, 6, 139
  preparation for, 62
adolescents
  and self-esteem, 300
  and sex education, 208
  and sexual behavior, 201
  need for mothers, 295
adopted children, 86–89
  and discipline, 86
adrenaline, related to violence, 288
adult children, living at home, 322
age and maturity in children, 176

age as factor in school placement, 176, 177
aggressiveness, 142
    linked to violence on television, 98
AIDS, 213–215
alcohol consumption during pregnancy, 56
Allens, Dr. Hugh, 60
anger, 27
    inappropriate use in discipline, 115
anorexia, 57
anxiety
    in children, 46, 164
    in parents, 77, 80
apologies, parents to children, 138, 286
athletic abilities related to sibling rivalry, 236
athletic accomplishment and peer pressure, 254
attention deficit disorder, 64–74, 181, 190
**Attention Deficit Disorder in Children and Adults, chapter 5,
    ques. #64–74**
attention deficit/hyperactivity disorder, 64, 70, 154, 190
attention getting, related to sibling rivalry, 238
attitude chart, 122
attitudes, 122
    of children toward themselves, 175
authoritarian parenting, 27
authority, 256
    challenged, 39
    in the home, 25
    tested by children, 33
authority figures, 111
authority of parents, 108, 110
    according to Scriptures, 133

B
babies
    moral state, 12
    personalities of, 3, 5
    temperaments of, 2, 5
baby-sitters, and children's safety, 102
balance of power in the home, 239
    related to sibling rivalry, 239
Barbie dolls, 304
Barkley, Russell, 67
beauty contests, 296
bed-wetting, 48–50
Beecher, Marguerite *(Parents on the Run),* 32, 234
Beecher, Willard *(Parents on the Run),* 32, 234
behavior, 1

affected by consequences, 125
indicative of ADD or ADHD, 65
behavioral boundaries, 14, 103, 107, 136, 238
Bessman, Dr. Sam, 250
Bible
  interpretation of, 226
  on authority of parents, 133
  on discipline misused, 133
  on discipline of children, 133
  on nature of discipline, 133
Bible Knowledge Commentary: Old Testament, 226
biblical principles in parenting, 81
bladder control, 48
blended families, 241–242
body image, 294
boredom, 264
brain damage
  related to child abuse, 288
  related to violence in children, 288
Bronfenbrenner, Dr. Urie, 251
Building Self-Confidence in Children and Teens, chapter 16,
  ques. #296–318
bulimia, 57
burnout, of mothers, 159

C
Cain and Abel, 234
cancer of the cervix, related to HPV, 215–216
car trips, 137
career, and motherhood, 160
censorship, 272
Charren, Peggy, 98
checkpoints used to modify behavior, 126
Chess, Stella *(Know Your Child),* 3
child abuse, 87, 147, 244
  and the law, 145
  and violence, 288
  related to spanking, 144
child care, church programs, 158
child-care centers, 17, 157
child-care support, 158
child development, 1
child neglect, related to violence, 288
child rearing, philosophy of, 140
childhood depression, 58
childhood trauma, 59
childish behavior, 39, 103

children
    and family traditions, 85
    and information about sex, 205–206
    and responsibility, 24
    differences between, 302
    learning from mistakes, 24
    salvation of, 231
    temperaments of, 6
Children's Health and Well-Being, chapter 4, ques. #44–63
Childrens Hospital Los Angles, 61
children's rooms, 239
chlamydia, 214
choice of belief, in children, 225
Christmas, 223
church activity and adolescent sexual involvement, 201
church-run child care, 158
churches' involvement in sex education, 204
churches' responsibility to single parents, 240
civility, 313
class clown, 183
classroom discipline, 166, 169
classroom disorder, 187
classroom structure, 166, 169
college, preparation for, 323
Columbia Children's Hospital (Ohio), 60
Columbia University College of Physicians, 46
communication skills
    during adolescence, 260
    with children, 260
competition, 298
compliant child, 3, 6, 9
condoms, 209–210, 214
    and disease prevention, 209
    distribution of, 209
confidence, 308
conflict
    between parent and child, 251
    between siblings, 236
confrontation, 33, 39
    in discipline, 103
consequences, 125
contraceptives, and adolescents, 63, 199
"contracts" and teen behavior, 289
Coopersmith, Dr. Stanley, 175
coping skills, 303
Cornell University, 251
corporal punishment, 30, 79, 142–143, 147–150, 152–153, 155, 170

and age of child, 153
and the law, 155
in schools, 170
cortisol, related to violence, 288
courtship, 267
"Cradles of Eminence" study, 59
creative writing, 182
cruel behavior in children, 51
cruelty to animals, 51
crying
after punishment, 151
in children, 34
in infants, 15
curriculum, 173, 192
cursing, 135
custody, 244
Cylert, 71

D

Dallas Theological Seminary, 226
Dare to Discipline, 27
date rape, 200
dating, 267–268
DeBlassie, Dr. Richard, 201
defiance, 25, 29, 39–40, 86, 104–105, 113, 117, 124, 129, 148
defined limits, 14
Delicate Art of Letting Go, The, chapter 17, ques. #319–323
demanding children, 34
dependency, 27, 32
created by overprotection, 125
depression
in children, 58
in parents, 34
deprivation and its effect on intellectual development, 174
development in infants, 16
developmental years, 29
devotions in the family, 219
Dexedrine, 71
dieting among girls, 294
differences between siblings, 302
dinnertime battles, 47
disabled children, and discipline, 86
disciplinary techniques, 109
discipline, 30, 39, 79, 103, 115, 175
agreement between father and mother, 111
and adopted children, 86
and disabled children, 86

    and sick children, 86
    and teenagers, 290
    for children's welfare, according to Scripture, 133
    for infants, 31
    for one-year-olds, 33
    for toddlers, 40
    in balance, 28
    in schools, 165, 168
    in the classroom, 169
    misused, 142
    most common error in, 115
    not to be harsh, according to Scripture, 133
    of others' children, 23, 119
    of the ADD child, 73
    purpose of, 28
    related to safety, 40
    related to Scripture, 133
    related to sibling rivalry, 239
    too much, 42
**Disciplining the Elementary School Child, chapter 7,
   ques. #103–141**
Disciplining the Preschool Child, chapter 3, ques. #25–43
disease prevention, and condoms, 209
dishonesty, 20
disobedience, 39–40, 106, 113, 143, 148
disorganization
    and school achievement, 190
    and school problems, 181
disrespect, 114, 124
distractibility, 66
divine forgiveness, 103
divorce
    and health of children, 248
    effect on discipline, 120
    impact on teen sexual involvement, 248
domination, 27
double standard, relating to sexual behavior, 269
dressing, schoolchildren, 82
Driven to Distraction, 65, 71
drug abuse
    and family influence, 265
    and peer pressure, 265
    symptoms, 292

E

eating disorders, 57, 250
eating habits in children, 47, 60

Education: Public, Private, and Homeschooling, chapter 10, ques. #165–197
educational burnout in children, 189
Effective Parenting Today, chapter 6, ques. #75–102
electronic media, 21
emotions, expression of, 114
emotions, related to premenstrual tension, 262
employment outside the home, 162
empty nest, 319, 321
entertainment, 21
enuresis, 48–50
environment, and human behavior, 4
ethnic groups, 194
evil, 10, 217
exercise in children, 60
expression of emotions, 114
extinction, in behavior modification, 131, 164

F

failures, in parenting, 232
family
   devotions, 219
   disruption, and health of children, 248
   dynamics, and power, 256
   heritage, 233
   traditions, 85
fantasy, 224
   in children, 20
father, child's need for, 244
Father of the Bride, 319
father-daughter relationship, 92, 282
father-son relationship, 280–281
fatherhood, 75
fatherless sons, and mentors, 245
fathers
   absent, 18, 279
   as peacemakers, 285
   dates with their children, 307
Fathers and Sons, 281
fatigue
   during puberty, 258
   in parents, 34
fear, 27, 117
   of failure, 237
   of the dark, 164
fetal alcohol syndrome, 56
fighting, with parents, 14

forgiveness, taught in the home, 138
free choice, 1
free will, 228–229
freedom, preparing children for, 273
frustrations of parenting, 76
Fuller, Cheri, 181
fun, as a family, 85

G

genetic heritage, 4
girls and dieting, 294
God
    concept of, 220
    concept of, taught to children, 225
    love and justice, 220–221
    parents represent to children, 220
    represented by earthly fathers, 221
God's will, 230
Goertzel, Mildred ("Cradles of Eminence" study), 59
Goertzel, Victor ("Cradles of Eminence" study), 59
gonorrhea, 214
Graham, Rev. Franklin, 139
grandparents, 81
    and spanking, 147
    impact on grandchildren, 233
growth, 45
growth hormones, 45
guilt, feelings in parents, 77, 227, 232

H

Halloween, 224
Hallowell, Edward, M.D., 71
Hammond, Dr. Vince, 99
Harbin, Dr. Henry, 286
harshness, 117, 146
Harvard University Preschool Project, 16
health of children
    related to divorce, 248
    related to family disruption, 248
    related to group-setting child care, 157
    related to single parenting, 248
height, in children, 45
height, related to anxiety, 46
**Help for Single Parents and Stepparents, chapter 14,
    ques. #240–247**
heredity, and human behavior, 4
heritage, passed on by grandparents, 233

high-risk behavior, associated with ADD, 69
holidays, 137
home-based business, 162
Homemade Business, 162
homemaking, 163
homeschooling, 176, 187, 195–196
  and socialization, 196
  for immature children, 176
  support groups, 196
homework, in elementary schools, 189
honesty, 194
HPV (human papilloma virus), 209, 214–216
  related to cancer of the cervix, 216
human papilloma virus (HPV), 209, 214–216
human suffering, 100
human will, 104
humanism, effect on discipline, 104
humiliation, 27
humor in the home, 37, 318
husband, support of mother at home, 160
Hyperactive Child, The, 71, 74
hyperactivity, 64, 66, 176
hysterectomies, related to sexually transmitted diseases, 214

I

idealism in parenting, 275
idols, and teenagers, 217
idols of the young, 214
illiteracy, 167, 173, 184
immaturity, in relation to age, 176
impulse control, 142
in-laws, 81
incentive-and-disincentive program, 289
independence, preparing children for, 32, 273
infants
  crying, 15
  early development, 16
  fussiness, 15
infertility, related to sexually transmitted diseases, 211, 214
innocence
  in children, 26
  of babies, 10
insecurity, in children, 46
Institute for Research and Evaluation, 198
instruction, in early years, 26
intellectual capabilities in children, 16
intellectual skills, development during infancy, 16

intellectual stimulation, during child's early years, 16, 174
intelligence, related to sibling rivalry, 236
intercessory prayer, 228–230
irresponsibility, 132
isolation, of mothers of small children, 159

J

jealousy
    between children, 235
    over new baby, 314
Jesus Christ
    faith in, 301
    teaching children about, 218
Journal of Marriage and the Family, 201
junior high, problems, 253
justice, 313
    in the home, 239
    related to sibling rivalry, 239

K

kidnapping, 102
Know Your Child, 3
Koop, Dr. C. Everett, comments on AIDS, 213

L

language development in infants, 16
Larson, Dr. David, 79
late bloomers, 178–179
    and grade retention, 179
laziness, 258
leadership, in the home, 25
learning environment in schools, 168
learning, related to self-discipline and self-control, 180
letting go of children, 320–321
Levine, Dr. Milton, 89
limits, used in training children, 8, 107, 126, 238
Living with a Teenager, chapter 15, ques. #248–295
loneliness, and motherhood, 156
low self-esteem, in ADD or ADHD children, 64
Lush, Jean (Mothers and Sons), 245
Luster, Tom, 201
lying, in children, 20
lyrics, profanity in, 272

M

MacIntosh, Mike, 139
Madden, Dr. Denis, 286

magic, 21
manipulation, 128
  of parents, related to sibling rivalry, 238
manners, 22, 26, 84
marijuana, 55
Martin, Grant, Ph.D., 71
masturbation, 266
  and guilt, 266
  and pornography, 266
materialism, and rewards, 130
maturity, 32
  in relation to age, 176
McDowell, Josh, 43
McIlhaney, Dr. Joe, 214
media, influence of, 271
medical exams, for adolescents, 63
Medical Institute for Sexual Health (MISH), 214
medical suppliers, in relation to sex education, 210
medication
  and ADD, 71
  and night terrors, 53
memorization, in learning process, 193
Menninger Foundation (Topeka, KS), 55
mental abilities, 16
mental block, 309–310
mental retardation, related to alcohol use during pregnancy, 56
mentors, for boys without fathers, 245
Michigan State, 201
middle child, 306–307
mistakes in parenting, 80, 115–116, 227, 232
mistakes, role in teaching children, 24
modesty, 316
Mom's Day Out, 156
Moms in Touch International, 156, 159
moodiness, 121
Moore, Dr. Raymond (School Can Wait), 195
MOPS (Mothers of Preschoolers), 156, 159
moral purity, 207
mother's impact on infant development, 16
mother-daughter conflict, 283
mother-daughter relationship, 283
motherhood and career, 160
mothers
  and child rearing, 157
  at home, 161
  feelings of isolation, 159
  of adolescents, 295

    of preschoolers, 295
    of small children, 163
Mothers and Sons, 245
Mothers of Preschoolers (MOPS), 156, 159
Mothers on the Move, 156
movies, 294
    and teenagers, 217
    and violence, 100, 288
    youth idols, 214
MTV, 270
    and teenagers, 217
    and violence, 270
music, 272
    and teenagers, 217
    lyrics, 272
    related to rebellion, 270
    rock, 83
myelinization, stage of neurological development, 178

N

name-calling, 124
National Advisory Commission to the Office of Juvenile Justice and
    Delinquency Prevention, 286
National Coalition on Television Violence, 99
National Institutes of Health, 79
negativism, 41
negativity, 122
neighbors, 119
neurological damage, caused by shaking infants, 30
New Age, 21
New York Longitudinal Study, 3
newborns, personality of, 3
night terrors, 52–53
    medication for, 53
nightmares, 52
nonessentials in parent-child conflicts, 275
nonnegotiables in parent-child conflicts, 276
nuclear family, 16

O

obedience, 13
occult, 21, 224
Olson, Joseph, 198
Oregon Social Learning Center, 248
overprotection, 125
overweight, 294
    related to children, 60

P

parent battering, 286
parent-child conflicts
  choosing the right battles, 275–277
  nonessentials, 275
  nonnegotiables, 276
parental authority, 25
parental guidance, 12
parental guilt, 227
parental involvement in public schools, 169
parental involvement in sex education, 201
parental leadership, 25, 31–32, 39, 256
parental mediation, related to sibling rivalry, 239
parental mistakes, 103, 115–116, 227, 232
parental pressure, 298
parental values, 7
parenting, 75
  biblical principles of, 81
  frustrations of, 76
  inadequacies, 76, 80
Parenting Isn't for Cowards, 6
parents, identified with God, 29
Parents in Pain, 226, 228
Parents on the Run, 234
parents' role, in children's behavior, 4
Partow, Donna *(Homemade Business)*, 162
pedophiles, 102
peer groups
  acceptance in, 251
  and power games, 254
  during adolescence, 252
peer pressure, 209, 254
  and athletic accomplishment, 254
  and physical attractiveness, 254
  and substance abuse, 265
peers, and school-aged children, 196
perfectionism in parenting, 275
permissive parenting, 27
permissiveness, 25, 146
  related to violence in youths, 286
personal responsibility, 59, 127, 227
personal worth, 298
personality, 1–2, 317
  in babies, 5
  in newborns, 3
physical attractiveness, 294, 296–297, 304

and peer pressure, 254
    related to sibling rivalry, 236
physical development in children, 249
physical punishment, 30, 142–143, 147–150, 152–153, 155
    and age of child, 153
    and the law, 155
    in schools, 170
Pine, Dr. Daniel, 46
Planned Parenthood, 198–199, 209
    and sex education, 210
pluralism, in schools, 197
pornography
    and masturbation, 266
Poussaint, Dr. Alvin, 62
power
    given to children, 257
    importance to teenagers, 256
    meaning for teenagers, 255
    need for, 255
    role in family dynamics, 256
power games, 124
    and peer groups, 254
power plays, 13
prayer, 230
    for children, 8, 228
    intercessory, 228–229
    persistence in, 230–231
prayer in schools, 197
prayer partners, and single parents, 240
pregnancy, 18
    and alcohol consumption, 56
premarital adolescent sexual activity, 201
premarital sex, 199
    and sexually transmitted diseases, 211
premenstrual tension, effects on adolescent emotions, 262
"Preparing for Adolescence" weekend, conversation, 62, 266
prescription drugs, and ADD, 72
privacy, and teenagers, 293, 316
private education, 187
profanity, 135
    in lyrics, 272
promiscuity, 297
    among teens, 210
promises, of God, 226
proverbs in the Bible, nature of, 226
puberty, 208, 274
    and fatigue, 258

public behavior, 38
public schools, 167
    and parental involvement, 169
punishment, 31, 37, 110, 117, 151
    and crying, 151
    appropriate, 40
    corporal, 30
    physical, 30
    related to bed-wetting, 49
punishment and reward, 122–123, 128

R

racial groups, 194
Raising the Preschool Child, chapter 2, ques. #15–24
rape, related to rock music, 270
Ratey, John, M.D., 71
reading
    and preschoolers, 185
    as a family activity, 85
reading difficulty, 178
reassurance with discipline, 103
rebellion, 12, 25, 27, 87, 113, 139, 226–228, 275, 286
    during adolescence, 6, 43, 139, 261–262
    related to culture, 270
    related to music, 270
rebellious nature, 106
regressive behavior in children, 314
Reid, Dr. Robert, 71
reinforcement, 131
    and report cards, 186
    in behavior modification, 164
rejection
    by opposite sex, 311
    by peers, 303
relationships
    mothers' need for, 156
religious liberty, 197
religious training, 225
remarriage, 241
Renshaw, Dr. Domeena, 74
report cards, 186
respect, 29, 114, 256, 313
    for children, 110
    for parents, 109–110, 270
    in the classroom, 169
    of parents toward children, 299
    related to racial and ethnic groups, 194

responsibility, 32, 125–126
    in children, 24
    of church to single parents, 240
retention, when appropriate, 179
reward and punishment, 122–123, 128
rewards, 127, 131
    and materialism, 130
    and report cards, 186
    and teen behavior, 289
    misuse of, 129
ridicule, 104, 110, 311–312, 318
Ries, Rev. Raul, 139
risky behavior in young people, 214
Ritalin, 71–72
rock music, 83, 294
    related to rape, 270
    related to suicide, 270
    youth idols, 214
role models, 21
    masculine, 245
routine, change of, 136

S

safe sex, 209, 212, 214–215
safety
    for children, 102
    related to order, 171
salvation, 226
    of children, 228, 231
Santa Claus, 223
sassiness, 40, 274
scholastic aptitude, 298
School Can Wait, 195
school choice, 184
schoolchildren, clothing, 82
schools, 165, 168
    and corporal punishment, 170
Scripture, misinterpretation of, 227
searching of teen's room, 293
segregation, of boys and girls for sex education, 200
self-arousal in children, 94–95
self-concept, 110, 299, 308
    in children, 104
self-confidence, 309
self-control, 112, 175
    related to learning, 180
self-discipline, 32, 112, 127

and school achievement, 190
as goal of structure in the classroom, 166
related to learning, 180
self-doubt, 296
during adolescence, 251
in parents, 77
self-esteem, 175, 183, 296
during adolescence, 300
related to sibling rivalry, 236
self-image, 308
self-reliance, 112
sex
designed for marriage, 214
on television, 98
sex education 198–200, 202, 204, 208, 210–211
in public schools, 203
sex-education counselors, 210
sex-education programs, 201
**Sex Education: Where, When, and How, chapter 11,
ques. #198–216**
sexes, differences between, 91
sexual abuse, 51, 102
sexual activity among teens, 212
sexual attitudes of children, 93
sexual development, 250
sexual differences between men and women, 269
sexual experimentation, 200
related to dating, 267
sexual intercourse, 209
sexual involvement among teens, related to divorce, 248
sexual molestation, 102
sexual nature of children, 93
sexual promiscuity, 269
sexual revolution, 269
sexuality, 62
and cultural conditioning, 91
information to children, 205–206
sexually transmitted diseases, 201, 210–211, 213–214
shaking, dangers of, with infants, 30
Sibling Rivalry, chapter 13, ques. #234–239
sibling rivalry, 234–239
and parental mediation, 239
sick children, and discipline, 86
SIDS, 44
SIECUS, in relation to sex education, 210
sin, 227
sin nature in children, 11, 26

single-parent families and adolescent sexual involvement, 201
single parenting and health of children, 248
single parents, 157, 240
    and prayer partners, 240
    support for, 247
sleep, in infants, 34
Slonecker, Dr. Bill, 31
slow learners, 174
    and retention, 179
Small, Stephen, 201
smoking
    and family influence, 265
    and peer pressure, 265
    dangers of, 265
social pressure, 309
    during adolescence, 252
social skills, development during infancy, 16
Society for Pediatric Research, 44
Sommers, Christina Hoff, 91
Spank or Not to Spank, To, chapter 8, ques. #142–155
spanking, 37, 79, 142, 144, 148–149, 152, 154
    and age of child, 153
    and teenagers, 289
    and the ADHD child, 154
    and the law, 155
    follow-up, 150
spirit, versus will, 104, 133
Spiritual Life of the Family, chapter 12, ques. #217–233
spiritual training, 218, 222, 225
stammering, 61
standards, inappropriate, 275
Stanley, Andy, 275
Stanley, Charles, 275
STDs, 201, 210–211, 213–214
stimulation
    effect on intellectual development, 174
    in formative years, 16
stress, in girls, 46
stress hormone cortisol, 46, 288
stress hormones, 46, 288
strong-willed child, 3, 6–8, 14, 25, 34, 38, 47, 104, 107–108, 124, 141
structure
    in schools, 165
    in the classroom, 169
structured time, 264
stuttering, 61
substance abuse

and family influence, *265*
and peer pressure, *265*
sudden infant death syndrome (SIDS), 44
suicide
among teens, *252, 270*
related to rock music, *270*
summer school, 179
supervision, 264
support, child care, 158
surrogate spouse, children of single parents, 242
swearwords, 135
syphilis, 214

T

targets, in behavior, 126
teachers, 167, 171
teaching through discipline, 103
teen pregnancy, 198, 201, 210, 291
teen sexual involvement, related to divorce, 248
teen suicide, 252, 270
teen years, 29
teenage behavior, across cultures, 217
teenage rebellion, 25
teenagers, 43
and marijuana use, *55*
and need for power, *255–256*
and rebellion, *261–262*
and sexual activity, *210, 212, 248*
and television, *217*
television, 96–98, 294
advertisers, *97*
and teenagers, *217*
and violence, *100–101*
and youth idols, *214*
temper tantrums, 25, 35, 37
temperament, 317
categories of, *3*
in babies, *2, 5*
terrible twos, 41
test scores, 167
testing authority, 33
Thomas, Alexander *(Know Your Child),* 3
time away from children, for single parents, 243
toddlerhood, 41
toddlers, 104, 131
and discipline, *37, 40*
and temper tantrums, *35*

  eating habits, 47
  nature of, 19
  stage of development, 19
toilet training, 36
Topeka Veterans Administration Medical Center, 55
Tough Love, 286
traditions in the family, 85
transition from home to college, 323
traumas during childhood, 59
trust, of parents toward children, 299
2 Live Crew, 272
Type I children, 190–191
Type II children, 190–191

U
Understanding the Nature of Children, chapter 1, ques. #1–14
uniqueness of babies, 2
University of California, 175, 294
University of Maryland's medical school, 286
University of Massachusetts Medical Center, 67
University of Nebraska, 71
University of Southern California, 250
University of Wisconsin–Madison, 201, 248

V
vacations, 136–137
values, 29
  taught to children, 301
verbal rejection, 104
video games, 99, 217
violence, 100, 142
  among the young, 286–288
  in cartoons, 21
  in schools, 167
  on television, 98, 101
  related to MTV, 270
  related to toys, 21
virginity, 200
  among teens, 209
virtues, 20
visitation rights, 246
Voth, Harold, M.D., 55
voucher system, 184

W
Weed, Stan, 198
What's a Mother to Do?, chapter 9, ques. #156–164

whining, 131
White, Dr. Burton, 16
White, Dr. John *(Parents in Pain)*, 226, 228
White, Dr. Sharon, 201
Who Stole Feminism? 91
will, as differentiated from spirit, 104, 133
will of God, 230
willful defiance, in toddlers, 104
willful disobedience, 143
Woodward, Dr. Luther, 25–26
work, appropriate for children, 172
writing skills, 182
Wu, Lawrence L., 248

Y

Yablonsky, Lewis *(Fathers and Sons)*, 281
year-round schools, 188
York, David (Tough Love), 286
York, Phyllis (Tough Love), 286
Your Child from Two to Five, 25, 89
youth culture, 217, 304

INDEX OF SCRIPTURE REFERENCES

Numbers refer to question numbers, not page numbers.

Genesis 25:22-27—*personhood in the womb* 5
Genesis 38:8—*sex misused* 266

Deuteronomy 6:7-9—*child discipline and training*. 218

1 Samuel 2:22-36—*parental guilt* 227

Psalm 37:7, 10-11—*reward and punishment*. 123
Psalm 51:5—*sin nature* 11

Proverbs 6:16-19—*truthfulness* 20
Proverbs 10:4, 22, 27—*nature of proverbs*. 226
Proverbs 12:21—*nature of proverbs*. 226
Proverbs 15:22—*nature of proverbs*. 226
Proverbs 16:31, 33—*nature of proverbs*. 226
Proverbs 22:3-4, 6, 9, 11, 16, 29—*nature of proverbs* 226
Proverbs 22:6—*child discipline and training* 7, 226
Proverbs 28:16—*nature of proverbs*. 226
Proverbs 29:17—*child discipline and training* 133

Ecclesiastes 8:11-12—*reward and punishment*. 123

Isaiah 1:17—*helping others* 245

Jeremiah 1:5—*personhood in the womb*. 5

Matthew 18:5—*welcoming children* 245
Matthew 25:40—*helping others* 240

Luke 18:1-8—*prayer* 230
Luke 18:17—*faith in children* 220

John 14:9—*knowing the Father*. 220

Romans 3:23—*sin nature*. 11
Romans 4:19-22—*God's promises* 231
Romans 9:13—*personhood in the womb*. 5

1 Corinthians 7:5—*sex in marriage* 266

2 Corinthians 4:4—*spiritual blindness*. 228

Ephesians 1:4—*personhood in the womb* 5
Ephesians 6:1-4—*child discipline and training* 133

Philippians 3:13-14—*dealing with failure* 232

Colossians 3:20-21—*child discipline and training*.................. 133

1 Thessalonians 5:17—*prayer* 230

1 Timothy 3:4-5—*child discipline and training* 133

Hebrews 12:5-11—*child discipline and training* 133

James 1:27—*helping others* 240

2 Peter 2:7—*sin and culture*................................... 272
2 Peter 3:9—*God's patience*................................... 228